Anderson Guide to
ENJOYING
GREENWICH
Connecticut
An insider's favorite places

*I've lived in Greenwich all my life and
I'm finding new places to go and
restaurants to try in* The Anderson Guide.
It's really a great resource.
- Dr. Robert L. Ailleo, DMD

A real insider's guide. I keep it next to my phone.
- Darius Toraby, Architect

The Anderson Guide *is my left hand and my right hand
since moving to Greenwich from London.*
- Paul Roberts

This is the best directory for town resources.
- Caroline Frano, RTM Chair District 8

This indispensable guide is invaluable for new residents
- Hillary Watson, Past President of
The Old Greenwich-Riverside Newcomers Club

Anderson Guide to
ENJOYING
GREENWICH
Connecticut
An insider's favorite places

Fourth Edition

Anderson Associates
Greenwich Specialists

with illustrations and maps
by Vanessa Y. Chow

IG
Avocet Press

Anderson Guide to
Enjoying Greenwich, Connecticut
An insider's favorite places

Written by:
Carolyn Anderson &
Anderson Associates, Ltd.
www.GreenwichRealtors.com
164 Mason Street, Greenwich, CT 06830
(203) 629-4519

Illustrations and maps by: Vanessa Y. Chow

Published by:
Ickus Guides, Avocet Press Inc
19 Paul Court
Pearl River, NY 10965
www.avocetpress.com
Designed by: Melanie Kershaw

Library of Congress Cataloging-in-Publication Data
Anderson, Carolyn, date
The Anderson guide to enjoying Greenwich, CT : an insider's favorite places /
written by Carolyn Anderson & Anderson Associates, Ltd. ; with illustrations and
maps by Vanessa Y. Chow.— 4th ed.
p. cm.
Includes index.
ISBN 0-9677346-0-6
1. Greenwich (Conn.)—Guidebooks. I. Title: Guide to enjoying Greenwich,
Connecticut. II. Anderson Associates (Greenwich, Conn.) III. Title.
F104.G8 A53 2000
917.46'9—dc21
00-008450

On the cover: Photographs by Carolyn Anderson ©2000

Printed in the United States of America

Dedicated to:
Our old and new friends in Greenwich

Disclaimer:
The purpose of this guide is to educate and entertain. Every effort has been made to make this guide accurate, however, it should not be relied upon as the ultimate source of information about Greenwich or about any resource mentioned in the Guide.

There may be mistakes both typographical and in content. We have done our best to lead you to spots we hope you will like. This is by no means a complete guide to every resource in Greenwich. Unfortunately, even the best are not always perfect. If you have tried one of our favorites and are disappointed, if we have missed your favorite, if we have made a mistake in a description—please let us know: fill out the feedback form in the back of the book and send it to us.

A note about "Hours":
The hours and days of operation are intended as a guide, but they should not be considered definitive. Establishments change their hours as business dictates. In addition, many change their hours for winter and summer and during holidays. Finally, just about every establishment takes a vacation.

WHAT KIND OF
GUIDE IS THIS ?

This is a guide to our favorites . . . simply that. It is *not* a book of advertisements. No place mentioned in this Guide had any idea that it would be included. Establishments are here only because we like them. Although this Guide is about enjoying Greenwich, you will note that some of our selections are outside of Greenwich's town limits. These easy-to-reach places complement our many in-town resources.

Finding favorite spots takes awhile. We have lived in Greenwich for many years. If you are just beginning life in America's number one town, we hope that some of the resources in this guide will give you a head start in feeling right at home.

Initially, we prepared this Guide for our private clients. Then the calls came in . . . their friends needed a copy. The Anderson Guide, the book we dedicated to our new friends who had selected Greenwich as their home, was published! We hope you will find it useful, too. Please let us know what you think of this guide. We love your comments!

Sincerely,

Carolyn Anderson   *Lisa Gessner*
Amy Purpora   *Jennifer O'Brien*
Jerry Anderson   *Maurice Hunt*
Marilyn Secord   *Caroline Ferrari*
Sarah Jane Cafiero   *Pat Johnson*

. . . and all of us at Anderson Associates.

ENJOY GREENWICH

Enjoy a gracious residential community only twenty-eight miles from New York City. By train (from one of Greenwich's four train stations) or car, New York is a short commute.

Enjoy the scenic New England stone walls, meadows and wooded parklands. Greenwich has 1,487 acres of public parks and beaches, including two islands in Long Island Sound.

Enjoy one of the nation's finest public school systems. Greenwich has excellent libraries, a full-service hospital, a superb museum, a professional symphony orchestra, and many art and cultural events. Choose among more than forty synagogues and churches.

Enjoy the many outdoor activities that Greenwich offers. Play tennis on one of more than 50 public courts. Golf at the Griffith Harris Memorial Golf Course, watch polo matches, or ride horses on the extensive Greenwich trail system. Learn how to sail or watch sailboat races on summer evenings. In the winter, skate at the Dorothy Hamill Rink or on a picturesque town pond.

Enjoy the sophisticated shopping and restaurants. Because of Greenwich's unique status, it has attracted world class shops which have blended with the small, specialty, New England stores. The downtown section of Greenwich remains vibrant and active. Restaurants abound, from the very casual to some of the best in the USA. Greenwich offers a great variety of cuisines: if you are hungry for clam chowder, curry, sushi, pad tai or veal saltimbocca, you can find it here.

Discover for yourself why Greenwich is so special!

CONTENTS

CONTENTS

CONTENTS

CONTENTS

CONTENTS

CONTENTS

CONTENTS

CONTENTS

CONTENTS

GREENWICH

AT A GLANCE

www.state.ct.us/munic/Greenwich

- Average age: 39.9
- Median family income: $82,900
- Median home sale price: $676,000
- Assessed value of all residences: $7.5 billion
- Average annual increase in the value of homes: 9.1%
- 50 square miles
- Population: 58,440
- 1,500 acres of public parks
- 32 miles of shoreline
- 150 miles of riding trails
- 37 houses of worship (34 churches, 3 synagogues)
- 9 yacht clubs, 8 country clubs and one tennis club
- 98 special interest organizations
- 15 garden clubs
- 40 languages spoken
- School system rated #1 in Connecticut
- Rated safest community in Connecticut

GREENWICH

RATED BEST TOWN IN CONNECTICUT

Time and again, Greenwich is rated as Connecticut's number one place to live. Greenwich is the premier town along what is called the Connecticut Gold Coast. The town's unique beauty has been preserved by very careful town planning and zoning. Like Beverly Hills, Greenwich has the rare distinction of being one of those recognizable names. But unlike Beverly Hills, which is a 5.7 square mile enclave, Greenwich extends over fifty square miles with rolling hills, woodlands, meadows and 32 miles of gorgeous shoreline bordering the Long Island Sound. Greenwich is not isolated—it is a real community and a wonderful place to raise a family.

Although Greenwich conjures up thoughts of stately country homes and waterfront estates reserved for the select few, Greenwich is much, much more. As you will discover, Greenwich offers a wealth of diversity, not only in real estate and architecture, but also in residents. Greenwich is home not only to a cosmopolitan group of executives, but to a great variety of professionals, artists, writers, diplomats, actors and sports figures.

In addition to being rated number one in safety and education by *Connecticut Magazine*, Greenwich is rated the number one city in Connecticut for quality of life. Greenwich has a vast wealth of attractions. Whether you look at the picturesque shopping areas, the personal service provided by its mix of elegant shops, its fantastic library (the most used in Connecticut), its ultra-modern hospital or its fifty fabulous restaurants, Greenwich has it all. Recently *Connecticut's Best Dining Guide*, which covers the entire state, gave 19 of Greenwich's restaurants top honors. Of the twenty best restaurants in the state, four were located in Greenwich. *The New York Times* recently declared that Greenwich has more Very Good and Excellent restaurants per capita than any other community in Connecticut. One of the many unique things about Greenwich can be found on Greenwich Avenue every day between the hours of 8 am and 6:30 pm: the police officers at the street corners directing traffic. These officers help to preserve the feeling of a small town and, of course, also help keep the town's crime rate low.

GREENWICH

TOWN FACILITIES

Greenwich is still 25% green. It has thirty-two miles of coastline, with its main beaches (open only to Greenwich Residents) at Greenwich Point (147 acres), Byram Beach and the two city-owned islands (Captain's Island & Island Beach). Greenwich has 8,000 acres of protected land, over 1000 acres of town parks, thirty-five town tennis courts (not including the YMCA and YWCA Courts), an indoor ice rink (open only to residents), fourteen public marinas and a 158-acre, 18-hole golf course (open only to residents). Music lovers enjoy the Greenwich Philharmonic, while the Bruce Museum appeals to everyone and is rated one of the best museums in Connecticut.

EDUCATION

Greenwich public schools (ten elementary, three middle and one high school) are rated number one in Connecticut - 40% of the graduates go to the "Most Competitive Colleges." The school budget is $70 million. The average class size is 20 and over 90% of the teachers have masters degrees. In addition, Greenwich has thirty independent preschools and nine excellent private and parochial day schools. For details, see section SCHOOLS.

GREENWICH

LIBRARY - GREENWICH

www.greenwich.lib.ct.us

The Greenwich Library is a special treasure - used by young and old alike. Last year the Library lent 675,000 customers an average of 4.5 books per minute. It is no wonder the library has been rated the best in the country. The library recently received a $25,000,000 bequest from Clementine Peterson. Based on this bequest and funds raised by the Friends of Greenwich Library, Architect Cesar Pelli has designed the 31,000 square-foot addition, as well as renovations to the original building. The Byram Shubert branch is also being enhanced and we have a wonderful new Cos Cob Library. These branches provide convenient neighborhood locations and serve as community centers. The library provides a large number of programs. These programs are noted in other sections of this guide.

Use the web site to check on books or phone 622.7910 to reserve items, and ask to have your reserved materials sent to one of the branches. There is no limit to the number of books you can check out.

Greenwich Library (Main Library)

101 West Putnam Avenue, 622.7900

Hours: Weekdays, 9 am - 9 pm (June - August, 5 pm); Saturday, 9 am - 5 pm; Sunday, 1 pm - 5 pm (Oct - April).

Byram Shubert Library (Branch)

21 Mead Avenue, 531.0426

Hours: Monday - Wednesday & Friday, 9 am - 5 pm; Thursday, 1 pm - 8 pm; Closed Saturday and Sunday.

Cos Cob Library (Branch)

5 Sinawoy Road, Cos Cob, 622.6883

Cos Cob has a new library, perfect for family enjoyment. While the youngest ones enjoy playing or reading in the children's corner, older ones can read favorite books or search the Internet. The dynamic staff organizes different events for children and adults. In just a short while it has become an important part of Cos Cob community life.

Hours: Tuesday - Saturday, 9 am - 5 pm, Thursday until 6 pm; Closed Sunday and Monday. Children story times at 10:45 am on Thursday.

GREENWICH

LIBRARY - OLD GREENWICH

Perrot Library of Old Greenwich
(Independent Library)
90 Sound Beach Avenue, 637.1066;
Children's Library, 637.8802

The Perrot Memorial Library is a non-profit institution independent of the Greenwich Library. It is open to all residents of Greenwich, although it principally serves the residents of Old Greenwich, Riverside and North Mianus. Perrot has recently completed a beautiful $3.3 million, 7,000 square-foot Children's Library.

Hours: Monday, Wednesday, Friday, 9 am - 6 pm; Thursday, 9 am - 8 pm; Saturday, 9 am - 5 pm; Sunday, 1 pm - 5 pm.

HOSPITAL

The 160-bed Greenwich hospital is an affiliate of Yale University School of Medicine. It is a world-class hospital, providing the town with excellent health care. Patients from all over Fairfield and Westchester seek treatment at Greenwich Hospital. Greenwich Hospital is carefully gearing up for the 21st century. The hospital has just built a state-of-the-art cancer center (Bendheim) as well as a $10,000,000 expansion to make it a high-tech diagnostic and healing center without the austere look, normal delays and "red-tape" often associated with hospitals. For more information on the Hospital and other medical services, see HEALTH.

GREENWICH

LOCATION

Greenwich is in the southwest corner of Connecticut, providing residents with the convenience of being close to a big city, while living in the comfort and security of the country. Greenwich has an excellent transportation system. Greenwich is just minutes from Westchester Airport, making convenient trips to nearby cities such as Boston or Washington. Greenwich is only twenty-nine miles from Times Square (forty-three minutes by one of the seventy-eight trains that operate daily between New York City and Greenwich). There are four train stations conveniently located throughout the town. U.S. Route 1, the historic Post Road, is the main commercial artery. Locally, it is named Putnam Avenue. In addition, Interstate 95 and the Merritt Parkway traverse Greenwich, giving it excellent regional accessibility. It takes about ten minutes to drive to Stamford, about sixty minutes to Danbury and approximately fifteen minutes to White Plains. Limousines provide easy and quick access to New York City's international airports; La Guardia Airport is about a 45-minute drive. The Merritt Parkway, built in 1935 for cars only, was placed on the National Register of Historic Places in 1993. For more information, see the section TRAVEL.

GREENWICH

POPULATION & HOUSING

The population of Greenwich grew until about 1970. Since 1970, the resident population has been stable or declining slightly. This has been accompanied by the construction or conversion of more dwellings to house the same number of people. In 1950, the population of 40,835 lived in 10,524 households, with an average of 3.9 persons in each. In 1990, the population of 58,441 persons lived in 23,515 households, with an average of 2.6 persons. Two-thirds of Greenwich homes are for single families, mostly detached, one to a lot. The town's residential zones provide a wide variety of housing types, from small condominiums to single-family homes of more than 10,000 square feet on four acres or more. Greenwich is divided into several strictly enforced zoning areas. In or near town, the density is high as a result of condominiums and apartments. Further from the center of town, the zoning changes to one acre per family, then to two acres per family and north of the Merritt Parkway it is a minimum of 4 acres per family. The population of the town continues to be diverse. One-sixth of all public school students, with thirty-eight different first languages, are learning English as a second language.

JOBS & INCOME

Greenwich is a job center where 33,093 people are employed. More people now come to work in Greenwich than go to work elsewhere. As a result of the many offices moving to the suburbs, Greenwich has become a net provider of jobs during the past twenty-five years. At the same time the median household income in Greenwich has been growing steadily. In 1979 it was $30,278. Ten years later, in 1989, it was $65,072. Today it is over $80,000.

GREENWICH

TAXES

The Town of Greenwich operates on a "pay as you go" basis and does not carry debt. This allows Greenwich to keep property taxes low while maintaining a budget of over $183,000,000. Real estate taxes are based on assessments limited by statute to 70% of market value (presently 17.70 cents + sewer .85 cents per thousand of assessed value (mill rate)). There are no separate school taxes. There is a personal property tax on cars equal to the mill rate. There is no town income tax. The state has an income tax of 0.044 (4.4%). By 2017, the state inheritance tax will be phased out.

CRIME

Greenwich is rated the safest community in Connecticut and one of the safest in the country - and it's no wonder: with fourteen police cars on the road at all times, traffic downtown directed by police officers, with a force of 158 police officers, the average response time to a call is less than four minutes.

TRENDS

Greenwich is in the largest metropolitan area of the United States, and is fortunate in its location, natural features, and historic development. Within the New York metropolitan area, Greenwich is the most desirable place to live. The migration of business and jobs from New York City to White Plains, Greenwich and Stamford has increased the demand for housing here. Greenwich intends to keep its place as the premier town to live in. To maintain control of its future, Greenwich has developed a new Plan of Conservation and Development. This plan, filled with maps and information on the town, will be very influential in preserving the town's goals. It can be purchased from the Planning & Zoning Commission at Town Hall, 622.7700. Greenwich is also bringing its information systems to meet the needs of the 21st century. The town is working on a Geographic Information System (GIS) which will allow the town and residents to access information such as property boundaries, assessments and building lines.

GREENWICH

GOVERNMENT

www.state.ct.us/munic/Greenwich

Unlike many towns and cities, there is a great feeling of community here. Greenwich is run primarily by volunteers, not politicians. The town is governed by a Board of Selectmen (one full time and two part-time) who are elected every two years. Although town departments are staffed by paid professionals, except for the Selectmen, all town boards (such as the Board of Estimate and Taxation, which serves as the town's comptroller) and the Representative Town Meeting, are made up of unpaid citizen volunteers. In addition to the volunteers in government offices, Greenwich depends on many residents who serve in unofficial capacities. The volunteer network supports and supplements the work of town departments and gives the town its unique cultural and social values.

REPRESENTATIVE TOWN MEETING

Greenwich still retains the traditional New England Representative Town Meeting (RTM). The RTM consists of 230 members selected by the voters in the town's 12 districts. It is larger than the State's House and Senate combined. Candidates run on a non-partisan basis and serve without compensation. As a result, the composition of the RTM is very egalitarian. The RTM serves as the town's legislative body and most issues of importance, including appointments, labor contracts, town expenditures over $5,000, town ordinances and the town budget, must be approved by the RTM. Any town issue may be brought before the RTM by a petition of twenty registered voters. Because many of the RTM members are quite successful in business and other careers, the town is run efficiently, honestly, conservatively and in the interest of its citizens.

RTM meetings are held at night about once every month. RTM meetings are open to everyone and are a good source of information about the town. Call the League of Women Voters (352.4700) for a schedule. The League is very active and is a great way to get involved. They publish an informative guide on Greenwich Government, *People Make it Happen*.

GREENWICH

VOTER REGISTRATION

622.7889, 7890

You must be registered at least fourteen days before a regular election and by noon of the last business day before a party primary. You must be registered by the day before a special election or referendum.

HISTORY

Greenwich is the tenth oldest town in Connecticut. Named after Greenwich, England, the town began as a temporary trading post founded by Captain Adrian Block in 1614. Greenwich was settled in 1640 when it was purchased from the Indians as part of the New Haven Colony, with allegiance to England. The settlers grew restless under the Puritan influence and, in 1642, the settlers withdrew their allegiance to England and transferred it to the more liberal Dutch. At this time, the Cos Cob section of Greenwich was occupied by the Siwanoy Indians and a toll gate was set up between them and the central part of Greenwich, called Horseneck. In about ten years the town was forced back under the domination of the New Haven Colony. Greenwich supported the British during the French and Indian War, but during the Revolution the town was sacked several times by the King's troops. The advent of the New Haven Railroad in 1848 began the transformation of Greenwich into a residential community. This period saw many wealthy New Yorkers, including Boss Tweed, building summer homes. In the twenties, the town began to grow rapidly and land values began to soar. By 1928, Greenwich led the nation in per capita wealth. In 1933 the town had grown so large that it had to abandon open town meetings and adopted the Representative Town Meeting (RTM). Although the population growth has abated (because of the scarcity of buildable land) the property values have continued to climb.

The Greenwich Library and The Greenwich Historical Society have developed an Oral History of Greenwich. This program records the memories of residents who were influential in the town's development or who observed important events in the town's history. The Library has more than 130 volumes of recorded conversations. These interviews are a unique and wonderful way to learn about the town.

GREENWICH LAYOUT

AREAS & VILLAGES

Greenwich is made up of a number of small villages and neighborhoods, each with it own character and charm. The largest of these are: Byram, Banksville, Back Country, Central, Cos Cob, Mianus, Old Greenwich, Glenville, Riverside. All parts of Greenwich share the same government, school system, property tax rate and access to public facilities.

AREA CODES

See Greenwich Telephone system under HOME, UTILITIES.

ZIP CODES

See POST OFFICES & ZIP CODES.

GREENWICH LAYOUT

MAIN STREETS

The central street connecting the main part of Greenwich with the Riverside, Cos Cob, and Old Greenwich sections is Putnam Avenue (aka Post Road, US 1). It runs essentially east to west through the town (of course out-of-town maps show US 1 running North/South from Stamford to Port Chester). Greenwich Avenue, the main shopping street, is the dividing line between East and West Putnam Avenue. Sound Beach Avenue on the eastern end of Putnam Avenue, is the main shopping street for Old Greenwich and runs to the Greenwich Beach.

HIGHWAY MAP

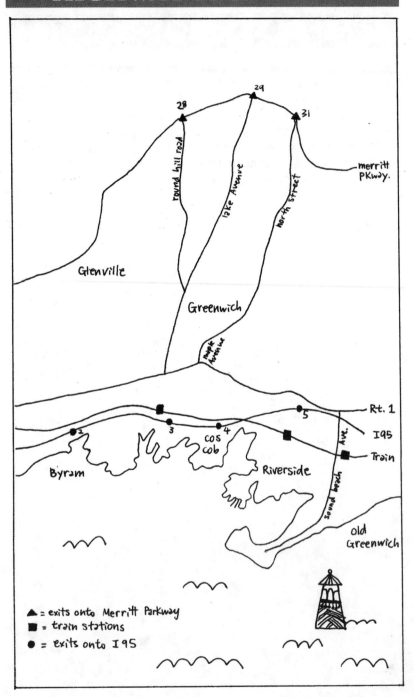

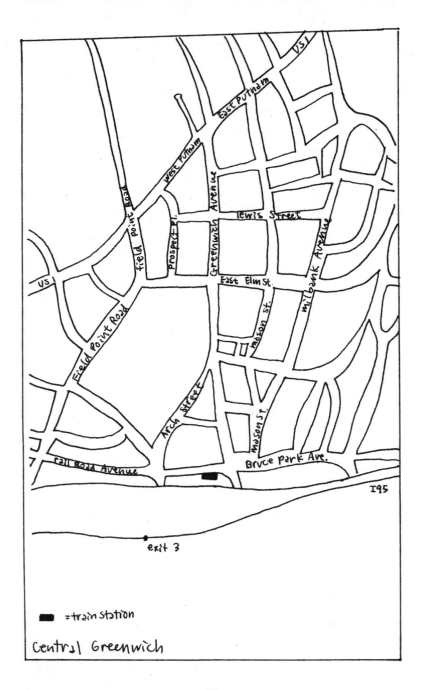

Central Greenwich

■ = train station

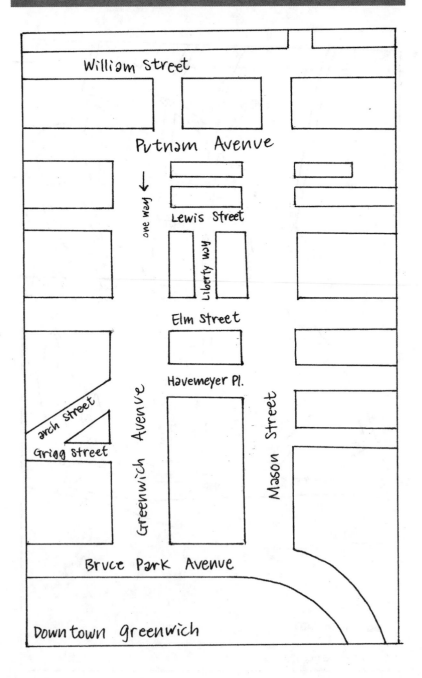

ANIMALS

INTRODUCTION

Pets, popular in Greenwich, bring great cheer to their owners and often assume the role of "Head of the Household." Over 1,600 dogs are masters of homes in Greenwich. If you hear someone calling - Maggie, Max, Sabrina, Buddy, Sam, Molly or Jake - chances are it isn't a child being summoned.

DOG OBEDIENCE

Invisible Fencing
Stamford, 800.628.2264
A safe way to keep your dog in your yard. Also works to keep your pet out of designated rooms in your home.
Hours: Weekdays, 8:30 am to 5 pm; Saturday, 8:30 am to 1 pm.

Dog Training
622.9695
Held at the Round Hill Community House, 397 Round Hill Road.
They offer very good dog obedience classes, conducted by Ken Berenson's Canine Services. For more information, call Ken at 914.699.4982.

ANIMALS

PETS

Adopt-A-Dog
629.9494
Since 1981, this unique, local, not-for-profit animal agency has helped over 7,000 homeless dogs find loving families. If you have a soft spot in your heart for animals, consider adopting or becoming a foster "parent." You are always welcome to call or visit their kennels. They hold the annual show, "Puttin' on the Dog."

Connecticut Canine Law
Dogs over six months of age must have a license issued by the Town Clerk's office (622.7897) in town hall (8 am to 4 pm), and the dog must be immunized against rabies.

Connecticut Humane Society
Stamford, CT 324.9269
Although the Greenwich Animal Shelter sometimes has pets to adopt, the Humane Society is the major area resource. They maintain a lost-and-found file and will come to your home to remove injured or sick wild animals or birds.
Hours: Weekdays, 10 am - 4:45 pm (Thursday to 5:45); Saturday, 10 am - 3:45 pm.

Greenwich Kennel Club
Cos Cob Community Center, 54 Bible Street,
Cos Cob, 203.426.6586 or 203.426.2881
The GKC is a non-profit organization whose membership is comprised of area dog enthusiasts with interests in conformation, obedience and performance events. The GKC holds an annual all-breed dog show every June. If you are not sure whether you want to bring a beagle or vizsla into your home, attend this show. It is a wonderful way to meet them all, as well as to find a suitable breeder.

House of Fins
99 Bruce Park Avenue, 661.8131
Everything you need to make a successful aquarium, and good advice as well.
Hours: Monday - Saturday, 10 am - 7 pm; Sunday, 10 am - 5 pm.

ANIMALS

PETS

Lost Pet Department of *The Greenwich Post*
861.9191
If you have lost a pet, send a picture with all information to The Greenwich Post, 22 West Putnam Avenue, Greenwich, CT 06830, or fax the description to 861.9442.

Pet Pantry
290 Railroad Avenue, 869.6444
Large store with a gigantic inventory. Friendly, helpful service.
Hours: Weekdays, 8 am - 6 pm; Saturday, 9 am - 5 pm.

Project Save-A-Cat
661.6855
A non-profit organization managed by volunteers.
Call to arrange an adoption.

Puttin' On The Dog - Annual Dog Show
Roger Sherman Baldwin Park, Late September
Run by Adopt-a-Dog, 849 Lake Avenue, 629.9494, this show is a great place to show your dog, learn about dogs, or adopt a new friend. Always a hit with children - of all ages.

Walkin' Dogs
203.322.3652
Laura and Aileen have been caring for pets in their homes for the last eleven years. They are a great alternative to kenneling. They will also keep your plants watered. $15- $20 per day.

PLEASE NOTE: All town parks require dogs to be on a leash.

ANIMALS

VETERINARIANS

Greenwich Animal Hospital
430 West Putnam Avenue, 869.0534
Here you'll find competent, compassionate doctors. Full service including boarding and bathing.
Hours: Weekdays, 8:30 am - 6 pm; Saturday, 8:30 am - 3 pm.

Just Cats Hospital
1110 East Main Street, Stamford, CT 327.7220
Located off of I-95 at exit 9. They provide excellent medical
services, boarding, grooming and TLC, just for cats.
Hours: Weekdays, 7:30 am - 8 pm (Friday until 6 pm); Saturday, 8 am - 5 pm.
Directions: I-95N to Exit 9; L at light; L on East Main.

Parkside Hospital for Animals
336 West Putnam Avenue, 661.6493
For over twenty years, Dr. Vitka has cared for many of Greenwich
resident's best friends with skill and loving care.
Hours: Available around the clock. All visits are by appointment.

Veterinarian Referral & Emergency Center
123 West Cedar Street, Norwalk CT, 203.854.9960
If your vet is not available, this is a wonderful emergency room for
your pet. During normal hours, appointments must be made for specialists.
Hours: 24-hours a day, 7 days a week.
Directions: I-95 N to Exit 13; R on US 1; L on W Taylor; L on W Cedar.

ANIMALS

WILDLIFE & ANIMAL RESCUE

Animal Control

Dog Pound, Museum Drive, 622.8299, 622.8081
A Town of Greenwich Police Department service that handles dead or sick animals as well as stray dogs. We have a kind animal control officer, Allyson Halm. If your pet is missing, call her first. A few dogs are available here for adoption.
Hours: Every day, 8 am - 3:30 pm.

Bats and Wildlife

323.0468
They carefully remove wildlife from your home and relocate it so you won't have unwanted pets. They can also help prevent furry intrusions.

Northeast Working Dogs

914.937.4421
If you have too many Canada Geese on your lawn this is the place to go for effective and humane control. A husband and wife team, Rob and Betsy Drummond, use border collies to herd the geese off your property. Treatment often takes six weeks or more.

Wild Life Trust

Contact: Jean and Buzz Seward, 869.5415
They take in orphaned and injured mammals and birds. This incredible Greenwich couple also breed endangered species.
Hours: Weekdays, 9 am - 5 pm.

Wild Wings, Inc.

637.9822 or 967.2121
Alison Taintor and Meredith Sampson are state and federally licensed wildlife rehabilitators who operate a wildlife rescue and rehabilitation center in Old Greenwich and Stamford. They respond to oil spill emergencies that affect wildlife.
Hours: They are on call 24 hours a day, 7 days a week for emergencies. For general information, call weekdays, 9 am - 5 pm.

AUTOMOBILES

Travel Information

Local commuters can untangle their morning commutes by consulting the following commuter transportation web sites:

> **MetroPool:** www.metropool.com
> The site offers news and information on commuting in and around Fairfield and Westchester counties:
>
> **TravTips** www.TravTips.net
> The latest traffic information for Connecticut.

Car Wash Center of Greenwich (SPLASH)

625 West Putnam Avenue, 531.4497
Hours: Weekdays, 9 am - 6 pm (Friday until 7 pm); Saturday, 8 am - 6 pm; Sunday, 9 am - 3 pm.

Classic Shine Auto Fitness Center

67 Church Street, 629.8077
This car detailing firm does not often advertise, but has been in business for many, many years. They operate on the strength of recommendations alone.

Concours of Elegance

To exibit a concours-quality car call Bruce and
Genia Wennerstrom, 661.1669 (Co-chairs)
The Concours takes place in the Roger Sherman Baldwin Park the weekend after Memorial Day is observed. This exciting event for all ages features an exhibit of outstanding motor-cars from the last decade of the nineteenth century through the late 1970's. It is one of the most prestigious Concours events in the country, attracting over 10,000 spectators.
Hours: 10 am - 5 pm.

Cos Cob Car Wash

73 Post Road, Cos Cob, 625.0809
A good place to have your car cleaned, inside and out.
Hours: Monday to Saturday, 8 am - 4:45 pm.

AUTOMOBILES

Department of Motor Vehicles Bureau

540 Main Avenue (Route 7), Norwalk, CT, 800.842.8222
860.263.5700   www.dmv.ct.org

New residents must obtain a Connecticut driver's license within sixty days, even if they hold a valid license from another state. Vehicles must also be registered within sixty days after the owner has established residency. The car must pass an inspection before being registered.

Hours: Tuesday - Saturday, 8 am - 4:30 pm (Thursday, until 7:30 pm, Saturday, until 12:30 pm); Closed Sunday, Monday and holidays.

Directions: I-95 N to exit 15, Rte 7 N; follow Rte 7 expressway to end, R and straight into the DMV.

Driver's License Renewals

Licenses can be renewed at the DMV in Norwalk or at the Connecticut License Bus, which stops in front of Town Hall the first Tuesday of every month from to 10 am - 6 pm.

Hank May's Goodyear

285 Boston Post Road (Route 1), Port Chester, NY, 914.937.0700

Eddie Jones, manager of this tire and service shop, can be trusted to give you the right information and great service.

Hours: Weekdays, 7 am - 6 pm; Saturday, 7 am - 5 pm.

Parking Meters

Parking meters in Greenwich are not expensive, but parking tickets are. Parking meters are a must weekdays from 9 am to 5 pm and Saturday 9 am - noon. On Sundays and holidays, parking is free. Old Greenwich is still free of parking meters.

Parking Permits

622.7730

Call for details about train station parking permits and the location of municipal lots.

Police Directing Traffic

We still have the privilege of having police direct traffic on Greenwich Avenue. They are always helpful and friendly. When you can't find something, they are a great source of information.

However, be warned - pedestrians and drivers alike are expected to pay attention. Follow their crossing instructions or face humiliation!

AUTOMOBILES

Vehicle Inspection

Automobiles must pass an emissions test annually. The nearest inspection station is located on I-95 between exits 9 and 10 in Darien. Call 800.842.8222 for directions and times.

VEHICLE RENTALS

Enterprise Rent-a-Car

16 Old Track Road   622.1611   www.Enterprise.com
They often have the lowest rates, but charge for mileage.
Hours: Weekdays, 7:30 am - 6 pm; Saturday, 9 am - noon.

Hertz Rent-a-Car

111 West Putnam Avenue, 800.654.3131   www.Hertz.com
At the Exxon Station next to the Library, 622.4044
Hours: Weekdays, 6:30 am - 6:30 pm; Saturday, 9 am - noon.

Ryder Truck Rentals

142 Railroad Avenue, 661.5548   www.Ryder.com
At the Mobil gas station. Hassle-free.
Hours: Every day, 7 am - 7 pm.

CHILDREN

INTRODUCTION

Children are our most treasured citizens. Greenwich has the top-rated school system in Connecticut and is ranked among the best in the country. Children nurtured in Greenwich have unique opportunities to develop their skills and to grow into happy, healthy, mature individuals. Young people in Greenwich have lots of fun.

AFTER-SCHOOL PROGRAMS

The following elementary schools have on-site after-school child care programs for students enrolled in that school:

Cos Cob School, 869.4670
Glenville School, 531.9287
Hamilton Avenue School, 869.1685 (2nd grade scholars)
Julian Curtiss School, 869.1896
New Lebanon School, 531.9139
North Mianus School, 637.9730
North Street School, 869.6756
Old Greenwich School, 637.0150
Parkway School, 869.7466
Riverside School, 637.1440

BANC
Byram Archibald Neighborhood Center
After School Program
289 Delavan Avenue, 622.7788
Ages: 5 - 13 yrs. Four days per week.
Follows public school calendar.

Children's Center of Cos Cob Inc.
300 East Putnam Avenue, 625.5569

CHILDREN

AFTER-SCHOOL PROGRAMS

Girls Inc.

Western Civic Center, 531.5699

Girls, grades 1 - 5, Hours: 2:45 - 4:45 pm.

An excellent four day-a-week, math and science-based enrichment program for girls. Girls are picked up from Julian Curtiss, Hamilton Avenue & New Lebanon Elementary Schools, taken to Western Civic Center and returned to the school by 4:45. They have an excellent summer camp.

Greenwich Boys and Girls Club

Horseneck Lane, 869.3224

Co-ed, Ages: 6 and up, Hours: 3 - 9 pm. On school holidays, the program starts at 8:30 am. Summer hours are 8 am - 6:30 pm.

Kaleidoscope - YWCA

259 East Putnam Avenue, 869.6501, x 225

Co-ed, Ages: K - grade 5, Hours: 2:30 - 6 pm. Follows the public school schedule, including early release days. Social, educational and recreational enrichment. Transportation is provided from all Greenwich schools. Kaleidoscope also provides childcare services during school closings for holidays and vacations.

Rainbow Express - YMCA

869.3381.

They run after-school childcare programs at Hamilton Avenue, New Lebanon, Julian Curtiss, North Street, North Mianus and Parkway Elementary Schools.

CHILDREN

BABYSITTING

Au Pair & Nannies Club
YWCA, 259 East Putnam Avenue, 869.6501 x 248
Area nannies meet to share care-giving ideas and to make new friends.

Babysitting Training
231 East Putnam Avenue, 869.8444
If your son or daughter wants to be a babysitter, the Red Cross sponsors a comprehensive five-hour babysitting course which is open to 11 - 14 year-olds.

Child Care and Parenting Services
A wonderful pamphlet compiled by Community Answers and Greenwich Early Childhood Council. Available at the Community Answers desk at the Greenwich Library.

Child Care Infoline
800.505.1000
They provide information on licensed daycare, summer camps and nursery school programs throughout Connecticut.

Helping Hands
869.9217
An au-pair/nanny service that has been in business for ten years and focuses on the local area. Their new Child Temp Service offers weekend, evening and occasional babysitting.

CHILDREN

BABYSITTING

Kid's Night Out
YMCA, 50 East Putnam Avenue, 869.1630
On the second and last Friday of every month, parents of children in grades K - 6 can enjoy an evening out, while their children enjoy an inexpensive, fun, safe night of activities, including gym games, swimming, movies, popcorn and board games.

Pumpkin Prep
24 Valleywood Road, Cos Cob, 869.5616
When you need to run an errand, use this licensed, drop-off childcare facility run by Loretta Polvere. She will take children from two months to five years. Call in advance, she is limited to six children at a time. Hours: 9 am - 1 pm.

Student Employment Service
Greenwich High School, 625.8008, 8000
The office has limited hours, keep trying. During the summer, the service is run through Community Answers, 622.7979.
Children, ages 3 - 4. Full-day, year-round child care; tuition based on need.

CHILDREN

CHILDCARE

Christian Day School
139 East Putnam Avenue, 869.5395
Children, Ages 6 weeks - 5 years; Hours: 7:45 - 5:30 pm.

Family Center
Joan Warburg Early Childhood Center
22 Bridge Street, 629.2822
Children, ages 6 weeks - 2 years; Hours: 7:30 - 6 pm.

Gateway School
2 Chapel Street, 531.8430
Children, ages 3 - 4. Full-day, year-round childcare; tuition based on need.
Hours: 7:30 am - 6 pm.

Little Angels Play Group
Greenwich Catholic School
471 North Street, 869.4000
Children, ages 3 - 4; hours: 1 pm - 3 pm. Pre-K program,
Ages 4 - 5; 8:30 am - noon.

Tutor Time
25 Valley Drive, 861.6549
Children, ages 6 weeks - 5 years; hours: 6:30 am - 6:30 pm.
Early drop off, 6:30 am; late pick-up, 6:30 pm.
Also 3- and 5-day programs, either half or full-day.

YMCA Magic Rainbow
2 Saint Roch Avenue, 869.3381
Children, ages: 6 weeks to 5 years.
All-day, year-round childcare. Hours: 7:30 am - 5:30 pm.

YWCA Playroom and Playroom Plus
259 East Putnam Avenue, 869.6501 x 221
Children, ages 15 months - 3 years. Professional on-site childcare services, either for parents attending Y classes or pursuing off-site activities. Morning or afternoon sessions available.

CHILD ENRICHMENT

ART

Art Workshop for Juniors

Greenwich Art Society, 299 Greenwich Avenue, 629.1533
Elaine Huyer teaches children a lively, creative course in all media: clay, paint and collage to children ages 7 to 11.
Hours: Classes are conducted year-round. In the winter, classes are held after school on Tuesdays and Wednesdays, 3:45 am - 5:30 pm.

Easel in the Gallery

Bruce Museum, 1 Museum Drive, 869.0376, x 325
Experts teach children from kindergarten through 5th grade. Children explore the current Bruce Museum exhibits, sketching in the galleries and creating art projects inspired by what they have seen.

Parent & Child Art Work Shop

YWCA, 259 East Putnam Avenue, 869.6501
Multi-media art projects from paints to clay for children 2½ to 4.

COMPUTERS

Children's Computer Corner

At YWCA, 259 East Putnam Avenue, 869.6501
For children ages 9 - 12, introduction to computers and programming.

Computer Tots

At YWCA, 259 East Putnam Avenue, 869.6501
Hands-on classes for ages 3 - 5.

PC Playhouse

321 Greenwich Avenue, 861.7510
www.pcplayhouse.com
For group or individual classes (or a concentrated computer camp) they teach beginning reader and young adults (ages 2 to about 12) the basics of computer operation placing an emphasis on academics—from story writing and art to math. A large selection of good children's software is available. They also offer basic computer training for adults.
Hours: Monday - Saturday, 9 am - 6 pm.

CHILD ENRICHMENT
DANCE & ETIQUETTE

Allegra Dance Studio
37 West Putnam Avenue, 629.9162
Claudia Fletcher has been teaching dance to children in Greenwich for over twenty-five years. Ages 3 - adult; classes in jazz, ballet, tap and modern.

Barclay Ballroom Dancing for Young Children
Lois Thompson, Director, 908.232.8370
Friday evening classes, starting in September, are held at the Round Hill Community Center. The one-hour classes teach ballroom dancing and polite socialization to children in grades 4, 5, & 6. Children's attire is dressy. Girls should apply early.

Dance Adventure
230 Mason Street, 625.0930
www.danceadventure.com
Programs for parent and child, 4 months to 2½ years; pre-ballet for ages 3 - 5; ballet, tap & jazz for 1st graders to teens.
See also Greenwich Ballet Workshop.

Magic Dance
YMCA, 50 East Putnam Avenue, 869.1630
Directed by Audrey Appleby, children have a wide choice of programs: fun and fundamentals, jazz, street dance or classical ballet for ages:15 months and up.
Magic Dance also offers singing, acting and vocal coaching for children auditioning for television or theater.

Mayfair Ballroom Dancing for Young Children
Dorina Link 869.7016 or call the Brunswick School (625.5800)
Mayfair is sponsored by the Brunswick Parents Association, but is open to all children in Greenwich. Like Barclay, they teach ballroom dancing and etiquette to children in grades 4, 5, 6. Friday evening classes start in September and are usually taught at Brunswick. If you have a boy who wants to attend, there is usually no problem. For girls, there may be a waiting list.

CHILD ENRICHMENT
DANCE & ETIQUETTE

Greenwich Ballet Workshop
Directed by Felicity Foote, 869.9373
Felicity coaches dedicated children who want to look their very best on stage. See her Ambassador in Leotard Program under Young Adults.

Young Etiquette
591 Riversville Road, 629.6123
To help tame the little monster in your house. A variety of classes on etiquette for young ladies and gentlemen, including how to behave in social gatherings, how to give a gift, and table manners.

CHILD ENRICHMENT

GYMNASTICS

Monkey Business
Greenwich Civic Center, 90 Harding Road
Contact Sandy Del Vecchio, 532.4911.
Classes for children, ages 18 months to 6 years. Summer camps for children 3 - 6 years. They also do fun children's parties.

US Academy of Gymnastics
6 Riverside Avenue, Riverside, 637.3303
Tumble Bugs and Snuggle Bugs for children 18 months to 5 years. Serious gymnastics training for children from 1st grade through high school.

YWCA Programs
259 East Putnam Avenue, 869.6501
Jelly Beans - ages 16 - 36 months.
Tumble Tots - ages 2½ - 3 years.
Pre-Gymnastics - ages 3 - 5 years.
Gymnastics - ages 6 - 8; 9 and over.
Advanced Gymnastics.

YMCA Programs
50 East Putnam Avenue, 869.1630
Baby Power - 12 to 24 months.
Toddler Gym - 24 to 36 months.
Rockers - 3 to 4 years.
Rollers - 4 and 5 years.
Beginner - 6 to 10 years.
Intermediate - 6 to 10 years.

CHILD ENRICHMENT

LANGUAGES

Alliance Française
299 Greenwich Avenue, 629.1240
Classes for beginners, intermediate and advanced are given in the French Center for children ages 3 - 13. Their latest program, "Total Body Response" for children ages 3 - 5, teaches French through games, songs and music. On Tuesdays French classes are offered for native French-speaking children who are enrolled in English-speaking schools.

German School
135 School Road, Weston, CT, 203.222.1228, 792.2795
50 Partridge Road, White Plains, NY, 914.948.6513
www.dsny.org
Saturday morning German language and cultural instruction for novice to native speakers. Available for children preschool through high school. They also have an adult program. Closed during the summer. Classes begin in September.

Language Workshop for Children
914.722.1537
Headquartered in NY at 888 Lexington Ave, 212.396.1369, they have a branch in Greenwich. Morning and afternoon programs for children 6 months - 3 years, accompanied by a caregiver: French for Tots, Spanish for Tots and Le Petite French. Preschool for children 3 - 5 years. Programs for children 3 - 12: French for Children, Spanish for Children, Japanese for Children. New York City only programs for children 3 - 12 during the summer. Winter & spring breaks: Le Club des Enfants (French-American Day Camp), El Club de los Niños (Spanish-American Day Camp). Classes are conducted in Greenwich at the First United Methodist Church across from the YMCA.

CHILD ENRICHMENT

MUSIC

Atelier Constantin Popescu
1139 East Putnam Avenue, Riverside, 637.7421
Sells, repairs and rents string instruments.
Hours: Weekdays, 10 am - 6 pm; Saturday, 10 am - 2 pm.

Kinder Music
23 Clark Street, Old Greenwich, 637.0461
Pre-instrumental programs for infants to 8 years. A delightful way to
begin a child's love of music.
Hours: Monday - Saturday, morning and afternoon sessions.

Music Academy
YWCA, 259 East Putnam Avenue, 869.6501
Contact: 914.761.3715
High-quality, individual instrumental instruction for children in violin,
Suzuki violin, piano, guitar and woodwinds, provided by the Music
Conservatory of Westchester. Music theory lessons also available.

Young Artists Philharmonic
PO Box 3301, Ridgeway Station, Stamford, CT 532.1278
A regional youth symphony organization for talented youngsters. They've
been playing for over forty years.

CHILD ENRICHMENT

READING

Preschool Stories

Preschool stories in the mornings most weekdays. During the summer, stories may be read in a nearby park.

Byram-Shubert Library, 21 Mead Avenue, Byram, 531.0426
Cos Cob Library, 5 Sinoway Road, Cos Cob, 622.6883
Greenwich Library, 110 West Putnam Avenue, 622.7900
Perrot Library, 90 Sound Beach Avenue, Old Greenwich, 637.1066

Tales at Twilight

Greenwich Library, 110 West Putnam Avenue, 622.7900
The Children's Desk, 622.7942
Thursday evenings in the summer at 7 pm are a special time for parents and children. Children, dressed in pajamas, bring their favorite teddy bear and listen to stories.

Young Critics Club

Perrot Library, 90 Sound Beach Avenue, Old Greenwich, 637.1066
Children in grades 5 - 7, who love to read and talk about books, gather on Friday afternoons with Kate McClelland and Mary Clark for a guided discussion.

CHILDREN

FAIRS & CARNIVALS

These annual fairs - complete with midway rides, food tents and games - provide excellent, safe entertainment for young children and raise funds for good causes at the same time. Church fairs tend to run for five days (Wednesday to Sunday), from 6 to 10 pm on weekdays, and noon to 10 pm on weekends, although some of the spring carnivals may only last for two to four days. Be sure to call for the exact dates and times.

Cos Cob School Fair
300 East Putnam Avenue (early May), 869.4670

Glenville School Carnival
33 Riversville Road (late April), 531.9287

Mianus School Pow Wow
309 Palmer Hill Road (early May), 637.1623

St. Catherine's Carnival
4 Riverside Avenue (middle August), 637.3661

St. Paul's Episcopal Church
200 Riverside Avenue, (late May), 637.2447

St. Roch's Bazaar
10 Saint Roch Avenue, Byram (early August), 869.4176

United Way September Fest
Roger Sherman Baldwin Park at Arch Street
(middle September), 869.2221

CHILDREN

FAMILY OUTINGS

Many family museums are included here, however for a complete list of Museums see, CULTURE, MUSEUMS.

Audubon Center

613 Riversville Road, 869.5272
485-acre sanctuary, including 15 miles of trails and exhibits. Gift shop.
Hours: Open year-round except for major holidays, Tuesday - Sunday, 9 am - 5 pm.

Bridgeport Bluefish

Harbor Yard, 500 Main Street, Bridgeport, CT, 203.334.8199
Professional Minor League Baseball in the new Atlantic League.
Hours: May to September, Monday - Saturday, 7 pm; Sunday 1 pm.
Verify hours and ticket availability before you go.
Directions: I-95 N to exit 27.

Bronx Zoo

www.wcs.org/zoos
Fordham Road at Bronx River Parkway, Bronx, NY, 718.367.1010
World-class zoo with terrific rides and exhibits. Easy to find. Wednesdays are free.
Hours: Open year-round, weekdays, 10 am - 5 pm; Weekends and holidays, 10 am - 5:30 pm; November - March, 10 am - 4:30 pm.
Directions: (30-minutes) I-95 S to Pelham Pkw W; or Merritt Pkw S to Cross County Pkw W, then Bronx River Pkw S.

Bruce Museum

1 Museum Drive, 869.0376
www.brucemuseum.com
Recently expanded, they have impressive rotating exhibits and many programs for adults and children. They have a terrific gift shop with a large selection of books. The Museum has been accredited by the American Association of Museums, as being in the top 10 percent of US museums. The Museum sponsors two fairs in Bruce Park every year: the mid-May Craft Fair and the Columbus Day Arts Festival have juried artists from around the country and draw visitors from all over the area.
Hours: Tuesday - Saturday, 10 am - 5 pm; Sunday, 1 pm - 5 pm.

FAMILY OUTINGS

Bush-Holley House Museum

39 Strickland Road, Cos Cob, 869.6899

Home of the Historical Society, this is the place to learn about Greenwich history. They also have a good library and a shop with books on Greenwich history, as well as reproductions of nineteenth century children's toys and books. While you are there, pick up a list of their always informative programs.

Hours: April - December, Wednesday - Friday, noon - 4 pm; Saturday, 11 am - 4 pm, Sunday 1 am - 4 pm; January - March, Wednesday, noon - 4 pm, Saturday, 11 am - 4 pm; Sunday, 1 - 4 pm.

Discovery Museum

4450 Park Avenue, Bridgeport, CT, 203.372.3521

www.discoverymuseum.org

Hands-on art and science exhibits for children of all age levels, including their parents. A special section is devoted to preschoolers with dozens of attractions based on principles of early childhood development. Families who have discovered the Discovery Museum go there on a regular basis.

Hours: Tuesday - Saturday, 10 am - 5 pm; Sunday, noon - 5 pm.

Directions: Merritt Parkway N to exit 47, L on Park Avenue (1 mile S on L).

Essex Steam Train & Riverboat

Essex, CT, 860.767.0103, 800.377.3987

www.essex-steam-train.com

Take a trip back in history through the scenic Connecticut River valley. Passengers board the 1920 steam train at the Essex station for a one-hour ride. At Deep River Landing the train meets the river boat for a one-hour cruise. The North Cove Express offers brunch, lunch and dinner during a two-hour excursion. Call 860.621.9311 for reservations on the Dinner Train.

Hours: Call for seasonal hours.

Directions: I-95 N to exit 69, Rte. 9 N to exit 3, W 1/4 mile.

CHILDREN

FAMILY OUTINGS

IMAX Theater

At the Maritime Aquarium, 10 North Water Street, Norwalk, CT,
203.852.0700, www.MaritimeAquarium.org
With a screen that is sixstories high and eight stories wide and with a
24,000-watt sound system, the experience is awesome.
Hours: Open daily; September - June, 10 am - 5 pm; July - Labor Day, 10
am - 6 pm.
Directions: I-95 N to exit 14, R at light on West Ave, l at 3rd light on
North Main, L at light on Ann.

Jones Family Farm

266 Israel Hill Road & Route 110, Shelton, CT, 203.929.8425
This pick-your-own farm is in its thirtieth year. They have strawberries
in June, followed by blueberries in July and August, and pumpkins in
the autumn. In December, come and cut your own Christmas tree. They
even have hayrides in October.
Hours: Best to call, hours change seasonally. Closed Sunday & Monday; Summer hours, Tuesday - Friday, 8 am - 7:30 pm; Saturday, 8 am
- 5 pm.

Maritime Aquarium

10 North Water Street, Norwalk, CT, 203.852.0700
www.MaritimeAquarium.org
Interactive exhibits often including a Shark Touch Pool. Cited as one of
the 10 Great Aquariums to visit.
Hours: Open daily; September - June, 10 am - 5 pm;
July - Labor Day, 10 am - 6 pm.
Directions: I-95 N to exit 14. See directions for IMAX Theater above.

CHILDREN

FAMILY OUTINGS

Mystic Seaport and Museum

Mystic, CT, 860.572.0711   www.mysticseaport.org

Mystic is a two-hour drive. The Mystic Seaport Museum has a world-renowned waterfront collection of ships and crafts that tells the story of America and the sea. Mystic also has a good aquarium, with exciting special exhibits.

While in the Mystic area, stop by Stonington, which is about five miles east on US 1. Stonington is a nineteenth century fishing village which has kept its charm and has become a center for antique shops.

Don't forget Mystic Pizza - which inspired the movie. There is one in Mystic, 860.536.3700 and one in North Stonington, 860.599.5126.

Hours: Open every day except December 25th; Ships & exhibits, 9 am - 5 pm; Museum grounds, 9 am - 6 pm.

Directions: I-95 N to exit 90. Rte 27 S.

NY Botanical Gardens

Bronx, NY, 718.817.8705   www.nybg.org

They have recently undergone a $25 million renovation and are considered the best in the country.

Hours: Open year-round, Tuesday - Sunday, 10 am - 6 pm. Wednesdays are free.

Directions: (30 minutes) Merritt/Hutchinson Pkw S to exit 15; Cross County Pkw W to exit 6; Bronx River Pkw S to exit 8W (Mosholu Pkw), at second light, L into Garden.

Philipsburg Manor

Sleepy Hollow, NY, 914.631.8200, 914.631.3992
www.HudsonValley.org

An eighteenth century working farm, with water-powered grist mill and livestock. Tours are conducted by interpreters in eighteenth century costumes.

Hours: April - December, open every day except Tuesday, 10 am - 5 pm. Open on weekends in March; closed January & February.

Directions: I 287/87 W to exit 9; follow signs for Rte. 9.

CHILDREN

FAMILY OUTINGS

Playland Park
Playland Parkway, Rye, NY, 914.925.2701
www.co.westchester.ny.us/parks/PLAY.htm
Recently renovated amusement park, just 15 minutes away. A wide variety of rides for older kids from Go-Karts to Zombie Castle and Old Mill. Kiddyland has 20 of Playland's 45 rides. Playland also has a beach, swimming pool, lake cruises, ice casino, miniature golf and sightseeing cruises on Long Island Sound.
Hours: Open May to mid-September. The ice rink is open from October to April.
Directions: I-95 S exit 19.

Putnam Cottage
243 East Putnam Avenue, 869.9697
Originally a tavern serving travelers along the Post Road, it is now a museum owned by the Daughters of the American Revolution. Each year on the last Sunday in February (1 pm -3 pm), the Putnam Hill Revolutionary War battle is recreated. A definite must-see for adults and children alike.
Hours: Wednesday, Friday, Sunday, 1 pm - 4 pm.

Renaissance Faire
Route 17A, Sterling Forest, Tuxedo, NY, 914.351.5171, 5174
www.renfair.com
Over 300 actors, in costume, mingle with the visitors (who can also don costumes) in a mock sixteenth century village. A wonderful way to enjoy a day of improvisation and learning.
Hours: August 1st to September 20th, weekends only; 10:30 am - 7 pm.

Stamford Museum & Nature Center

39 Scofieldtown Road (corner of High Ridge Rd), Stamford, CT, 322.1646, www.StamfordMuseum.org

118-acres, with a 10-acre working farm, pond life exhibit, boardwalks, natural history exhibits, planetarium and observatory. If your child hasn't grown up on a farm, this is the perfect place to learn about farming and farm animals.

Hours: Open year-round except for major holidays, Monday - Saturday, 9 am - 5 pm; Sunday, 1 pm - 5 pm; planetarium shows Sunday at 3 pm; Observatory, Friday, 8 pm - 10 pm.

Directions: Merritt Parkway N, exit 35 (Rte 15).

United States Military Academy

West Point, NY, 914.938.2638

www.usma.edu/Tour

Start at the visitors center to get a free map and information on self-guided tours. Don't miss the military museum.

Hours: Open all year, dawn to dusk.

Directions: I-95 to I-287/I-87 (NYS Thruway). Over bridge, take exit 13N onto the Palisades Interstate Parkway heading north. Take the PIP north to its end (Bear Mountain traffic circle). Follow signs for Route 9W north (3rd exit off traffic circle). Exit 9W via West Point exit, Stony Lonesome exit, or Route 293 exit.

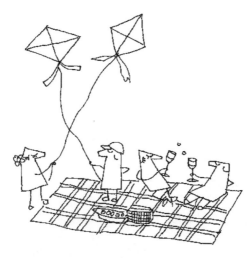

CHILDREN

PARENTING SERVICES

ARC Greenwich
531.1880
Family support services and after-school programs for families of children with special needs.

Center for Wellness and Preventive Medicine
Greenwich Health at Greenwich Hospital, 863.4444
Parents Exchange, parenting classes, infant car-seat loan program, preschool vision screening, Totsaver CPR, First Aid, anti-smoking education, TEL-MED.

Child Guidance Center of Southern Connecticut
259 East Putnam Avenue, 869.7187
Professionally-staffed mental health center for children and adolescents. Individual, group and family therapy, parent guidance, 24-hour crisis services, and community education programs.

Community Answers
622.7979
www.greenwich.lib.ct.us (click on the Community Answers link)
Information on parent education programs, support groups, crisis programs, counseling services, nannies, au-pair and babysitting services.

Family Health
Greenwich Department of Health, 622.6495
Prenatal and postpartum home visits, well-child clinics (birth to age 5), immunization and hypertension screening clinic (5 years to adult); school health services; early childhood/daycare licenses.

Kids in Crisis
622.6556
Crisis intervention counseling and short-term shelter.
Ages: Newborn - 17 years.

Le Leche League
869.5344, 637.7621
Support groups and information on breastfeeding.

CHILDREN

PARENTING SERVICES

Parents Exchange
Greenwich Health at Greenwich Hospital, 637.3771, 863.4444
Weekly discussion groups led by child development specialists. A good environment to stimulate and provide parents with opportunities to exchange ideas. Parents are grouped by their children's age from infants to adolescents. Babysitting is available.

Parents Together
P.O. Box 4843, Greenwich, CT, 06831-0417, 869.7379.
An independent, non-profit organization working in cooperation with the PTA Council and public and independent schools in Greenwich. They publish two newsletters: Birth to Age 10 and Ages 11 - 15. Consider their newsletter a must! For an annual subscription, send a check for $10 and indicate the newsletter you want to receive.

Parent to Parent Network
50 Glenville Street, 531.1880, ext. 2300.
Information network for families with children who have special needs.

Tender Beginnings
At Greenwich Hospital, 863.3655
Expectant parent classes, Lamaze classes, baby care and breastfeeding classes, nutrition, prenatal exercise, newborn parenting groups, grand parenting, baby food preparation, babysitting, sibling classes.

CHILDREN

PARTIES AT HOME

Many fabulous, fun parties are documented in Greenwich picture albums. Making children feel special on their birthday is not unique to Greenwich, but Greenwich parents find unique ways to do so. Many of the best parties are hosted by imaginative parents at home or in a town park. However if you want to consider assistance, the following may be of help:

Awesome Science Parties
203.227.8112, 800.311.9993
Hands-on, interactive parties - each child is involved with every experiment. Children have lots of science fun making edible gummy drops, or volcanos and launching rockets. Parties are age appropriate. They also do after school programs in our elementary schools.   Ages: 5 - 11.

Little Cooks
888.695.2665
They have a variety of upscale parties for different age groups and themes, including holidays and international cuisine (youngsters cook recipes from - and learn about - a country). Parties include invitations, party favors, chef hats, aprons and all ingredients.   Ages: 5 - 18.

Mad Science of CT
888.381.9754
Interactive experiments for children, combining science with entertainment. Party programs are tailored to the age group and can include: chemical magic, vortex generators, indoor fireworks, or model rocket launchings.   Ages: 5 - 12.

Pied Piper Pony Rides
203.431.8322
You may want to invite one of their gentle ponies and friendly staff members to your party. The children will have a good time and the pony droppings will be removed. Closes for the winter.

PARTIES AWAY FROM HOME

Adventure Kids

16 Old Track Road, 861.2227, 629.5641

www.AdventureKids.com

A fun, indoor place for young children to play. Combines play with learning. Cafeteria where parents can relax while their children run amuck safely.

Ages: 6 months - 12 years.

Hours: Daily 10 am - 7 pm; closed last two weeks of August and December 25th.

Elmsford Raceway

17 Raceway Lane (formerly North Payne Street), Elmsford, NY, 914.592.5375

For 33 years the del Rosario family has entertained children and their parents with 6½" slot car racing. They have recently relocated to a newer, better building - about twice the size of their old location.

Ages: 4 to 99.

Hours: Weekdays, noon to 9:30 pm; Saturday, 11 am - 9:30 pm; Sunday, noon - 7 pm.

Directions: I-95 South to I-287 West, exit 2, R at light, N ½ mile, L onto Raceway.

CHILDREN

PARTIES AWAY FROM HOME

Magic Dance
622.0744
Magic Dance tailors parties for 1 to 5 year olds to the child's favorite music themes and characters, with dance, improvisation and lots of imagination. 6 years through teen parties may feature street dance/hip hop or dancing & acting Broadway or movie themes. Parents provide refreshments. Parties can be in their studio or in your home.
Ages: Programs for all ages.   Hours: Call for scheduling.

Nimble Thimble
19 Putnam Avenue, Port Chester, NY, 914.934.2934
Choose a project for your age group - for instance, make a fabric covered bulletin board or a vest. Parents can bring cake and ice cream.
Ages: 5 and up.
Hours: Monday - Saturday, 10 am - 7 pm.

Paintin' Place
79 East Putnam Avenue, 203-629-0263
Discover the artist in your child and in yourself. A paint-your-own pottery studio with numerous clay pieces to choose from and a variety of colors. Perfect for chasing away the rainy day blues.
Hours: Monday - Tuesday 10 am - 6 pm, closed Wednesdays, Thursday 10 am - 10 am, Friday - Saturday 10 am - 6 pm, Sunday 12 - 6.

PC Playhouse
321 Greenwich Avenue, 861.7510,   www.pcplayhouse.com
Learn and have fun on computers. Every child designs their own tee shirt or mouse pad. Ages: 4 to 12.
Hours: Monday - Saturday, 9 am - 6 pm.

United Studios of Self Defense
202 Field Point Road, 629.4666
A party where children can learn karate.   Ages: 4 to 7.
Hours: Saturday parties, noon - 2 pm.

CHILDREN

PARTIES AWAY FROM HOME

YWCA

259 East Putnam Avenue, 869.6501

Rent a party room and/or hire one of their special instructors to teach the children activities such as swimming, gymnastics or climbing their rock wall. Parents provide the refreshments. All ages.

Hours: Parties are held during regular Y hours: weekdays, 6:30 am - 10 pm; Saturday, 7:30 am - 5 pm (Summer Saturday hours are shorter).

YMCA

50 East Putnam Avenue, 869.1630

Rent the gym, pool, roller blade or tennis court for your party with cake and presents in the Rendevous room. The Y can even provide a clown or magician.

Hours: Weedays, 5 am - 10 pm; Saturday, 6:30 am - 7 pm; Sunday, 8 am - 5 pm (Summer hours may be shorter).

All ages.

CHILDREN
PARTY SUPPLIES

Party City
535 Boston Post Road,
Port Chester, NY, 914.939.6900
A giant store with an impressive inventory of party supplies. Like the Strauss Warehouse Outlet, they have a very large assortment of Halloween costumes during the season.
Hours: Monday - Saturday, 9:30 am - 9 pm; Sunday, 10 am - 6 pm.

Party Paper and Things
403 East Putnam Avenue (Cos Cob Plaza), 661.1255
A good selection of high-quality party paper goods, wrapping paper, picnic take-out dishes and lots of balloons. Whether you need just one balloon to send to a friend in the hospital or several dozen for a birthday party, they will deliver for a very modest fee.
Hours: Monday - Saturday, 10 am - 5:30 pm.

PM Amusements
36 Bush Avenue, Port Chester, 914.937.1188
This is the ultimate party rental source. If you want to turn your backyard into an amusement park or just rent a cotton candy machine, they have it all. Ask about sumo wrestling, a velcro wall, miniature golf, karaoke, clowns, inflatable rides, or perhaps just an Abe Lincoln or Mick Jagger look-a-like /impersonator. Call and ask for their catalog.
Hours: Weekdays, 8 am - 5 pm; open sometimes on Saturday; call before going.
Directions: Post Road W to Main Street in Port Chester, R on Westchester, R on Haseco, R on Bush.

PARTY SUPPLIES

Strauss Warehouse Outlet

140 Horton Avenue, Port Chester, NY, 914.939.3544, 7132

Gift wrapping, party favors, balloons, paper goods, just about anything you might want for a party at great prices. They carry a huge selection of Halloween costumes during October.

Hours: Weekdays, 8 am - 7 pm; Saturday, 8 am - 5 pm; Sunday, 10 am - 3 pm.

Directions: Post Road to Main Street in Port Chester, R on Wilkins, L on Locust, R on Horton (Horton is a one-way).

Smith Party Rentals

133 Mason Street, 869-9315

A good source for children's tables, chairs and other party needs, just as they are for adult parties.

Hours: Monday - Saturday, 9 am - 5 pm.

CHILDREN

PLAYGROUNDS

Town playgrounds are open from 9 am - 4 pm. From late June through early August, the Greenwich Department of Parks and Recreation conducts supervised activities at the playgrounds for children ages 7 to 15. There are a number of small playgrounds scattered throughout the town (Binney Park, Bible Street Park, Christiano Park, Eastern and Western Greenwich Civic Centers, Island Beach and Loughlin Avenue Park), however, only a few are worth a trip if you don't live in that area. Our favorites are:

Bruce Park

60 acres, across from the Bruce Museum on Museum Drive. One of Greenwich's prettiest parks, with excellent play equipment.

Byram Park

30 acres, located on Ritch Avenue and Byram Shore Road in Byram. The park has an attractive beach area and the town's only public fresh water pool. (The playground is tucked behind the Byram Shore Boat Club.) How can you go wrong?

Greenwich Common

16 acres, located adjacent to Greenwich Avenue, with an entrance on Greenwich Avenue next to the Havemeyer Building (Board of Education). This is a wonderful place to rest during a busy shopping day and let your children play. The Common has a small, but attractive playground area.

Public Elementary Schools

These playgrounds are well-kept and extensive. They are available to residents during the weekends and summer when school is not in session. For more information on the location of the elementary schools, see the Public Elementary School section under SCHOOLS.

Western Greenwich Civic Center

10 acres, located on the corner of Glenville Road and Pemberwick Road, this playground is a favorite with kids.

CHILDREN

SCOUTING

Boy Scouts of America, Greenwich Council #67

63 Mason Street, 869.8424

www.bsa.scouting.org, www.scouts.com

This is the headquarters of the local chapter of the nonprofit organization dedicated to instilling ethical values in young people. The Scouts are fortunate to own the Seton Reservation, a large preserve located at 363 Riversville Road. It serves as the site for the Cub Scout day camp as well as many other scouting outdoor programs. Call to check on a troop near you. The chapter sponsors the following programs:

Programs open to boys: Tiger Cubs, age 6; Cub Scouts, ages 7 - 10; Boy Scouts, ages 11 - 18.

Programs open to boys and girls: Explorers, ages 14 - 20 (specialties: aviation, scuba, emergency rescue.)

The Greenwich office has a small store for uniforms. A larger selection is available at the Darien Sports Shop (1127 Post Road, Darien, CT, 203.655.2575), and the Connecticut-Yankee Council #72, Boy Scouts of America (in Norwalk, CT, exit 40A on the Merritt Parkway, 362 Main Avenue, 203.847.2445.

Hours: Greenwich Scouts office is open weekdays, 8:30 am - 4:30 pm.

Girl Scout Council of Southwestern Connecticut

529 Danbury Road, Wilton, CT, 800.882.5561, 203.762.5557

www.gsusa.org/

This is the headquarters of the local chapter of the nonprofit organization dedicated to addressing girls' current interests and their future roles as women. The current Executive Director is Betsy Keefer, the Greenwich Unit Manager is Joan Karasick.

Programs: Daises, kindergarten; Brownies, grades 1 - 3; Junior Girl Scouts, grades 4 - 6; Cadettes, grades 7 - 9; Seniors, grades 9 - 12.

Uniforms are available from Best & Co. in Greenwich and from the Darien Sports Shop, 1127 Post Road, Darien, CT, 203.655.2575.

Hours: Weekdays, 9 am - 5:30 pm, Thursday until 8:30 pm.

Indian Guides and Princesses

YMCA, 50 East Putnam Avenue, 869.1630

Outings and campouts for fathers and their kindergarten to 2nd grade children.

CHILDREN

SHOPS - CLOTHING & SHOES

Beame & Barre

260 Greenwich Avenue, 622.0591

Dance wear to suit even the most discriminating ballerina's tastes.

Hours: Weekdays, 10 am - 5:30 pm; Saturday, 10 am - 5 pm.

Best & Co.

289 Greenwich Avenue, 629.1743

Susie Hilfiger (wife of designer, Tommy Hilfiger) and Ellen Keogh, are a perfect team. They are mothers who know what children need and what's in style. They carry good quality basic clothing as well as high-end garments. The second floor carries wonderful children's furniture. If there were a best-dressed children's list, this would be their shop. Elegant, sophisticated clothing for newborns and youngsters. They also carry girl scout uniforms.

Hours: Monday - Saturday, 9 am - 5:30 pm.

Candy Nichols

68 Greenwich Avenue, 622.1220

Attractive children's clothing with a European flair.

Hours: Monday - Saturday, 9:30 am - 5:30 pm.

Children's Classics

254 Sound Beach Avenue, Old Greenwich, 698.3255

A delightful collection of first-rate children's clothing. Greenwich mothers frequent this shop for basic as well as beautiful garments.

Hours: Monday - Saturday, 9:30 am - 5:30 pm.

CHILDREN

SHOPS - CLOTHING & SHOES

Chillybear

401 Greenwich Avenue, 622.7115   www.chillybear.com

A store for the hip young adolescent. Filled with the latest garb as well as skateboards, in-line skates and accessories.

Hours: Monday - Saturday, 10 am - 6 pm; Sunday, noon - 5 pm.

Flight of Fancy

255 Greenwich Avenue, 661.1188

Children love this shop because it carries the latest in accessories and clothing.

Hours: Monday - Saturday, 9:30 am - 6 pm; Sunday, 11 am - 5 pm.

Gap Kids

264 Greenwich Avenue, 625.0662

Traditional children's denim and rompers for outdoor fun.

Hours: Monday - Saturday, 9 am - 7 pm; Saturday, 9 am - 6 pm; Sunday, 9 am - 6 pm. Holiday hours may vary.

Greenwich Exchange for Women's Work

28 Sherwood Place, 869.0229

This small shop, whose mission is to help others help themselves, has reasonably-priced, handmade items by local residents. If you want to give a gift to a newborn or young child, you will like their handknit sweaters and smocked dresses.

Hours: Weekdays, 9:30 am - 2:30 pm.

L'Enfance Magique

236 Greenwich Avenue, 625.0929

Pretty French clothes accent this shop.

Hours: Monday - Saturday, 10 am - 5:30 pm; Sunday, noon - 4 pm.

Little Eric

15 East Elm Street, 622.1600

A children's shoe store with high quality dress and play wear. A helpful sales staff eliminates the usual shoe shopping hassles.

Hours: Monday - Saturday, 10 am - 6 pm; Sunday 11 am - 5 pm.

CHILDREN

SHOPS - CLOTHING & SHOES

Monica Noel
23 Benedict Place (use back entrance), 661.0505
Expensive but charming children's clothing. The beautiful smock dresses and adorable sailor suits are enough to melt any parents heart.
Hours: Weekdays, 9 am - 5 pm.

Otto's
68 Water Street, South Norwalk, CT, 203.857.4717
This small discount fine-quality clothing store, primarily for men, also has boys' dress jackets and blazers for dress-up occasions and private and parochial school uniforms.
Hours: Tuesday - Saturday, 10:30 am - 5 pm; Sunday, noon - 5 pm.
In the summer and during holidays, hours are usually extended.
Directions: I-95 N to exit 14, R on West, bear left at fork onto North Main, cross intersection with Washington street, L on Haviland.

Petit Patapon
271 Greenwich Avenue, 861.2037
www.petitgift.com
Lovely playwear for young children. The whimsical and pastel-colored outfits will make you smile.
Hours: Monday - Saturday, 10 am - 5:30 pm;
            Sunday, noon - 5 pm or 11 am - 4 pm.

CHILDREN

SHOPS - FURNITURE & EQUIPMENT

Amish Outdoor Living

346 Ethan Allen Highway (Rte 7), Ridgefield, CT, 203.431.9888

Amish craftsmen from around the country are supplying this shop. This is the perfect place to find your child's "starter home." Your children will love the outdoor playhouses and you will like the reasonable prices and look of the sturdy children's furniture.

Hours: Summer hours, Monday - Saturday, 9 am - 5 pm; Sunday, noon - 5 pm; Closed Wednesdays. Call for winter hours.

Directions: Merritt Parkway N to exit 39 (or I-95 N to exit 15) (Norwalk), N about 13 miles on Route 7.

Go to Your Room

234 Mill Street, Byram, 532.9701

Children's rooms do not have to be boring. Fernando Martinez, an Argentine furniture designer, creates colorful, whimsical furniture to make any child smile.

Hours: Monday - Saturday, 10:30 am - 5 pm.

Great Outdoor Toy Company

249 Rail Road Avenue, 629.9188

Their main showroom is in Westport, 203.222.3818. Interchangeable parts allow you to design fun redwood play sets.

Hours: Monday - Saturday, 9 am - 5 pm (closed Wednesday).

TOY SHOPS

Diane's Doll Shoppe

227 Mill Street, 531.3370

A darling collection of play and collector dolls. Sweet faces so lifelike, they encourage you to pick them up and cuddle them. A delight for the little girl in your life.

Hours: Tuesday - Saturday, 10 am - 5 pm.

(The) Funhouse

236 Sound Beach Avenue, Old Greenwich, 698.2402

This is a store where you happily take your children. They have a great variety of small, inexpensive fun items. Parents fill their party bags here. The staff couldn't be more friendly.

Hours: Monday - Saturday, 10 am - 6 pm; Sunday, 11 am - 5 pm.

Hobby House

405 East Putnam Avenue (Cos Cob Plaza), Cos Cob, 869.0969

For years, kids in Greenwich have been rewarded for cleaning their room or finishing their homework with a trip to the Hobby House. Rockets and radio-controlled boats are current favorites.

Hours: Monday - Saturday, 10 am - 5:30 pm

Kay-Bee Toy

75 Greenwich Avenue, 622.6081

A friendly store with tons of toys for kids who must have what is advertised on TV.

Hours: Monday - Friday, 9 am - 7 pm; Saturday, 9 am - 6 pm;
Sunday, 11 am - 5 pm.

CHILDREN

TOY SHOPS

Smart Kids Company
17 East Elm Street, 869.0022,   www.SmartKidsToys.com
The toys in Mary De Silva's shop may look like a lot of fun, but most have been selected to help in your child's growth and educational development through play. Through her web site, this local shop has a global clientele.
Hours: Monday - Saturday, 9 am - 6 pm; Sunday, 11 am - 5 pm.

Toys "R" Us
59 Connecticut Avenue, Norwalk, CT, 203.852.6988
A typically mega-toy store.
Hours: Monday - Saturday, 9:30 am - 9:30 pm; Sunday, 10 am - 6 pm.
Directions: Just off I-95, exit 14.

Whimsies Doll House & Miniature Shop
18 Lewis Street, 629.8024
The ultimate dollhouse store.
Hours: Monday - Saturday, 10 am - 5 pm.

CHILDREN

SUMMER CAMPS

No need to travel to New Hampshire or Maine, the Greenwich area has all sorts of camps. For a more complete list, call Community Answers at 622.7979. Ask for their list of Summer Camps and Programs. It provides good information about everything from sailing programs to intensive educational programs. If your child is interested in a specific sport, check the section of FITNESS & SPORTS for specialized camp information.

Allegra Summer Stock Performing Arts Camps
37 West Putnam Avenue, 629.9162
Drama, theater, jazz, tap and other fantastic art programs.

American Camping Association
New England Section, 800.446.4494   www.acacamps.org
A national non-profit educational organization that accredits children's summer camps. Call to get a copy of their directory.

Art Scampers
First Presbyterian Church, 37 Lafayette Place, 869.7782
Focus on art, music, drama, ages 3 - 6 years.
Audubon Center, 613 Riversville Road, 869-5272, ext. 227
For the little explorer in your home. A day camp with sessions such as Creepy Crawlies and Wetland Waders.

Banksville Community House Summer Camp
12 Banksville Road, 622.9597
A perfect camp for those living in the Banksville area, featuring summer fun activities such as archery and swimming.

CHILDREN

SUMMER CAMPS

Boy Scouts of America

Greenwich Council, 63 Mason Street, 869.8424

The Seton Reservation at 363 Riversville Road, is a great treasure. Day camp is available for boys in grades 1 - 4 with no prior Scouting experience. The camp does a good job of teaching outdoor sports such as swimming, archery, canoeing and fishing.

Bruce Museum

(held at Greenwich Point), 869.0376

Weeklong summer workshops. Ages 6 - 9 years.

Brunswick School

100 Maher Avenue, Greenwich

Summer Baseball camps for boys ages 6 to 12 as well as co-ed summer play camps for ages 3 - 5.

Camp Pelican

471 North Street, Greenwich, 869.4000

Contact: Pat Hellwig, 869.4242 or 914.232.5089

Established in 1965, this day camp provides instruction in a variety of outdoor and indoor activities. The camp begins in June and ends in August. Sessions are four to six weeks. Coed ages 3 -13. Capacity 500. The camp is located on the campus of Greenwich Catholic School.

Camp Simmons

Run by the Boys and Girls Club of Greenwich, 869.3224

Two-month session includes canoeing, swimming, field sports, archery, and nature hikes. Ages 6 - 18 years.

Camp Sunbeam

869.6600

Run by Christ Episcopal Church and Temple Sholom. Two 3-week sessions focus on crafts, sports, games and music for ages 5 - 8 years.

CHILDREN

SUMMER CAMPS

Computer Ed High-Tech Camps

1-888-226-6733   www.computered.com

Email: camp@computered.com

For the kid who can think of nothing but computers. Like-minded children come from all over the world to learn programming, computer graphics and rocketry. There are three camps - the closest just outside Boston.

Connecticut All-Star Lacrosse Clinic

Held at Greenwich Country Day School, Old Church Road, 863.5675

Lacrosse for beginners and intermediate boys in grades 2 - 8.

Connecticut Children's Musical Theater

at Arch Street Teen Center, Arch Street, 852.9275

Co-ed day camp for ages 8 - 13. Children create a musical which they perform for their parents.

Country Day School

Old Church Road, 863.5600

Summer day camps for ages 4-12. Many programs for each age group.

Department of Parks and Recreation

622.7830

There are a great variety of town-sponsored co-ed camps, such as Kamp Kairphree for ages 5-12 and the Music and Art Program for children 8-15 who have had, at least, one year of study with an instrument. Don't forget to ask for their program bulletin.

First Church Day Camp

First Congregational Church, 108 Sound Beach Avenue, 637.5430

Co-ed day camp for ages 3-9. Beach activities, games, music and sports.

Gan Israel Camp

75 Mason Street, 629.9059

Run by Chabad Lubavitch of Greenwich, this co-ed July camp provides traditional camp activities for ages 20 months - 3 years, and 4 - 9 years.

CHILDREN

SUMMER CAMPS

Girls Inc. Summer Camp
At Western Greenwich Civic Center, 531.5699
Camp for 6 - 8th grade girls. Girls can sign up for individual weeks or longer sessions. The camp presents science and math in a fun atmosphere. Several campers have won science awards.

Greenwich Public Schools Summer Program
Western Middle School, 531.7977
Enrichment and review courses for all students from pre-K to grade 12.

Greenwich Sports Camp
869.4444
Held at the Greenwich Academy. Open to boys and girls ages 7 to 14, the camp offers 11 different sports including baseball, golf, lacrosse, soccer, tennis and volleyball.

Manhattanville College
2900 Purchase Street, Purchase, NY, 914.323.5214
The college (914.692.2200) provides a summer writing workshop for young people in grades 4 - 11, and hosts a number of sports camps, including soccer, basketball and tennis.

Norwalk Community College
"College for Kids" - Norwalk, CT, 203.857.3337
A mix of athletic activity and academic challenge for children in grades 1 - 6.

Performing Arts Conservatory
Convent of the Sacred Heart, 1177 King Street, 869.2924
Co-ed day camp for children entering grades 7 -10. Training in music and acting (plays by Shakespeare).

Purchase College
735 Anderson Hill Road, Purchase, NY, 914.251.6500
The State University of New York (SUNY) at Purchase offers a number of Summer Youth Programs in the Arts (art, music, acting) for ages 6 - 17. They have early drop-off and extended-day options.

CHILDREN
SUMMER CAMPS

Robin Hood Camp
Herrick Road, Brooksville, ME, 207.359.8313
One of the best all-around camps in the US. It has a strong Greenwich connection.

Silvermine School of Art
New Canaan, CT, 203.966.6668, 866.0411
Creative summer camp for the artistically inclined, ages 2 - 17. Learn painting, drawing, photography and sculpture on an attractive 4-acre campus.

Summer Camp Fair
Greenwich High School, 625.8000
http://www.greenwich.k12.ct.us/high/ghs/ghs.htm
Known as "Summerfare," this event is sponsored by the Greenwich High School PTA and draws hundreds of camps from around the USA. The fair is usually held in February.

Summer Camp Expo
Greenwich Academy, 625.8990   www.greenwichacademy.org
Their Summer Opportunity Fair is usually held at the end of January.

U.S. Academy of Gymnastics
6 Riverside Avenue, 637.3303
Tumble Bugs Day Camp.

Whitby School Summer Camp
969 Lake Avenue, 869.8464
Co-ed, ages 4-6. Montessori staff teaching gardening, cooking, arts and crafts and nature study.

CHILDREN

SUMMER CAMPS

Wideworld Children's Corner

521 East Putnam Avenue, 629.5567

A Japanese-English camp with festivals, water play and games. For children ages 3 - 6 years.

YMCA

50 East Putnam Avenue, 869.1630

Summer Fun Clubs - four 2-week co-ed sessions begin at the end of June. They include field trips, sports, and environmental education.

YWCA

259 East Putnam Avenue, 869.6501, ext. 225

Camp Ta-Yi-To is a co-ed camp for grades K - 8; includes swimming and tennis.

CLUBS/ORGANIZATIONS

COMMUNITY

Does this partial list of Community Clubs and Organizations give you an idea of the multitude of interests in Greenwich? The energy, enthusiasm and brilliance of individuals in each of these organizations is always remarkable, as is the astonishing abundance of good works they accomplish. For more information about these clubs and organization go to the web site: http://www.greenwich.lib.ct.us/ and click on Community Answers.

American Association of University Women
Greenwich Branch
37-5 Sheephill Road, Riverside
Joan Carter, President - 637.1825

American Legion
Greenwich Post 29
248 Glenville Road, 531.0109
Emile Smeriglio, Commander

American Red Cross
Greenwich Chapter
231 East Putnam Avenue, 869.8444
Rosemary Calderato, Director
Contact: Sarah Mobilia, Director of Communication

Art Society of Old Greenwich
PO Box 103, Old Greenwich 06870
John Tatge, President - 637.9949 / Marjorie Wolfe, Office - 637.3084

Audubon Society of Greenwich
613 Riversville Road, 869.5272
Ann Sawyer, President
Tom Baptist, Executive Director of State Office (x 222)

Boys & Girls Club of Greenwich
4 Horseneck Lane, 869.3224
Robert DeAngelo, Executive Director
Jeffrey Starcher, Director of Operations

CLUBS/ORGANIZATIONS

COMMUNITY

Byram Garden Club
Byram Schubert Library
21 Mead Avenue, Byram
Margaret Wiener, Co-President - 531.7120
Betty McKenna, Co-President - 532.1688

Children of the American Revolution
Mary Bush Society, Putnam Cottage
243 East Putnam Avenue
Catherine Bohrman, Senior President - 629.8533
Contact: Katie Bacon, Senior Registrar - 637.6789

Chinese Association of Fairfield County
PO Box 506, Riverside, CT 06878, 921.0130
Tak Eng, President - 637.5512

Church Women United of Greenwich
5 Somerset Lane, Riverside
Alice Dais, President - 637.3473
Contact: Kate Bryner, Publicity - 869.6261

Council of Churches and Synagogues
628 Main Street, Stamford, CT, 348.2800
Rev. James Carter, Executive Director

Daughters of the American Revolution
Putnam Hill Chapter
243 East Putnam Avenue, 869.9697
Helen Anderson, Regent - 637.0364

Friends of Binney Park
92 Wesskum Wood Road, Old Greenwich
Robert E. Horton III - 637.8334
Contact: Linda Butler - 637.3558

Garden Club of Old Greenwich
11 Somerset Lane, Riverside
Marcia Livingston, President - 637.9708

CLUBS/ORGANIZATIONS
COMMUNITY

Garden Education Center
Bible Street, Cos Cob
Liza Haywood MacLeish, Administrative Director
869-9242
Contact: Maureen Fitzpatrick and Brookie Mc Culloch, Co-Presidents

Glenville Senior Citizens
110 Pilgrim Drive, Byram
Contact: Celine Crothers - 531.6784

Green Fingers Garden Club
PO Box 4655, Greenwich 06830
Robin Browning, President - 661.2670

Greenwich Adopt-A-Road
PO Box 4716, Greenwich, CT, 06831-0413
Robert A. Hack, President - 661.0397

Greenwich Daffodil Society
38 Perkins Road
Nancy B. Mott, President - 661.6142

Greenwich Chamber of Commerce
21 West Putnam Avenue, 869.3500
Managing Director, Mary Ann Morrison
Chairman, Jack Moffley

Greenwich Democratic Town Committee
PO Box 126, Greenwich 06836
Sigmund "Pete" Beck, Chair - 869.3643
Contact: Betty Bonsal, Vice-Chairman - 637.1352

Greenwich Democratic Women's Club
Midge Bacon, Co-President, 58 Winthrop Drive, Riverside, 637.3327
Betsie Halkins, Co-President, 45 Lockwood Avenue, Old Greenwich - 637.7550
Contact: Barbara Bloch - 637.3830

CLUBS/ORGANIZATIONS

COMMUNITY

Greenwich Garden Club
PO Box 4896, Greenwich 06831
Valerie Stauffer, President - 869.7451

Greenwich Green & Clean
Yantoro Community Center, 113 Pemberwick Road, 629.8439 or 531.0006
Mary G. Hull, Executive Director

Greenwich Hospital Auxiliary
Greenwich Hospital
5 Perryridge Road
863.3222 - auxiliary office
863.3335 - Medicare Assistance
Suzanne Rand, President
Contact: Marguerite Heithaus, Director of Volunteer Services - 863.3221

Greenwich Jaycees
PO Box 232, Greenwich 06836
Carl Groppe, President - (H) 622.4459, (W) (212) 398.0200

Greenwich Kiwanis Club
PO Box 183, Greenwich 06836
Jim Creber, President - 351.9300

Greenwich Land Trust
PO Box 1152, Greenwich 06836-1152
Daniel Barrett, Executive Director
629.2151
Contact: George Jost, President

Greenwich Old Timers Athletic Association
PO Box 558, Greenwich 06836
Nino Sechi, President - 661.7134
Contact: Jeffrey D. Harris, Secretary - (H) 869.8762

Greenwich Police Silver Shield Association
PO Box 1123, Greenwich 06836
Charles Mahood, President
869.2830

CLUBS/ORGANIZATIONS

COMMUNITY

Greenwich Recycling Advisory Board (GRAB)
234 North Maple Avenue
Mariette A.Badger, Chairman - (H)869.4623, (W) 869.8100

Greenwich Republican Roundtable
15 Upper Cross Road
H. Arthur Bellows, Jr., Chairman - (H) 869.7024, (W) 627.9700

Greenwich Republican Town Committee
74 Greenwich Avenue, 869.2983
David Hopper, Chair - (W) 629.1100
Contact: Elaine Lee, Office Administrator

Greenwich Riding and Trails Association, Inc.
PO Box 1403, Greenwich 06836, 661.3062
Walter L. Statton, President
Contact: Mary Jane Wallace, Secretary

Greenwich Seniors Club
Sheila Shea Russo, President - (W) 622.1500, (H) 531.4345
Contact: Wilma Kasprak, Membership - 531.7753

Greenwich Square Dance Club
48 Carroll Street, Stamford 06907
Ralph Lupo, President - 324.5210
Contact: Doris and John Penn, Vice Presidents - 655.1530

Greenwich Women's Civic Club
PO Box 26, Greenwich 06836
Gwendolyn Petitt, President - 968.2821

Greenwich Woman's Club Gardeners
89 Maple Avenue, 869.2046
Jane Boutelle, President - 869.7341

Greenwich Women's Exchange
28 Sherwood Place, 869.0229
Helen Chester, Chairman and President - 869.4488

CLUBS/ORGANIZATIONS

COMMUNITY

Hadassah, Greenwich Chapter
Temple Sholom, 300 East Putnam Avenue
Alma Rutgers, President - 531.1385
Contact: Natalie Garr, Membership, Vice President - 532.0490

Historical Society of the Town of Greenwich
39 Strickland Road, Cos Cob
Debra Mecky, Executive Director - 869.6899
Contact: Karen Blanchfield, Curator (x12)
Jane Hoder, Curator of Education (x 17)

Hortulus
PO Box 4666, Greenwich, CT 06830
Karen Tell, President
Contact: Letitia Potter - 869.6069

Improved Order of Red Men
17 East Elm Street, 862.9213 (answering machine)
Contact: Anthony Scarnati, Building Manager - 943.2168

Japanese Volunteer Group
c/o Japan Education Center
15 Ridgeway, 629.5922 x 2 or 3

Junior League of Greenwich
48 Maple Avenue, 869.1979
Karen Royce, President
Contact: Lynn Benson, Office Manager

Junior League of Greenwich
Sustainer's Garden Club
Junior League of Greenwich
48 Maple Avenue, 869.1979
Emily Toohey, President - 661.7988

Knollwood Garden Club
170 Clapboard Ridge Road
Paula Burton, President - 869.1315

CLUBS/ORGANIZATIONS
COMMUNITY

League of Women Voters of Greenwich
PO Box 604, Greenwich 06836-0604, 352.4700
Jo Ann Messina, President - 869.1464
Contact: Miriam Mennim, Membership Director - 637.3183

Lions Club of Greenwich
PO Box 1044, Greenwich 06836-1044
Steve Gordon, President - (W) 869.7000, (H) 598.1258
Contact: Dave Noble - 661.2540

Lions Club of Old Greenwich
PO Box 215, Old Greenwich 06870
John Corrado, President - (H) 637.4244

Lions Club of Western Greenwich
101 Glenville Street, Greenwich 06831
Roy Zold, President - 531.9495

National League of American Pen Women, Connecticut
8 Dartmouth Road, Cos Cob 06807
Catherine Bohrman, President - 629.8533
Connie Walton, Membership Chair - 637.7620

National League of American Pen Women
Greenwich Branch
2 Putnam Hill, Greenwich
Bette Willis, President - 661.1417 / Anita Kiere, Vice President - 869.4228

National Society of New England Women
365 Round Hill Road
Joan Ingersoll, President - 661.6314

NOW, Greenwich Chapter
PO Box 245, Cos Cob, CT 06807
Contact: Carolyn Hopley, Information - 622.1372

P.E.O. Sisterhood, Greenwich Chapter
Carol Scott, President - 968.1974

CLUBS/ORGANIZATIONS
COMMUNITY

Retired Men's Association
YMCA
50 East Putnam Avenue
Gene Waggaman, President - 637.9924
Contact: Dom DiMaio, Program Chairman - 661.3833

Riverside Garden Club
PO Box 11
Riverside 06878-0011
Terry Lubman, President - 637.8221
Contact: Joan Denne, Membership Chairman - 637.1350

Rotary Club of Byram-Cos Cob
PO Box 4632, Valley Drive Station, Greenwich 06831
Tomas Menten, President - 622.0458

Rotary Club of Greenwich
PO Box 1375, Greenwich 06836
Annette Markley, President - 869.7329

Rotary Club of Old Greenwich-Riverside
PO Box 335, Old Greenwich 06870
Jeff Parker, President - (H) 637.9329

Round Hill Community Guild
397 Round Hill Road, 869.1091

Round Hill Country Dances
Round Hill Community House
Bernie Koser, President - 914.736.6489
For Information call 381.9509

Travel Club of Greenwich
56 Birch Hill Road, Newton CT 06470
Edith Szatai, President - (203) 270.1285
Contact: Mary Jane Watson, Membership Chair - 637.9439;
Virginia Obrig, Program Chair - 661.4456

CLUBS/ORGANIZATIONS
COMMUNITY

UJA Federation of Greenwich
One Holly Hill Lane, Greenwich 06830-6080 , 622.1434
Pamela Zue, President

United Way of Greenwich
1 Lafayette Court, 869.2221
Stuart Adelberg, President and C.P.O

Veterans of Foreign Wars
Cos Cob Post 10112   PO Box 8, Cos Cob 06807
Vincent Mitchell, Commander - 869.7249

Veterans of Foreign Wars
Greenwich Post 1792
James Clifford, Quartermaster - 531.9557
Paul Jablonski, Commander - 531.9557

Woman's Club of Greenwich
89 Maple Avenue, 869.2046
Martha Kreger, President

YMCA
50 East Putnam Avenue, 869.1630
John P. Eikrem, Executive Director
Contact: Pamela Hearn, Director of Development and Marketing

YWCA
259 East Putnam Avenue, 869.6501
Dr. Donna M. Nickitas, President

CLUBS/ORGANIZATIONS

COUNTRY CLUBS

Greenwich has a number of country clubs. Costs to join a country club vary from about $5,000 to $30,000 for the initiation fee with annual dues ranging from approximately $2,000 to $4,000. Country clubs with golf courses are typically the most expensive. Clubs with dining rooms usually require a quarterly food minimum. In addition, country clubs may have assessments for capital improvements. Membership in most private clubs usually requires a proposer and one or more seconders who are members. Therefore, the more members you know, the easier it is to join. Clubs which serve a particular area, such as Belle Haven or Milbrook, often give preference to area residents. The waiting period to join a club can be several years.

Bailiwick Club of Greenwich
Duncan Drive, 531.7591 (Summer)
Bob Caie, Manager
Swimming and tennis.

Belle Haven Club
100 Harbor Drive, 861.5353
Neil P. Mac Kenzie, Manager
Dining, boating, tennis, swimming, sailing.

Burning Tree Country Club
120 Perkins Road, 869.9004
Roger Loose, Manager
Dining, golf, swimming, tennis, paddle tennis.

CLUBS/ORGANIZATIONS
COUNTRY CLUBS

Fairview Country Club
1241 King Street, 531.6200
Andrew Campbell, Manager
Dining, golf, tennis, paddle, swimming.

Field Club
276 Lake Avenue, 869.1300
Martina A.Halsey, Manager
Dining, tennis (grass & indoor), squash, paddle, swimming.

Greenwich Country Club
19 Doubling Road, 869.1000
Dan Denetry, Manager
Dining, golf, tennis, squash, paddle, swimming, skeet.

Innis Arden Golf Club
120 Tomac Avenue, Old Greenwich, 637.3677
Jim Mc Gannon, General Manager
Dining, golf, tennis, paddle, swimming.

Milbrook Club
61 Woodside Drive, 869.4540
John Zerega, Manager
Dining, golf, swimming, paddle, tennis.

Round Hill Club
33 Round Hill Club Road, 869.2350
Dennis Meermans, Manager
Dining, golf, swimming, tennis, skeet.

Stanwich Club
888 North Street, 869.0555
Peter Tunley, Manager
Dining, golf, swimming, tennis, paddle.

Tamarack Country Club
55 Locust Road, 531.7300
Tom Tuthill, Manager
Dining, golf, swimming, tennis.

CLUBS/ORGANIZATIONS

NEWCOMERS CLUBS

Several organizations are designed to help new residents make friends and feel welcome.

Chinese Association of Fairfield County

Contact: Tak Eng, 637.5512
Wide variety of social and educational programs. They are planning to publish a directory of Chinese-speaking resources for newcomers.

Greenwich Newcomer's & Neighbors Club

YWCA, 259 East Putnam Avenue, 869.6501
www.GreenwichNewcomers.com
Contact: Randy Rituno, President - 869.6501
The club has a comprehensive program of coffees, luncheons, dinners and special interest groups. Be sure to ask for their excellent newsletter. The Y playroom is available for baby-sitting during daytime events. A good resource whether you have lived in Greenwich for two weeks or twenty years.

International Club of the YWCA

YWCA, 259 East Putnam Avenue
Hilary Jarman, President - 869.9811
Contact: Patricia Eggert, Membership and Reservations Chairman - 532.1677
Founded in 1975, the club holds monthly functions to help women of all nationalities who are new to Greenwich make friends in the community. New members, including Americans, are welcome.

Old Greenwich-Riverside Newcomer's Club

PO Box 256, Old Greenwich, CT 06870
www.GreenwichNewcomers.com
Connie Ramachandran, President - 637.2284
Contact: Bridget Barket, Membership - 698.1388.
The club is 37 years old and hosts a great variety of functions, from house renovation to gourmet dinners. They have events of interest to everyone, and they welcome new or established residents. Be sure to ask for their excellent newsletter.

CLUBS/ORGANIZATIONS
YACHT CLUBS

As one might expect for a town on the water, Greenwich has a number of excellent yacht and boating clubs. Many yacht clubs have long waiting lists (some as long as 12 years) but are considerably less expensive to join than a country club.

Belle Haven Club
100 Harbor Drive, 861.5353
Neil P. MacKenzie, Manager
Dining, boating, tennis, swimming. A combination yacht and country club.

Byram Shore Boat Club
PO Box 4335, Greenwich CT 06830
Byram Park, 531.9858 (clubhouse)
Jim Polvere, Commodore - 531.6141
Mooring/docking adjacent to town park and beach.

Cos Cob Yacht Club
PO Box 155, Riverside CT 06878.
Frank X. Reichert, Commodore - 637.2959
Social club for people interested in boating. Membership is by invitation. Meets the fourth Wednesday of the month at Ponus Yacht Club in Stamford.

CLUBS/ORGANIZATIONS
YACHT CLUBS

Greenwich Boat & Yacht Club
PO Box 40 Greenwich, CT 06830
Grass Island
Frank J. Lanzarone, Commodore - 637.3637
Club House, Mooring/docking and picnic areas.

Indian Harbor Yacht Club
710 Steamboat Road, 869.2484
Jason Powell, Manager
Dining and boating facilities including mooring/docking.

Mianus River Boat & Yacht Club
98 Strickland Road Cos Cob, 869.4689
Joe Benoit, Commodore - 637.1225
Boat and yacht club open to any Greenwich resident. Meets the first Monday of the month at 7:30 pm at the clubhouse. The clubhouse may be rented for private functions by anyone who is sponsored by a member (but it is unavailable on weekends from May to September. Accommodates a sit-down dinner for 75 people.

Old Greenwich Yacht Club
Tod's Driftway, Old Greenwich, 637.3074
Bill King, Commodore - 637.1788
Contact: Ann Riley, Secretary - 698.0308
Club house, launch and moorings are handled through the town hall.

Riverside Yacht Club
102 Club Road, Riverside, 637.1706
Gary Ashley, Manager
Dining, swimming and boating.

Rocky Point Club
Rocky Point Road, Old Greenwich, 637.2397
John Davidson, President - (H) 698.0933, (W) 224.1940
Clubhouse, mooring, salt water pool (Open in summer only).

COOKING

COOKING SCHOOLS

Bella Cucina

New Canaan, CT, Carol Borelli, 966.4477
Established in 1996, the school has one to six session courses covering basic techniques and seasonal menus. The emphasis is on fine Italian cooking. Excursions to markets and restaurants, as well as travel programs to Italy. Courses conducted at the owner's home. Average class size is 5 - 20 and costs vary from $45 to $270.

Complete Kitchen Cooking School

410 Main Street, Ridgefield, CT, 203.431.7722
www.TheCompleteKitchenLLC.com
A cooking store that provides a wealth of hands-on and demonstration cooking lessons provided by a variety of guest instructors. Although they have a store in Greenwich, the classes are usually held in Ridgefield. Classes are limited to 20. The average price is $40 - $70 per class.

Cooking with Class

Chief Instructor, Colin Walker, 961.9765 (203)
One-on-one or small group instruction in your own kitchen. Colin is a pastry chef who enjoys teaching others to make delicious full-course dinners, including the presentation. An affordable way to have a fun evening. Class size is limited to the size of your kitchen. A lesson for one costs $100 plus cost of ingredients (which he will pick up for you, once the menu is set).

COOKING

COOKING SCHOOLS

Greenwich Continuing Education

Greenwich High School, 625.7474, 7475
www.GreenwichSchools.org/gce
Well-priced, well-taught classes. Besides their specialized courses, they
often have classes in basic cookery for beginners. Check the Culinary
Arts section of their catalog.

Lauren Groveman's Kitchen

55 Prospect Avenue, Larchmont, NY, 914.834.1372
www.laurengroveman.com
Established in 1990, the school provides 5-session participation courses
as well as individual classes for adults and young people. The emphasis is on techniques and the preparation of comfort foods, breads and
appetizers. The average class size is 6. Cost is $450 for a five-session
course and $100 for a specialty course.

Peter Kump's New York Cooking School

50 West 23rd Street, NY, NY, 800.522.4610, 212.847.0700
www.pkcookschool.com
Although this school is in New York City, it has from time to time conducted courses in the Greenwich area. It has been in business since
1975 and has established a large Greenwich following. The school provides hands-on courses and workshops from 5 to 25-hours. The emphasis is on techniques of fine cooking. The average class size is 12 for
hands-on instruction and 30 for demonstrations. The school has a staff
of 15 who operate from a 27,000 sq-ft facility with 9 kitchens. Hands-on
classes range from $85 - $485. For additional cooking schools in New
York City try www.ShawGuides.com.

COOKING

COOKING SUPPLIES

Greenwich is fortunate to have two complementary cookware shops right across from each other on Greenwich Avenue.

Complete Kitchen

118 Greenwich Avenue 869.8384
www.TheCompleteKitchenLLC.com
This shop caters to passionate cooks who want the best.
Hours: Monday - Saturday, 9:30 am to 6 pm.

Harris Restaurant Supply

25 Abendroth Avenue, Port Chester, NY, 914.937.0404
Commercial restaurant supplier which also allows the general public to buy supplies. Cooks go crazy here.
Hours: weekdays, 9 am to 4 pm; Saturday, 9 am to 2 pm.

Lechters

125 Greenwich Avenue, 869.7698
A housewares shop that carries all of the basic cooking paraphernalia.
Hours: Weekdays: 9 am - 6 pm (Thursday until 8 pm);
Saturday 9am - 7 pm; Sunday, noon - 5 pm.

CULTURE

INTRODUCTION

Rarely is a community so fully appreciative as Greenwich is of the value of the arts. Note the peaceful expressions on the faces in the audience of the Greenwich Symphony, or the joyful chatter of a family in the Bruce Museum, or the smiles surrounding the Grace Notes, and you may discover how many of our high-powered, busiest residents relax and refresh themselves.

For art museums see CULTURE, MUSEUMS; for art education see SCHOOLS, ADULT CONTINUING EDUCATION or CHILDREN, ENRICHMENT.

ART

Art Society of Old Greenwich

Contact: John Tatge, 637.9949

An organization of amateur and professional artists with membership open to everyone. We always enjoy their Sound Beach Avenue sidewalk art show in September.

Barney's Place

107 Greenwich Avenue, 661.7369

British Art as well as fine art, craft and drafting supplies.

Hours: Monday - Saturday, 9 am - 6 pm.

Cavalier Galleries

405 Greenwich Avenue, 869.3664

www.artnet.com/cavalier.html

Ronald Cavalier specializes in painting and sculpture by contemporary artists working in a representational style. You may already have smiled at one of the gallery's life-like sculptures on a sidewalk in Greenwich or Stamford.

Hours: Monday - Thursday, 10:30 am - 6 pm;

Friday & Saturday, 11 am - 9 pm; Sunday, noon - 5 pm.

CULTURE

ART

Flinn Gallery

At Greenwich Library, 101 West Putnam Avenue, 622.7900
This attractive gallery, sponsored by the Friends of Greenwich Library, has rotating exhibits selected by a jury. In addition the Gallery hosts the annual juried exhibition of the Greenwich Art Society.

Friedman, A.I.

431 Boston Post Road, Port Chester, NY, 914.937.7351
Discount art and craft supply store frequented by many local artists. Their custom framing hours may be different.
Hours: Weekdays, 9 am - 8:30 pm; Saturday, 9 am - 6 pm; Sunday, 10 am - 6 pm.

Greenwich Arts Council

299 Greenwich Avenue, 622.3998
Betsy Hand, executive director in combination with an outstanding board, is keeping this nonprofit organization dynamic. They are celebrating twenty-five years of support for the arts. They manage the Arts Center on the two top floors of the old Town Hall which houses two art galleries, a large dance studio, a small theater/recital hall and several artist studios. It is home to many Greenwich organizations, such as the Choral Society and the Art Society, as well as the Alliance Française. The Council publishes a newsletter with a good calendar of music and art events in town. The Council maintains a talent bank of all types of music and art teachers. It is also a good resource for classes as disparate as Tai Chi Chuan, classical ballet or acting. You can even rent a darkroom for black and white printing.

Greenwich Art Society

299 Greenwich Avenue, 629.1533
The Art Society has been stimulating interest in the arts since 1912. Greenwich has many talented artists. While walking along Greenwich Avenue, stop in the Greenwich Art Center to see the latest show.
Hours: Weekdays, 9:30 am - 5:30 pm.

CULTURE

ART

Greenwich Gallery

6 West Putnam Avenue, 622.4494

www.artnet.com/greenwich.html

This gallery specializes in nineteenth and early twentieth century paintings. Besides being a pleasure to visit, they also offer appraisal, restoration and framing services.

Hours: Monday - Saturday, 10 am - 5 pm.

Left of the Bank

185 Sound Beach Avenue, Old Greenwich, 637.4000

This quality framer does a lot of framing for local artists. Recently he has expanded his studio to include a gallery.

Hours: Tuesday - Saturday, 9 am - 5 pm.

Lois Richards Galleries

54 Greenwich Avenue, 661.4441

We are pleased to see this gallery, which has many European artists, carrying the work of favorite Greenwich artists such as Margaret Bragg.

Hours: Monday - Saturday, 10 am - 5 pm. Sunday and evenings by appointment.

(The) Red Studio

39 Lewis Street, 861.6525

The frames are often works of art in themselves. They also sell prints and old drawings.

Hours: Monday - Saturday, 10:30 am - 6:30 pm.

Union Church of Pocantico Hills

555 Bedford Road, North Tarrytown, NY, 914.631.8200, 2069

Stained glass windows created by Henri Matisse (1869-1954) and Marc Chagall (1887-1985).

Hours: April - October, open daily except Tuesday, 11 am - 5 pm; Saturdays, 10 am - 5 pm; Sundays, 2 pm - 5 pm.

Directions: I-95 to I-287 W, Exit 1; R on Rte 119 W, R on Rte 9 N; R on Rte 448.

CULTURE

MOVIES

Not many towns still have movie theaters left in their downtown area. Greenwich has two. Enjoy the luxury of strolling from a nice restaurant to one of these theaters. See Movie Phone under CULTURE, THEATER TICKETS for an easy way to buy your movie tickets. Also see CULTURE, VIDEO.

Clearview Twin Cinema
356 Greenwich Avenue, 869-6030

Crown Plaza Three
2 Railroad Avenue, 869-4030

Greenwich Library Friday Films
101 West Putnam Avenue, 622.7910
At 8 pm (doors open at 7:40) in the Cole Auditorium, the Library presents award-winning US and foreign films. Admission is free. Call to get a schedule and verify that a film is being shown.

Nearby Greenwich:

Crown Avon Two
272 Bedford Street, Stamford, CT, 324.9205

Crown Landmark Nine
5 Landmark Square, Stamford, CT, 324.3100

Crown Majestic Six
118 Summer Street, Stamford, CT, 323.1690
The newest theater in Stamford.

Crown Ridgeway Two
Ridgeway Shopping Center, 52 Sixth Street, Stamford, CT, 323.5000

CULTURE

MOVIES

IMAX Theater

At the Norwalk Aquarium, 10 North Water Street, SoNo, 203.852.0700

With a screen that is six stories high and eight stories wide, the visual effects are stunning. See full description under CHILDREN, FAMILY OUTINGS.

Hours: Open daily, 10 am - 5pm.

Rye Ridge Twin Cinema

1 Rye Ridge Plaza, Rye Brook, NY, 914.939.8177

SoNo Cinema

SoNo Plaza, Norwalk, CT, 203.869.9202

mbgoodman@snet.net

If you like foreign, independent or art films that have won film festival awards, this small theater is your ticket. It is well worth the trip. Just give them your email address and they will provide you with their upcoming features and show times. They even have a discussion group that meets at the Hunan Harmony across the street to analyze the films.

Directions: I-95 exit 14. Turn Right, located behind the SoNo Plaza.

Movie Phone Express Code: 505

State Cinema

990 Hope Street, Stamford, CT, 325.0250

One of the least expensive theaters in the area. A good place to take a group of children and your best bet for avoiding long lines.

CULTURE

MOVIES: VIDEO & DVD

Reisdents of Greenwich campaigned against the establishment of a chain vido store in town. As a result, the local video stores have survived and thrived.

Academy Video

80 East Putnam Avenue, 629.3260

A good selection in a convenient location with average service.
Hours: every day, 10 am - 10 pm.

Glenville Video

1 Glenville Street, 531.6030

A small store with a friendly staff who can help with your movie selection.
Hours: Weekdays, 9 am - 9 pm, weekends, 10 am - 9 pm.

Sam Goody

145 Greenwich Avenue, 862.9630

www.samGoody.com

A chain store with a wide selection of videos and DVDs for sale, a pleasant staff and great hours. Good music web site.
Hours: Monday - Saturday, 9 am - 9 pm; Sunday, 11 am - 6 pm.

Video Station

160 Greenwich Avenue, 869.8543

A large selection with all the recent videos. A family run business. They know their movies. They can be extremely helpful if you are wondering what you should rent. The best selection of foreign films. They also have more than 1,100 DVDs for rent.
Hours: every day, 10 am - 9 pm.

CULTURE

MUSEUMS

Bruce Museum

1 Museum Drive, 869.0376

www.BruceMuseum.com

This year the Bruce attracted over 90,000 visitors to their eighteen exciting exhibitions. In addition, the Bruce sponsored over 50 lectures and gave educational programs to over 18,000 children. No wonder the Bruce is placed in the top 10% of US museums. The Museum sponsors two fairs in Bruce Park every year. The mid-May Craft Fair and the Columbus Day Arts Festival have juried artists from around the country and draw visitors from all over the area. When you become a member, you will be informed about their wonderful events.

Hours: Tuesday - Saturday, 10 am - 5 pm; Sunday, 1 am - 5 pm.

Bush-Holley House Museum

39 Strickland Road, Cos Cob, 869.6899

Home of the Historical Society, this is the place to learn about Greenwich history. They also have a good library and a shop with books on Greenwich history, as well as reproductions of nineteenth century children's toys and books. While you are there, pick up a list of their informative programs.

Hours: April - Dec: Wednesday - Friday, 12 - 4 pm; Saturday, 11 am - 4 pm; Sunday, 1 - 4 pm; Jan - March: Wednesday, 12 pm - 4 pm; Saturday, 11 am - 4 pm; Sunday 1 pm - 4 pm.

CULTURE

MUSEUMS

Donald M. Kendall Sculpture Gardens

At Pepsico, 700 Anderson Hill Road, Purchase, NY, 914.253.2000
One of the world's finest sculpture gardens is located right next to Greenwich. The collection includes forty pieces by such twentieth century artists as Noguchi, Moore, Nevelson, and Calder. The sculptures are set on 168 carefully landscaped acres. Pick up a map at the visitors parking lot. There are some picnic tables.
Hours: every day from dawn to dusk, except for Saturday in August.
Directions: From Glenville, R on King, L at light on Anderson, L at light into Pepsico.

Historical Society of the Town of Greenwich

39 Strickland Road, Cos Cob, CT, 869.6899
Their mission is to collect, preserve and disseminate the history of Greenwich. The society conducts a wide variety of adult and children's educational programs, exhibitions and workshops. Their extensive archives are open to anyone wanting to research town history. We sincerely appreciate this organization's dedication to preserving our community's historical roots.

Museum Trips

Greenwich Continuing Education, 625.0141
One of the more popular programs offered are group trips to New York City, Boston and other fine art museums.

Neuberger Museum

735 Anderson Hill Road, Purchase, NY, 914.251.6100
The museum is located on the 500-acre campus of the State University of New York (SUNY) at Purchase. It has 25,000 sq. feet of gallery space, a cafe, a store and an interactive learning center. It houses a well respected collection of modern art.
Hours: Closed Monday; Tuesday - Friday, 10 am - 4 pm; Saturday and Sunday, 11 am - 5 pm.
Directions: From Glenville, King Street N, L at light on Anderson, R at light into SUNY.

CULTURE

MUSEUMS

Putnam Cottage
243 East Putnam Avenue, 869.9697
Originally a tavern serving travelers along the Post Road, it is now a museum owned by the DAR. Each year on the last Sunday in February (1-3 pm) the Putnam Hill Revolutionary War battle is recreated. A definite must-see for adults and children alike.
Hours: April - December; Wednesday, Friday, Sunday, 1 pm - 4 pm. Special tours anytime.

Storm King Art Center
Old Pleasant Hill Road, Mountainville, NY, 914.534.3115
Take a walk or picnic in this leading outdoor sculpture museum with 120 masterworks set in a stunning 400-acre landscaped park. Great place to take the kids for a picnic. Open April 1 - November 15th.
Hours: 11 am - 5:30 pm; June, July & August open until 8 pm.
Directions: New York State Thruway, I-87 North to exit 16, Harriman; N on Route 32 for 10 miles; in Cornwall follow signs for the center.

CULTURE
THEATER/DANCE/MUSIC

Guide to Arts & Entertainment in Fairfield County
Published by Greenwich Time, 324.9799
This weekly guide provides a nice calendar of events as well as restaurant reviews.

Cameo Theater
Contact: Lori Feldman, 203.316.0262 or Pat Brandt, 637.4870
Theater company in its 20th season, performs at the First Congregational Church in Old Greenwich. A friendly group, open to anyone who is interested in acting or helping put on a show.

Caramoor Center for Music and Arts
Girdle Ridge Road, Katonah, NY, 914.232.5035, 1252
www.caramoor.com
Caramoor has wonderful music programs in a very intriguing setting. It should be on everyone's "must-do" list. For their evening performances, it is fashionable to bring a fancy picnic supper and eat on one of the lawns before the show. Caramoor has 100 acres of parklands and formal gardens. Most performances are open air, unless it rains. Mosquitoes are sparse but bringing some bug spray in the summer can't hurt. The main season is June through August although Caramoor provides fall, winter and spring indoor programs on a more limited schedule.
Directions: About 20 minutes from Greenwich. Take North Street N to the end (Bedford Village), R at the end, L on Route 22 N, R on Girdle Ridge Road; or I-684 N to exit 6, E on Rte 35, R on Rte 22 S.

Connecticut Playmakers
637-2298
Live theater open to adult participants from age 16. In addition to their major productions, the monthly meetings include dramatic presentations. The Playmakers Young People's Theater puts on a musical each summer. This is an enjoyable way for young people to meet each other and learn about the theater.

CULTURE
THEATER/DANCE/MUSIC

Emelin Theater
153 Library Lane, Mamaroneck, NY, 914.698.0098
Speakers, Cabaret, Jazz, Classical Music, Musical Theater, Children's Theater and more. Wonderful programs. Call for a catalog.
Directions: I-95 S to exit 18-A (Mamaroneck Ave), R on US 1, R on Library Lane.

Fairfield County Chorale
61 Unquowa Road, Fairfield, CT, 254.1333
scsu.ctstateu.edu/~Northcutt_J/chorale.html
Founded in 1963, the Chorale's repertoire consists of more than 100 classic works by composers from the 16th through the 20th century. Most performances are held at the Norwalk Concert Hall.

Fairfield Orchestra
50 Washington Street, Norwalk, CT
For information: 838.6995, For tickets: 622.5937
A well-respected, professional ensemble performing classical selections (usually in Norwalk). The Orchestra of the Old Fairfield Academy is the historical instrument affiliate. The Fairfield Orchestra is also known as the American Classical Orchestra.

Grace Notes
Contact: Kaia Fahrenhda, 595.0476
A women's "a cappella" singing group that has been entertaining Greenwich audiences for over thirty years. Singing with this group is a rewarding experience.

Greenwich Symphony Orchestra
869.2664
This professional orchestra is in its forty-first season. They play consistently excellent music at a low ticket price. Ask for a CD of their music highlights. Concerts are Saturday evenings and Sunday afternoons at the High School. To inquire about the Symphony's Chamber Players, call 869.5734.

THEATER/DANCE/MUSIC

Greenwich Choral Society

622.5136

Entering its seventy-fourth season, the society performs throughout the area during the winter months. Their annual Christmas concert held at Christ Church is a very popular event.

Long Wharf Theater

222 Sargent Drive, New Haven, CT, 203.787.4282, 800.782.8497
www.longwharf.org

Professional theater which produces traditional plays as well as plays by new playwrights. Over the last thirty-two years, Long Wharf has presented thirty-three world premiers, forty American premieres and twenty-three transfers to Broadway.

Directions: I-95 N to exit 46.

Palace Theater

61 Atlantic Street, Stamford, CT, 325.4466, 358.2305
www.onlyatsca.com, 325.4466

The Palace, along with the Rich Forum, is part of the Stamford Center for the Arts. The Palace is a 1,584-seat vaudeville theater that was acclaimed as "Connecticut's most magnificent" when it opened in 1927. The recently renovated Palace and the Rich Forum are a formidable duo.

Box Office Hours: Monday - Friday, 10 am - 5 pm.

Directions: I-95 N to exit 8, L on Atlantic.

Rich Forum

307 Atlantic Street, Stamford, CT, 325.4466, 358.2305

This theater has excellent facilities and an eclectic program of high quality events. Rich Forum, like the Palace, is committed to presenting the best of live theater, concerts, comedy and dance entertainment.

Box Office Hours: Weekdays, 10 am - 5 pm.

Directions: I-95 N to exit 8, L on Atlantic.

CULTURE

THEATER/DANCE/MUSIC

SUNY
Anderson Hill Road, Purchase, NY, 914.251.6200
The Performing Arts Center at the State University of New York at Purchase has wonderful music and dance performances, as well as plays. They have a number of summer offerings although the main season is September to May.
Directions: From Glenville, R on King Street, L at light on Anderson, R at light into SUNY Purchase.

Town Concerts and other summer events
622.7830
During July and August the Department of Parks and Recreation arranges free Tuesday afternoon and Wednesday evening concerts. In addition, the Fourth of July fireworks displays at the Greenwich High School and at Binney Park are always spectacular.

Westport Country Playhouse
25 Powers Court, Westport, CT, 203.226.0153, 203.227.4177
www.WestportPlayhouse.org
A six-play, summer season starting in June. Very professional. Only a twenty minute trip. Good seats matter here. If you cannot get seats in the first fifteen orchestra rows or in the first four rows of the balcony consider another theater. They also have a children's series. While there, try dinner at the Splash Cafe. See the restaurant section for details.
Directions: I-95 N to Exit 17, L on Rt. 33, R on Rte 1,
L on Powers Court, Playhouse on left.

Yale University Repertory Theater
149 Elm Stteet, New Haven, CT, 203.432.1234
www.yale.edu/drama/performance/conventions2.html
It is a drive—about an hour, but it's well worth it. Often as good as Broadway, but with much less hassle, better seats and lower prices. You can park right next to the theater for free. Subscribers can get front row seats.
Directions: I-95 N to exit 49, I-91 N to exit 3 (Trumbull Street). Stay in the middle lane and continue straight, L on Prospect Street (College Street), L on Elm.

TICKETS

Movie Phone

323-FILM (3456)

On Friday and Saturday nights, the demand for tickets is high and the lines can be very long—they often run out of tickets before you can get in. Call to hear previews and to buy your tickets in advance with your credit card. You should still arrive early for the best seating, but when you arrive you don't have to wait in the line. Just show your credit card and get your tickets.

When calling Movie Phone, their advertisements can sometimes be a nuisance. To get around this: press "*" to repeat or change your previous selection; "***" to start over; if you already know the theater you want, "#" plus the Theater Express Code will get you there immediately.

www.MovieLink.com

Purchase tickets for local theaters using the web. First choose New York City as your area, then choose Greenwich as your neighborhood. The same Express Codes used by Movie Phone apply here.

Cafe Rue

95 Railroad Avenue, 629.1056

They will buy tickets from Crown Plaza Three Theater (across the street) for those who dine there before the movie. Just call a couple of hours in advance and pay for your tickets with your dinner. (See description under RESTAURANTS).

Ticket Services

34 East Putnam Avenue, 661-5000

Private ticket services that can get you tickets for just about any event anywhere.

Ticket Affair/Ticket Box

www.TheTicketBox.com

869.9822, 800.331.9822

ENTERTAINING

CATERERS

These caterers have delicious food, they arrive on time and are dependable. As a result, they are often in high demand. Reserve early. For wine and other party foods, see FOOD STORES.

Eileen Grossman
Victorian teas and dinner parties, 323.5043
For an elegant event, be sure to give her a try.

Fjord Fisheries
137 River Road, Cos Cob, 661.5006
If you are invited to a clam bake or lobster party, chances are Fjord is the provider. They are a full-service caterer. You must try their salmon. From May through September, Fjord can cater a party of 40 to 120 on one of their four ships. Breakfast, lunch and dinner cruises lasting two to three hours are available.

Libby Cooke Catering
1 Boulder Avenue, Old Greenwich, 698.0545
Known for her fabulous presentations, she is equally competent with an intimate dinner party or a grand affair. You can sample her foods in her take-out shop.

Patricia Blake Catering
108 River Road, Cos Cob, 661.9676
Many choices on her catering menu from comfort foods to exotic delicacies. She has an impressive repertoire of hors d'oeuvres. She especially enjoys customizing the menu to meet your needs.

Watson's
201 Pemberwick Road, 532.0132
You will want to have a cocktail or dinner party, just to have Sue Scully's good food. Large parties are her forte.

ENTERTAINING

SERVICES

Greenwich Police
622.8015
If you are having a large party, consider hiring an off-duty policemen to help your guests know where to park safely. Be sure to call well in advance and to confirm back that someone has signed-up to help you.

Smith Party Rentals
133 Mason Street, 869.9315
If they don't have it, you probably don't need it.

SUPPLIES

For Chocolates, see FOOD STORES, CHOCOLATES
For Wine and other party foods, look under FOOD STORES.

Party Paper and Things
403 East Putnam Avenue (Mill Pond Shopping Center), 661.1355
A good selection of high quality party paper goods, wrapping paper, disposable serving dishes and lots of balloons. They will deliver for a very modest fee.
Hours: Monday - Saturday, 10 am - 5:30 pm.

Tallows End
41 East Elm Street, 661.5903
The largest selection of candles in the area, all shapes, sizes and scents. They also have a nice selection of gifts.
Hours: Monday - Saturday, 9 am - 5 pm (Friday - 5:30 pm).

FITNESS & SPORTS

INTRODUCTION

Fans and players of almost every imaginable sport live in Greenwich. Paddle tennis was even invented in Greenwich. Best of all, whether you are a professional or an amateur, finding a place to fish, skate, golf, sail or play ball is easy in our town.

ARCHERY

Cos Cob Archery Club
205 Bible Street, 625.9421 or Bob Harris, 869.6137
Twenty-four regular targets—members must have their own equipment and be over 18. Members have a key to the range and can practice any time. To join, visit the range Saturday or Sunday or attend the meeting on the second Wednesday of each month at 7:30 pm.

BADMINTON

Greenwich Badminton Club
Contact: Steve Edson, 637.2623
An affiliate of the US Badminton Association, www.usabadminton.org, they play at the YWCA.

YWCA
259 East Putnam Avenue, 869.6501
The Y provides supervised round robin youth badminton for all skill levels on Tuesday and Thursday evenings. The Y hosts tournaments sanctioned by the US Badminton Association.

BASEBALL

Babe Ruth League

Contact: Vinnie Gullotta, for the Bambino Division, 869.4132
Tina Carlucci, for the Junior Division, 531.9223
Bob Spaeth, for the Senior Division, 661.2386
Nonprofit organization sponsoring baseball. The Bambino division is for children 10 to 12; Junior division is for children 13 to 15; Senior division is for ages 16-18. Teams play from late May through mid-July at the Greenwich High School and Julian Curtiss Elementary School. Registration is in early April.

Blue Fish Professional Baseball

Listed as "Bridgeport Bluefish" under CHILDREN, FAMILY OUTINGS.

Brunswick Baseball Camp

Brunswick School, 100 Maher Avenue, 622.5800
The school offers six one-week baseball camps for boys ages 7 to 13.

Cos Cob Athletic Club

Contact Toni Natale, 869.0281
This community organization sponsors spring co-ed T-Ball for beginners in grades K-2.

Greenwich Department of Parks and Recreation Programs

Town Hall, 101 Field Point Road, 622.7830
Indoor baseball clinics January through March, at Dundee School for children ages 7 to 13. Co-ed spring outdoor clinics for Small-Fry age 7; Midget for age 8. Doyle Baseball School for ages 7-12, during school vacation in April; July & August co-ed baseball league for ages 9-12.

FITNESS & SPORTS

BASEBALL

Grand Slam USA

327 Main Avenue, Norwalk, CT, 203.847.3700, 203.849.0849
Located in a warehouse, this indoor baseball/softball training center can provide challenging batting practice for the beginning to the advanced player. Grand Slam can also provide expert batting and pitching instruction. During the summer the facility is relatively unused. During the winter it can be quite busy.
Summer hours: Monday - Saturday, 9 am - 9 pm; February - June: 9 am - 10 pm.
Directions: I-95 N to exit 15; Route 7 N to exit 2 (New Canaan Avenue); L off the Ramp; L on Main.

Old Greenwich-Riverside Community Center Programs

90 Harding Road, 637.3659
They sponsor a variety of baseball and softball teams and instruction programs for girls and boys from kindergarten through 8th grade. Evaluations are usually in March.

Uniforms and Equipment

See FITNESS & SPORT, TEAM SPORTS EQUIPMENT.

YMCA Baseball Programs

50 East Putnam Avenue, 869.1630
The Y provides sessions for boys & girls, ages 4 - 5, 7 and 6 - 8 to learn the fundamentals of baseball, as well as clinics for children in grades 1-5.

FITNESS & SPORTS

BASKETBALL

Business People's Lunch Time Pick-Up Basketball
At the Greenwich Civic Center, call 637.4583.

Greenwich Basketball Association
Contact Joe Curreri at 661.4641

Now in its 6th season, the Association is a town-wide instructional and competitive basketball program for 5th to 10th graders. It is designed to encourage and stimulate each child to build basketball skills. Players on high school teams are prohibited from league involvement. Registration and evaluation start in October.

Hoop Start USA, Summer Basketball Camp
800.771.3555, 637.4583

Sponsored by the Greenwich Parks and Recreation Department and run at the Greenwich Civic Center, it provides high quality instruction for boys and girls, Pre-K through the 5th grade. Camps begin in June.

Men's Basketball League
Call 622.7830 for information.

A recreation program from January through March at the Greenwich Civic Center.

FITNESS & SPORTS

BASKETBALL

OGRCC Basketball Programs

Old Greenwich - Riverside Community Center,
90 Harding Road, 637.3659
Starting in October, OGRCC sponsors a number of basketball programs for young children through adults: Youth Basketball for boys and girls in the 3rd and 4th grades; Boys' Basketball and Girls' Basketball for 5th to 8th graders; Adult Pick-Up Basketball for 18 and over.

Parks and Recreation Basketball

Greenwich Parks and Recreation Department, 622.7830
Co-Ed Clinics, K to 6th grade at the Glenville and Dundee Schools.
Girls' Clinic, K to 6th grade at the Dundee School.
Men's League at the central and Eastern Middle Schools.

Uniforms and Equipment

See FITNESS & SPORTS, TEAM SPORTS EQUIPMENT.

YMCA Programs

50 East Putnam Avenue, 869.1630
The Y provides clinics in Basketball for children in grades 1 - 5. They also sponsor A and B levels and an Adult Summer Outdoor Basketball League for ages 19 and up.

FITNESS & SPORTS

BICYCLING

Buzz's Cycle Shop
(1 Boulder Avenue) Post Road, Old Greenwich, 637.1665
Good advice, selection and repair for the serious (and not so serious) cyclist. They sponsor a number of local races.

Connecticut Department of Transportation
2800 Berlin Turnpike, PO Box 317564
Newington, CT 06131-7564.
The Connecticut Bicycle Map is published by the State. Write for a copy.

Connecticut Bicycle Newsletter
PO Box 121, Middletown, CT 06457
Published seasonally by the Coalition of Connecticut Bicyclists.

Dave's Cycle and Fitness
78 Valley Road, Cos Cob, 661.7736
www.davecycle.com
Bike rentals and exercise equipment.

Greenwich Department of Parks & Recreation
622.7830
A tour map/guide of the 7.5-mile town bike route is available at the Recreation Division Office.

Sound Cyclists
203.840.1757
www.SoundCyclists.com
This social cycling club offers, at no cost, rides for all levels of ability led by experienced cyclists. Routes are along scenic coast lines and country roads and vary from 12 miles to 60+ miles.

Threads and Treads
17 East Putnam Avenue, 661.0142
Entry forms for the latest races are available here. This is a good source for biking, swimming and running attire.

FITNESS & SPORTS

BOATING

Boat Master Services

Yacht Haven Marina, Washington Blvd, Stamford, CT, 203.348.1441

You can trust your treasure to this full-service boat cleaning company.

Greenwich Marine Facilities

622.7818

Assigns boat moorings for the town. To apply for a slip (as always, bring in a utility bill as proof of residency and a photo ID) you must own a boat and know the vessel's length, draft and beam. Boats are categorized as sail or power and over or under 20 feet; 20 feet and over receive deep-water moorings. After registering, you are put on a waiting list. The list is never short, but the amount of time varies with the vessel's type and size, as well as the location you request. The town has moorings at Greenwich Point, Cos Cob, Grass Island and Byram.

Greenwich Power Squadron

The Power Squadron is an all-volunteer civic organization with 200 Greenwich members; its present commander is John Giddings (869.9474). The Squadron's primary goal is education and boating safety - both sailing and power boating. The Squadron teaches two courses at the Greenwich High School through the Continuing Education program (625.7474) and depending upon demand, runs additional courses throughout the year. All boaters - even jet skiers - must have a Connecticut Boating License. The Power Squadron course qualifies you for your Connecticut license. This course is the first step for anyone who wants to enjoy the miles of coastline available to Greenwich residents.

Indian Harbor Yacht Club

710 Steamboat Road, 869.2484

One of the few private clubs with a sailing program open to the public. The program has such a good reputation that it is usually filled by February.

John Kantor's Longshore Sailing School

Westport, CT, 203.226.4646

If you or your children (ages 9-16) want to learn to sail and can't get into one of the Greenwich programs, try this school in Westport. It provides instruction from basic sailing to racing techniques.

FITNESS & SPORTS

BOATING

Landfall Navigation

354 West Putnam Avenue, 661.3176, www.landfallnav.com
Henry Marx, the owner, is very knowledgeable and helpful. He has what you need—charts, supplies or just information. Be sure to get a copy of his catalog.

Old Greenwich Yacht Club

Greenwich Point, Old Greenwich, 637.3074
This club is open to all residents with beach cards. It has deep water moorings as well as Mercury sailboats for member use. The club provides sailing lessons on weekends and trophy races during the summer. See the section on CLUBS for details on other yacht clubs.

Sound Sailing Center

South Norwalk, CT, 203.838.1110
Selected to manage the Old Greenwich Yacht Club sailing program, SSC focuses on adult education at its Norwalk Harbor facility.
After hours, call 203.454.4394.

Yachting Magazine

625.4480   www.yachtingmag.com
Published in Greenwich, this is the magazine for those who really want to get in the sailing swing.

BRIDGE

Lest you wonder why bridge is in this section, we regard it as fitness for the brain.

YWCA

259 East Putnam Avenue, 869.6501
The Y provides a variety of bridge lessons from beginning to advanced. Each Monday at noon, up to 100 serious players gather at the Y to participate in three and a half hours of duplicate or tournament bridge, played under the oversight of Steve Becker, who writes a syndicated bridge column. The game is franchised by the American Contract Bridge League and players can earn master points toward becoming life masters.

FITNESS & SPORTS

CANOEING/KAYAKING

The Mianus River in Greenwich is a good place to practice canoeing. There is no need to worry if you fall in - the water is very clean. For the more adventurous, the Housatonic River has class I and II rapids, and is a center for trips and instruction. Outfitters come and go, but check out the following:

Clarke Outdoors
West Cornwall, CT, 860.672.6365

Kittatinny Canoes
Dingmans Ferry, PA, 800.356.2852
www.kittatinny.com
Canoeing, kayacking or rafting the Delaware. Calm water for families or beginners, white water for experts.

Mountain Workshop
Ridgefield, CT, 203.438.3640

North American Whitewater
Madison, CT, 800.727.4379

River Running Expeditions
Main Street, Falls Village, CT, 203.824.5579

CROQUET

Greenwich Croquet Club
Greenwich has enjoyed an active Croquet Club for many years. William Campbell (661.9122) is the contact person. The Club is open to everyone and plays on the Bruce Park Green. Besides providing instruction, the Club holds the Greenwich Invitational Tournament every July 4th, and in August, hosts the Connecticut State Championship.

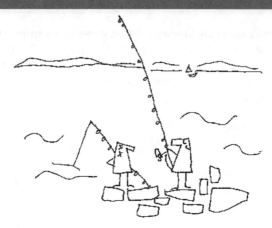

Bedford Sportsman

25 Adams Street, Bedford Hills, NY, 914.666.8091
Specializes in fly-fishing equipment.
Hours: Tuesday - Saturday, 9:30 am to 5:30 pm.
Directions: North Street to Banksville Road, becomes Rt 22. R at the end of Rt 22 into Bedford Village. L of village green, still on Rt 22 past Bedford Golf & Tennis Club, past Ripawam School. Take L fork; across from RR Ctr.

Compleat Angler

987 Post Road, Darien, CT, 203.655.9400
www.complete-angler.com
A large selection of fly-fishing and light tackle spin-fishing equipment as well as outdoor clothing.
Hours: Monday - Saturday, 9:30 am - 6 pm (Thursday until 8 pm); Sunday, 11 am - 4 pm.

Connecticut Angler's Guide

Connecticut Department of Environmental Protection
860.424.FISH
Ask for this comprehensive guide, which provides a summary of the rules and regulations governing sport fishing in Connecticut, descriptions of places to fish, the kinds of fish found there, and license information.

FITNESS & SPORTS

FISHING

Fishing Licenses
Licenses can be obtained from the Town Clerk's office, 622.7897

Mianus River Park
Merrybrook Road (Cognewaugh Road), 622.7814
Good trout fishing. Be sure you have your license, they do check.
See section on PARKS & RECREATION, PARKS & NATURE PRESERVES
for directions.

Orvis
71 Ethan Allen Highway (Route 7), Ridgefield, CT, 203.544.7700
Clothes, luggage and fishing equipment for the well-attired fisher. They
also have a large book and video selection.
Hours: Monday - Saturday, 10 am - 6 pm (Thursday until 8 pm);
Sunday, 11 am - 3 pm.
Directions: Merritt Pkw N to exit 39 (Norwalk), N on Rte 7; at end of
connector R at light, L at next light, continue on Rte 7.

Sound Fishing Charters
Contact: Kevin Reynolds, 622.0522
In business since 1997, they plan four-hour to all-day fishing trips for
groups up to six, complete with rods and bait. Call several weeks in
advance for weekend trips.

Sportsman's Den
33 River Road, Cos Cob, 869.3234
Supplies and classes on angling and fly tying.
One visit and you will be hooked.
Hours: Weekdays, 9 am - 5 pm (Monday until 2 pm); Saturday, 8 am - 5
pm; Sunday, 8 am - 2 pm.

FITNESS

Dave's Cycle and Fitness
78 Valley Road, Cos Cob, 661.7736   www.davecycle.com
A good source for exercise equipment.
Hours: Monday - Wednesday, Friday, 10 am - 6 pm; Thursday, 10 am - 8 pm; Saturday, 9 am - 5 pm; Sunday, 11 am - 3 pm.

Greenwich Fitness Center
1 Fawcett Place, 869.6189
Your standard, well-equipped fitness center with classes and weight rooms. Summer members welcome. Initiation fee approximately $200.
Hours: Monday - Thursday, 6 am - 9:30 pm; Friday, 6 am - 8:30 pm, Saturday, 9 am- 5 pm; Sunday, 11 am - 3 pm (Closed Sundays in the winter).

NY Sports Club
6 Liberty Way, 869.1253
In addition to a 6,000 sq. ft. state-of-the-art fitness center, the aerobics and Spinning™ studios offer classes seven days a week. Medically based health and wellness programs include nutrition, massage, personal training and a Medicare certified physical therapy department. Childcare available. Initiation fee $100 - 650.
Hours: Weekdays, 6 am - 9:30 pm; Saturday, 8 am - 5 pm;
Sunday, 8 am - 4 pm.

FITNESS

Omni Fitness
465 Canal street, Stamford, CT 203.327.0303
20 Railroad Avenue, 422.2277
A wide selection of high-end fitness equipment at reasonable prices.
Hours: Monday - Saturday, 10 am - 6 pm, Sunday, 11 am - 5 pm.
Directions to Stamford location: I-95 N to exit 8, R on Canal (at second light).

Spin Gym
280 Railroad Avenue, 552.0098
Studio cycling is a hot new trend in cardiovascular training. Run by Olympic competitor Darcy Ramsey, Spin Gym cyclists feel better and have a great time.
Hours: Monday, Wednesday & Friday, 7:30 am - 7:15 pm;
Tuesday & Thursday, 6 am - 7:15 pm; Weekends, 8 am - 10:45 pm.

Sportsplex
49 Brownhouse Road, Stamford, CT, 358.0066
On the border of Stamford and Old Greenwich is a complete training facility for adults and children. Morning programs for pre-schoolers and after-school programs for ages 6-8. Supervised nursery for children. In addition to machines, and spinning, they have an Olympic length pool, four squash courts and one racquetball court. Swimming and squash lessons are available. The aerobics room has a specially designed exercise floor. Call for an enthusiastic tour by Diane Lauer.
Hours: Weekdays, 5:30 am - 10 pm; Saturday 7 am - 8 pm, Sunday 8 am - 8 pm. (Different summer hours).

Thompson Method Exercise Classes
At the Mill, 128 Pemberwich Road, Glenville, 531.8762
Thompson Method classes work on stretching, strength and stamina (including combinations). Associates who attend the school swear by it. The cost for six months is $1,100, although there are a variety of different plans at different rates.
Hours: Tuesday & Wednesday, 8 am - 6 pm; Friday and Saturday, 8 am - 10 pm, Friday until noon.

FITNESS & SPORTS

FITNESS

United Studios of Self Defense

202 Field Point Road, 629.4666

Kick boxing is the hot new way to exercise, especially for women. This is a workout that will leave your muscles screaming and you asking for more. United Studios combines aerobic boxing with weights and floor stretches for a terrific all-around activity. $8 per class.

Hours: Weekdays, noon - 9 pm; Saturday 8 am - 2 pm.

YMCA

50 East Putnam Avenue, 869.1630

Renovated facility with an impressive weight room. The Y also provides aerobics, swimming, studio cycling, tennis, basketball, yoga, etc. Nice indoor track. Good outdoor tennis courts. Both Ys are open to men and women. You should consider joining, but you don't have to be a member to use their facilities.

A guest pass is $10.

Hours: Weekdays, 5 am - 10 pm; Saturday, 6:30 am - 7 pm; Sunday, 8 am - 5 pm.

YWCA

259 East Putnam Avenue, 869.6501

Gymnasium, climbing wall, badminton, tennis, racquet ball, weight room, classes, etc. Very good indoor pool and swimming programs.

Hours: Monday - Thursday, 6:30 am - 10 pm; Friday, 6:30 am - 9:30 pm; Saturday, 7 am - 5 pm; Closed on Sunday.

FITNESS & SPORTS

FOOTBALL

Cos Cob Athletic Club

Contact: Ed Kempfle, 661.5414 or Toni Natale, 869.0281
A community organization sponsoring midget football teams for
ages 8 - 13.

Gateway Youth Football League of Greenwich

Contact Carl Moeller, 531.8058 or Ernie Craumer, 532.1351
Town-wide instructional/competitive tackle football league for children
ages 8 -13. Registration takes place in August. The season runs from
September to November. Practices are held 2 - 3 times a week. Games
are on Sunday.

Uniforms and Equipment

See FITNESS & SPORTS, TEAM SPORTS EQUIPMENT.

YMCA Programs

50 East Putnam Avenue, 869.1630

GOLF

Public Golf Courses

There are a number of nearby courses open to non-residents. Some of these have limited times for non-residents; the greens fees listed are for weekday/weekend. However, many facilities have discounts for seniors, juniors, early morning or late afternoon play, or for 9-hole rounds. If you like the course, check out their policy on season passes. In any event, be sure to book before you go.

Brennan

451 Stillwater Road, Stamford, CT, 324.4185
Par 71, fee $25/$30. You can reserve seven days in advance.

Griffith Harris Memorial Golf Course

1300 King Street, 531.7200, 6944, 7261.
www.golfweb.com/gwid/15825.html
Open only to town residents (including tenants). This par 71, 18-hole golf course designed by Robert Trent Jones has a club house, pro shop, putting green and driving range. Call for details about obtaining a membership card. You will need to bring proof of Greenwich residency (such as a current phone bill) and a photo ID (such as a driver's license). Greens fees for adult members are $14/$15 for 18 holes. Membership is $75 for an adult permanent resident or $135 for a summer resident. Bring a guest.

FITNESS & SPORTS

GOLF

Maple Moor
1128 North Street, White Plains, NY, 914.242.4653
Par 71, fee $39/$44. You can reserve seven days in advance.

Oak Hills
165 Fillow Street, Norwalk, CT, 203.838.1015
Par 71, fee $29/$34. You can reserve seven days ahead for weekdays only.

Pound Ridge
Route 137, Pound Ridge, NY, 914.764.5771
Par 35, Fee $25/$40. On weekends, non-members can play
after 1 pm. A cart must be rented on the weekends. Cart rental is about $25.

Ridgefield
545 Ridgebury Road, Ridgefield, CT, 203.748.7008
Par 70, Fee $35/$35. You can reserve up to two days ahead for weekends.

Saxon Woods
Old Mamaroneck Road, Scarsdale, NY, 914.242.4653
Par 71, fee $39/$44. You can reserve up to seven days ahead.

Sterling Farms
1349 Newfield Avenue, Stamford, CT, 461.9090
Par 72, Fee $35/$40. On weekends, non-residents can play after 2:30 pm. You can reserve up to seven days in advance.

Vails Grove
Peach Lake, North Salem, NY, 914.669.5721
Par 66 (9-hole, double-tee). Fee $20/$20.
On weekends, non-members can play after 1 pm.

FITNESS & SPORTS
GOLF CLUBS/CLOTHING

Custom Golf of Connecticut

2802 Summer Street, Stamford, CT, 323.7888

Wide variety of golf clubs for sale or rent - some clothing. They do repairs and re-gripping.

Hours: Weekdays, 9 am - 6 pm (Thursday until 8 pm); Saturday, 9 am - 5 pm; Sunday, noon - 3 pm.

Directions: I-95 N to Atlantic Street exit 8, L on Atlantic (becomes Bedford), past Stop & Shop, L and next L onto Summer.

Darien Golf Center

233 Post Road, Darien, CT, 203.655.2788

Excellent selection of golf equipment and men's clothing.

Hours: Weekdays, 8 am - 5:30 pm; Saturday, 8 am - 5 pm; Sunday, 9 am - 4 pm.

Directions: I-95 N to exit 13, L on Post Rd.

De Mane's Golf, Inc.

35 Chapel Street, 531.9126

Golfers in-the-know visit Rick's shop for custom clubs and repairs.

Hours: Tuesday - Friday, 10 am - 6 pm; Saturday, 11 am - 4 pm.

FITNESS & SPORTS
GOLF PRACTICE

If you need a little practice before playing, use the golf range at Griffith Harris Memorial Golf Course or one of these:

Golf Training Center in Norwalk

Norwalk, CT, 203.847.8008

They provide indoor practice for your pitching and putting techniques, including driving bays with computer replay, virtual reality golf and exercise areas.

Hours: Monday - Thursday, 10 am - 10 pm; Friday, 10 am - 6 pm; Saturday, 8 am - 4 pm; Sunday, 10 am - 4 pm.

Directions: I-95 N to exit 15, Rte 7 N to exit 2, L at bottom of ramp, R on Main.

Nike Golf Schools and Junior Camps

800.645.3226

www.us-sportscamps.com

Nike sponsors a great number of adult and junior golf camps. The closest are Williams College, Williamstown, MA; Stowe, VT; and Loomis Chaffee, Windsor, CT.

Westchester Golf Range

701 Dobbs Ferry Road, White Plains, NY, 914.592.6553.

You can practice here until late.

Hours: Open every day, 8 am - 9 pm.

Directions: I-287 W to exit 3, Sprain Brook Pkw S to Rte 100B.

FITNESS & SPORTS

HOCKEY

Department of Parks and Recreation Ice Hockey Programs

At Dorothy Hamill Skating Rink, 622.7830
Prep League for boys and girls ages 13 and 14. Junior Hockey League ages 15 to 17. Sunday evening games, weekly practices. High school varsity participants are not allowed.

Department of Parks and Recreation Field Hockey Programs

Pemberwick Park, Moshier Street & Pemberwick Road
Contact: Claudia Collins, Recreation Supervisor, 622.7830
Co-ed field hockey clinics for grades 2-8 on Saturday mornings from late September through October.

Dorothy Hamill Skating Rink

Sherman Avenue, 531.8560, September - March; 622.7830, off-season.
An excellent municipal skating facility for Greenwich residents and their guests. You will need proof of residency such as a beach card. The Rink offers a full schedule of ice hockey programs for children, teens and adults.
Hours: September - March, weekends, 2 pm - 4 pm. Daily schedules are available.
Directions: US 1 W, L on Western Junior Highway, R on Henry, R on Sherman Avenue.

Greenwich Blues Youth Ice Hockey Association

PO Box 1107, Greenwich, CT 06836
Contact: Joe Rogers, 698.0542
Non-profit organization sponsoring competitive travel teams for boys and girls: Mites, under age 9; Squirts, 9-11; Peewees, 11-13; Bantam, 13-15. Dorothy Hamill Rink is their home rink. Season is from September through March, tryouts are in early September.

FITNESS & SPORTS
HOCKEY

Old Greenwich-Riverside Community Center
In-Line Roller Hockey
90 Harding Road, Old Greenwich, 637.3659
Adult pick-up roller hockey as well as spring and summer instruction and games for boys and girls ages 6 - 14. Call for times and details.

Uniforms and Equipment
See FITNESS & SPORTS, TEAM SPORTS EQUIPMENT.

YMCA Programs
50 East Putnam Avenue, 869.1630
In-line skating and hockey instruction for children and adults. Roller hockey for children ages 6 - 14.

FITNESS & SPORTS
HORSEBACK RIDING

For insurance reasons most stables will not rent horses for unaccompanied trail rides unless you have been taking a series of lessons and they know you are a skilled rider. Bedford, Wilton and Weston are centers for horseback riding in this area.

Arcadia Farm
69 Stone Hill Road, Bedford, NY, 914.234.6706
Set on 100 acres with indoor and outdoor riding areas, they give lessons from beginner to advanced.
Directions: North St. to the end, R onto Rte 22. Go thru Bedford Village, the road will bear L. R onto Rte 121. Go 2 miles, R onto Rte 137. The farm is 1/4 mile on the R. Sign says Coker Farm.

Greenwich Polo Club
Conyers (White Birch) Farm, North Street, 203.454.9604
People interested in playing polo should call the club for information about membership and events.

Greenwich Pony Club
Contact: Nancy Fertig, 661.6878 or Maria Fisher, 914.238.4179
Greenwich chapter of a national non-profit organization which promotes horse management and equestrian skills for young people, ages 8-21. You provide the pony or horse.

Greenwich Riding and Trails Association
661.3062
Greenwich has an extensive trail network which you can take advantage of if you own your own horse. For information and help, call them. A great organization to join for riders.

Lionshare Farm

404 Taconic Road, 869.4649, 552.0677

pleone@haven.ios.com

An excellent riding academy with programs for children and adults. The farm, owned by Peter Leone, an Olympic silver medalist, has two indoor rings and an outdoor ring, as well as access to the Greenwich trails. It is the premier show jumping stable in the Greenwich area. This is the first place to go if you want to buy a jumper.

On The Go Farms

550 Riversville Road, 661.1513

A friendly stable, focused on safety, with horses that are well-cared-for. Participants like the comradery and enjoy the end-of-the-year barbecue.

Ox Ridge Hunt Club

512 Middlesex Road, Darien, CT, 203.655.2559

There are many places to learn to ride, but serious riders will like Ox Ridge. This private hunt club offers riding lessons to the public. They have good horses, indoor and outdoor facilities and top instructors. Directions: Merritt Pwy exit 37, R onto Rte 124S. Stay on for 1.5 miles. At rotary, R onto Middlesex. At stop sign, L. Entrance on L.

Riders Up

1068 North Street, 618.9286

Leslie Stevenson believes that riders and their horses should be well dressed. Our favorite equestrian says, *"Leslie is a real horse woman, and I am completely hooked on her. You can count on her advice."* Her tack shop carries equipment for jumping, dressage and Western riding. Hours: Closed Sundays in summer; Monday - Saturday, 10 am - 5:30 pm.

Windswept Farms

107 June Road, Stamford, CT, 322.4984

Outdoor riding lessons for boys and girls 6-17. No previous riding experience is required. At the Greenwich/Stamford border, the stable has access to the 150 miles of Greenwich riding trails. Directions: Merritt Pkw exit 33, go straight. R at intersection. R at next intersection. Go over parkway bridge, turn L onto Riverbank. Second L onto June Rd. Go over bridge. Farm is on the R.

FITNESS & SPORTS

ICE SKATING

Binney Pond
Sound Beach Avenue, Old Greenwich
This is the prettiest pond for skating and it is town-tested for safety.

Dorothy Hamill Skating Rink
531.8560
We expect more Dorothy Hamill's to graduate from this rink!
Ask about figure skating lessons and hockey clubs.

Mianus River
Park off of Valley Road, bring your skates and hockey sticks (a shovel, too!)

Rink and Racquet
24 Railroad Avenue, 622.9180
Hockey and figure skating equipment.

Skating Club
Cardinal Road, 622.9583
The Skating Club, set inconspicuously off Fairfield Road, has an outdoor rink and offers a strong skating program for children. Because of its small membership, it is one of the more difficult clubs to join.

KARATE

Old Greenwich School of Karate
242 Sound Beach Avenue, 698.1057, 637.2685
Ages 4 and up.

Soo Bahk So
YMCA, 50 East Putnam Avenue, 869.1630
A Korean-style karate incorporating influences from China.
Classes are open to all ages.

United Studios of Self Defense
202 Field Point Road, Cos Cob, 629.4666

FITNESS & SPORTS

LACROSSE

Gilman Lacrosse Camps
800.753.2268, 203.834.7597
Summer camps in Greenwich for boys and girls, grades 1 - 11.

Greenwich Youth Lacrosse
www.gyl.idsite.com
PO Box 4627, Greenwich, CT 06831-0412
Contact: Bryan Tunney, 618.1970
A non-profit organization sponsoring lacrosse teams. House League for boys and girls in grades 1 - 6; Travel teams for boys and girls in grades 3 - 4 and 5 - 6. Boys travel teams for grades 7 - 8. Registration is usually in March.

Women's Summer Lacrosse League
Sponsored by the Greenwich Academy.
Contact: Angela Tammaro, 625.8959
Women's lacrosse league playing evenings from mid-June through July. Membership is open to any player who has completed grade 9.

Uniforms and Equipment
See FITNESS & SPORTS, TEAM SPORTS EQUIPMENT.

PADDLE TENNIS

Loughlin Avenue Park
Loughlin Avenue, Cos Cob
This 6-acre park has the town's only paddle tennis courts. The courts are lighted and open year-round. A small playground adjoins the tennis and paddle tennis courts. Call the Department of Parks & Recreation (622.7830) for a card to use the courts and for information on using the lights.

FITNESS & SPORTS

POLO

Greenwich Polo

Conyers (White Birch) Farms, North Street, 203.454.9604
Greenwich has a world-class polo facility. Most summer Sundays you can watch a good polo match in a beautiful setting. Matches begin at 3 pm, the gates open at 1 pm. General admission is $20 per car.

RACING - AUTO

Lime Rock Park

Lakeville, CT, 800.Race.LRP   www.limerock.com
About two hours north of Greenwich is the Lime Rock Race Track. The track is closed on Sundays, but most Saturdays (from early April to November) there are formula and sports car races. Lime Rock has no grandstands, and therefore there is no formal ticket system. Call to find out about the race schedule or to get a copy of their free newspaper, Track Record. The biggest race days are usually Memorial Day and Labor Day.

Skip Barber Racing School

Lime Rock Park, Lakeville, CT, 860.435.1300, 800.221.1131
www.skipbarber.com
Skip Barber is the largest racing school in the country. If you have always wanted to learn to race, this is the place to learn. The School offers two basic driving courses, with a lot of variations for each course: Advanced Driving School—one and two-day courses driving three different cars supplied by the School; Racing School—three hours to eight days. The School supplies the formula cars.

FITNESS & SPORTS

ROCK CLIMBING

Go Vertical
727 Canal Street, Stamford, CT, 358.8767
8,000 square feet of safe, challenging, indoor climbing surfaces, with on-site equipment. Lessons for beginners aged 13 and over. All necessary equipment can be rented. Be sure to call in advance if you are a beginner.
Hours: Weekdays, 10 am - 10 pm;
weekends, 10 am - 8 pm.
Directions: I-95 N to exit 8. R on Canal (2nd Light).

YWCA
259 East Putnam Avenue, 869.6501
The Y provides training workshops for beginning climbers.

ROLLER SKATING

See FITNESS & SPORTS, HOCKEY.
For skate boards and in-line skates, try Chili Bears or Rink & Racquet.

Eastern Civic Center
90 Harding Road, Old Greenwich, 637.4583
The Greenwich Civic Center offers roller skating from October to April. Call for details.

Stamford Skate Park
81 Camp Avenue, Stamford, CT, 322.2673
In-line skating, skate boarding, BMX biking, batting cages, arcade.
Hours: Tuesday - Thursday, 3 pm - 8 pm; Friday, 3 pm - 10 pm; Saturday, noon - 10 pm; Sunday, noon - 6 pm.
Directions: Merritt Pkw N to exit 36, R on Rte. 106, second light R on Camp.

FITNESS & SPORTS

RUNNING

Babcock Preserve

North Street, 622.7824

Two miles north of the Merritt Parkway, 297-acres of well-marked running trails.

Greenwich Point (Tod's Point)

Entrance at the south end of Shore Road in Old Greenwich.
This 147- acre beach has lots of jogging and biking trails.

Jim Fixx Memorial Day Race

Greenwich Recreation Office, 622.7830

This five-mile race, which starts and ends on Greenwich Avenue, begins the running season. If you run in no other event, you should consider it. It is always well-attended and attracts a great variety of talented and not-so-talented runners.

Threads and Treads

17 East Putnam Avenue, 661.0142

A good source for running gear, as well as a place to find out about the local races.

FITNESS & SPORTS
SOCCER

Greenwich Soccer Association
PO Box 1535, Greenwich, CT 06830, 352.5864
They field girls' and boys' travel soccer teams for ages 9 to 14. They play travel teams from other Fairfield County towns on Sunday afternoons. Tryouts are required and usually begin in November for the spring season.

Greenwich Soccer Club
PO Box 332, Cos Cob, CT 06807, 661.2620, 863.1936
The Greenwich Soccer Club is a volunteer based, all-inclusive, recreational and instructional program with a firm commitment to safety, fun and fairness. The GSC is a town-wide recreational program open to every boy and girl, ages 6 - 14, who either resides in or attends school in town. In the fall, over 1,700 boys and girls participate on Saturdays (coached by some 350 parent volunteers) with mid-week clinics taught by professional instructors. There are separate leagues for the boys and girls. The GSC is a privately funded, non-profit community service organization founded in 1976. Ken Irvine is the President.

Indoor Soccer
Greenwich Parks and Recreation, 622.7830
Winter co-ed training for children K to 6th grade. Limited to twenty-five children, so apply early. Registration by mail only: Greenwich Parks & Recreation, Recreation Division, 101 Field Point Road, Greenwich, CT 06836-2540.

Old Greenwich-Riverside Soccer Association
637.6776
Part of the Old Greenwich-Riverside Community Center and the Connecticut Junior Soccer Association, the club provides a comprehensive soccer program for over 700 youngsters who just wish to play for fun, as well as for those who wish to compete.

Uniforms and Equipment
See FITNESS & SPORTS, TEAM SPORTS EQUIPMENT.

YMCA
50 East Putnam Avenue, 869.7252
The Y provides spring training in the basics for youngsters ages 4 to 5 and 6 to 8. The emphasis is on sportsmanship and having fun.

FITNESS & SPORTS

SHOOTING

Cos Cob Revolver & Rifle Club

451 Steamboat Road, 622.9508

For those looking for a safe way to practice target shooting, this Greenwich club (despite its Cos Cob name), just across from the train station, has terrific facilities and a very helpful membership (including the Greenwich Police, many of whom practice here). To join, call and listen to the recorded announcement. Usually, all you have to do is attend a meeting (the second Wednesday of each month at 8 pm). To transport a gun to and from the club you need a Connecticut handgun license, which they can help you obtain.

EuroChasse

398 Greenwich Avenue, 625.9501

www.eurochasse.com

Two floors of fascinating gifts and fashionable men's and women's sporting apparel. If you plan to hunt in Europe, this is a must. They also have serious fly fishing equipment.

Hours: Monday - Saturday, 10 am - 5 pm.

Griffin & Howe

340 West Putnam Avenue, 618.0270

www.griffinhowe.com

Excellent sporting firearms, clothing and accessories. This is the place serious skeet and trap shooters buy their shotguns. They also have shooting schools and coaching.

Hours: Monday - Wednesday, 10 am - 6 pm; Thursday, 11 am -o 8 pm; Friday, 10 am - 6 pm; Saturday, 9 am - 5 pm.

FITNESS & SPORTS

SKIING

Old Greenwich-Riverside Community Center
90 Harding Road, 637.3659
Day ski trips for members in grades 5-8.

There are a great variety of ski areas in the Northeast. For fun on the slopes try some of the following areas:

LOCAL FAMILY SKI AREAS

Hunter
Hunter, NY, 518.263.4223   www.huntermtn.com
Difficulty: Beginner, Intermediate, Advanced.
Size: 12 lifts, 53 trails, snowmaking, snowtubing.
Distance: 2.5 hrs, I-87 N exit 20, Rte 32 N, Rte 23A W.

Mohawk
Cornwall, CT, 860.672.6100, 800.895.5222
www.mohawkmountain.com
Difficulty: Beginner & Intermediate.
Size: 5 lifts, 24 trails, snowmaking, night skiing.
Distance: 1.5 hrs, I-95 N to Rte 8 N to exit 44.
At the second light, left onto Rte 4 W (about 20 minutes).

Mount Southington
Southington, CT, 860.628.0954
www.MountSouthington.com
Difficulty: Beginner & Intermediate.
Size: 7 lifts, 14 trails, snowmaking, night skiing.
Distance: 2 hrs, I-84 N exit 30.

Powder Ridge
Middlefield, CT, 800.622.3321, 860.349.3454
www.powderridgect.com
Difficulty: Beginner & Intermediate, snowtubing.
Size: 7 lifts (2 for tubing), 5 wide runs, 14 trails, night skiing.
Distance: 45 minutes, Merritt Pkw N exit 67.

SKIING

Windham

Windham, NY, 518.734.4300, 800.342.5116, 4766
www.skiwindham.com
Difficulty: Beginner, Intermediate & Expert.
Size: 33 trails, 7 lifts, snowmaking.
Distance: 2.5 hrs, I-87 N exit 21, Rte 23 W.

Winding Trails Cross Country Ski Center

Farmington, CT, 860.678.9582, 677.8458
www.WindingTrails.com
Difficulty: Beginner, Intermediate.
Size: 20 Kilometers of trails.
Distance: 2.5 hrs, I-84 N exit 39, Rte 4 W.

LARGE REGIONAL SKI AREAS
CATERING TO FAMILIES

These areas also have extensive summer family activities.
Check their web sites for details.

Killington

Killington, VT, 802.422.3499, 800.621.6867
www.killington.com

Mount Snow

Dover, VT, 802.464.3333, 800.245.7669
www.mountsnow.com

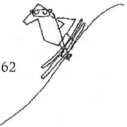

Stowe

Stowe, VT, 802.253.3000, 800.253.4754, 8562
www.Stowe.com

Stratton

South Londonderry, VT, 802.297.2200
www.stratton.com

FITNESS & SPORTS

SKIS/SKI CLOTHING

Hickory & Tweed
410 Main Street, Armonk, NY, 914.273.3397
A ski store with a wide selection of skis to buy or rent. Good technical help.
Hours: Weekdays, 10 am- 5:30 pm (Thursdays open until 8 pm); Saturday, 9:30 am - 5:30 pm; Sunday, noon - 4 pm

St. Paul's Episcopal Church
200 Riverside Avenue, 637.2447
Skate and ski swap for growing children. Call for details and dates.

SQUASH

Field Club
276 Lake Avenue, 869.1309
A private club which offers a weekly Junior Summer Squash Camp often open to the public. They have international singles and doubles courts.

Greenwich Academy Squash Training Camp
200 North Maple Avenue, 625.8900 x 7287
During the summer, the Academy uses their five international squash courts to provide training for children in grades 5 and above.

Sportsplex
49 Brownhouse Road, Stamford, CT, 358.0066
Right on the border of Old Greenwich and Stamford. The Sportsplex provides a complete training center, including four hardball squash courts, one racquetball court and squash instructions.

FITNESS & SPORTS
SWIMMING

For Greenwich Beaches see PARKS & RECREATION, BEACHES.

Department of Parks and Recreation
622.7830
They organize Family Swims at Greenwich High School.

Gordon's Gateway to Sports
217 East Putnam Avenue, Cos Cob, 661.1824
Swimming attire for serious swimmers.

Nike Swim Camps
800.645.3226
www.us-sportscamps.com
Nike runs a number of swim camps around the country for boys and girls ages 10 to 18. The Peddie School program (June and July) in Hightstown, NJ is the closest.

Town Swim Team: The Dolphins
In addition to the high school swim team, the town has a superior competition swim team, the Dolphins (YWCA - 869.6501). The Dolphins are for serious swimmers. Kids start early - swim practice is every day, with meets held on most Sundays. All that is required to join is parental consent and the ability not to sink. Some children start as early as four.

YMCA Programs
50 East Putnam Avenue, 869.1630
Skippers - for parents and babies 6 months to 2 years.
Perch - for ages 2 - 3. Children, with help of parent, propel themselves using flotation aids.
Progressive youth lessons: Polliwog, Guppy, Minnow, Fish, Flying Fish, Shark, for ages 5-12.
Private swimming lessons are available.
Marlins Swim Team, ages 5-18, September to March.

FITNESS & SPORTS

SWIMMING

YWCA Programs

259 East Putnam Avenue, 869.6501

Aqua Babies - for parents and babies 6 months to 3 years;
Aqua Tots/Kids - for ages 2½ to 4 years who are ready to participate without the parent. Both are ideal introductions to swimming and safety in and around the water. Junior Aquatics - K to 12 years. Progressive learn-to- swim lessons.

Dolphins Swim Team - K to high school - competitive technique instruction. Private swimming lessons are available.

TEAM SPORTS EQUIPMENT

Rink & Racquet

24 Railroad Avenue, 622.9180

Hockey (field & ice), Figure Skating, Baseball, Softball, Lacrosse, Rollerblades, Team uniforms.

Hours: Weekdays, 9 am - 5:30 pm; Saturday, 9 am - 5 pm.

Bruce Park Sports

104 Mason Street, 869.1382

Team uniforms and equipment for most sports.

Hours: Weekdays, 10 am - 6 pm (Thursday to 7:30);
Saturday, 10 am - 5:30 pm; Sunday, 10 am - 3:30 pm.

Gordon's Gateway to Sports

(Mill Pond Shopping Center)
217 East Putnam Avenue, Cos Cob, 661.1824

Large Lacrosse dealer.

Hours: Monday to Thursday 9 am - 8 pm; Friday 9 am - 5:30 pm;
Saturday, 9 am - 5 pm; Sunday 11 am - 4 pm.

FITNESS & SPORTS
TENNIS

Gordon's Gateway to Sports
217 East Putnam Avenue, Cos Cob, 661.1824
Nice selection of tennis wear; demo racquets and re-stringing.
Hours: Monday to Thursday, 9 am - 8 pm; Friday, 9 am - 5:30 pm;
Saturday, 9 am - 5 pm; Sunday, 11 am - 4 pm.

Greenwich Racquet Club
1 River Road, Cos Cob, 661.0606
4 indoor Har-Tru courts. They have good instruction and adult clinics.

Greenwich Tennis Headquarters
54 Bible Street, Cos Cob, 661.0182
There are 38 all-weather courts available throughout Greenwich, as
well as a paddle tennis court location. The town runs junior and adult
clinics for all levels and provides private lessons. It also sponsors a
junior and adult town tennis tournament which attracts some very good
players. Call for information, a map of the courts and a tennis permit.

Grand Slam
1 Bedford-Banksville Road, Bedford, NY, 914.234.9206
Five Har-Tru courts, five hard surface (Deco Turf II) courts. During the
winter, eight are indoor, during the summer, five are outside. Excellent
junior and adult programs including USTA League Play.

Nike Adult and Junior Tennis Camps
800.645.3226   www.us-sportscamps.com
Nike sponsors a great number of adult and junior tennis camps. The
closest are Amherst College, Amherst, MA; Loomis-Chaffee, Windsor,
CT; Peddie School, Hightstown, NJ; Lawrenceville School, Lawrenceville,
NJ.

Old Greenwich Tennis Academy
151 Sound Beach Avenue, 637.3398
5 indoor Har-Tru courts. Mainly used by groups who contract for court
time. Open September to May.

FITNESS & SPORTS

TENNIS

Personal Pro Services
May - October, Greenwich, 962.2673;
November - April, Scottsdale, Arizona, 480.575.9702.
email: personalpro@earthlink.net
Tim Richardson is a USPTA Pro 1 tennis instructor. During the playing season, Tim will help you perfect your tennis game in the privacy of your own court and on your own schedule. Tim has been teaching on private Greenwich courts for almost 20 years.

Sound Shore Tennis
303 Post Road, Port Chester, NY, 914.939.1300
Twelve indoor hard surface courts. Open September to May and rain-only weekends after May.

Wire Mill Racquet Club
578 Wire Mill Road, Stamford, CT, 329.9221
Just off exit 35 of the Merritt Parkway, Wire Mill (four outdoor red clay courts) is owned by the pros who teach in the winter at the Greenwich Racquet Club. Inexpensive to join.

YMCA Programs
50 East Putnam Avenue, 869.1630
The Y provides a number of tennis clinics as well as private lessons for women, men and children, from beginner to advanced.

YWCA Programs
259 East Putnam Avenue, 869.6501
Beginner and intermediate lessons for adults and children as young as six.

FITNESS & SPORTS

VOLLEYBALL

Department of Parks and Recreation Volleyball Programs

Contact: Frank Gabriele, 622.7830

The town sponsors adult co-ed volleyball games at the Western Greenwich Civic Center in Glenville. They also sponsor the Greenwich Volleyball League, an adult, winter co-ed volleyball league for A and B flight teams. They play at Glenville Elementary School on Tuesday & Thursday nights. Greenwich residents 16 years and older may participate.

Nike Volleyball Camps

800.645.322

www.us-sportscamps.com

Nike sponsors a number of volleyball camps around the country for ages 13 to 18. The closest camp is at Cornell University, Ithaca, NY.

Uniforms and Equipment

See FITNESS & SPORTS, TEAM SPORTS EQUIPMENT.

YMCA Volleyball Programs

50 East Putnam Avenue, 869.1630

The Y sponsors informal, co-ed volleyball games for adults.

FITNESS & SPORTS

WALKING

Audubon Guidebook to Walking Trails

A 63-page guide to 26 area walking trails is available for $17 from the Greenwich Audubon Society, PO Box 7487, Greenwich, CT 06831.

Audubon Center

613 Riversville Road, 869.5272

280 acres of well-kept trails, a delightful place to walk. The entrance is on the corner of Riversville Road and John Street.

Babcock Preserve

North Street, Greenwich

297 acres stretching between North Street and Lake Avenue. The entrance is on North Street about 2 miles north of the Merritt Parkway. An extensive network of trails which range in length from 1 to 3.5 miles.

Greenwich Point

Shore Road, Old Greenwich

147 acres at the end of Sound Beach Avenue. Greenwich Point is a popular spot for water sports, as well as walking, bicycle riding, roller blading and running. A network of trails leads along the changing coastline and through the woods. A trail guide is available at the Seaside Center of the Bruce Museum. During the summer a beach pass is required.

Mianus River Park

Cognewaugh Road, Cos Cob

220 acres stretching from Greenwich into Stamford. The entrance is ½ mile east of Stanwich Road on Cognewaugh Road. The two trails of most interest are the Pond Trail and the Oak Trail.

Montgomery Pinetum

Bible Street, Cos Cob

91 acres, just off of Bible Street in Cos Cob. The entrance is on the west side directly opposite Clover Place. Obtain a map and tree guide from the Garden Center office, then enjoy the extraordinary diversity of trees and plantings. One path leads to the 22-acre Greenwich Audubon Society's Mildred Bedard Caldwell Wildlife Sanctuary.

FITNESS & SPORTS
YOGA

Greenwich Continuing Education
At Greenwich High School, 625.0141, 625.7474
Beginning and advanced yoga courses as well as t'ai chi ch'uan classes.

Greenwich Health at Greenwich Hospital
Greenwich Hospital Cohen Pavilion, 77 Lafayette Place, 863.4444
They offer a number of wellness programs including yoga and t'ai chi ch'uan classes.
Hours: Weekdays, 9 am - 5 pm.

Old Greenwich-Riverside Community Center
90 Harding Road, Old Greenwich, 637.3659
They offer a beginning yoga program.

YMCA
50 East Putnam Avenue, 869.1630
The Y offers a beginning course in yoga techniques to reduce stress.

YWCA
259 East Putnam Avenue, 869.6501
The Y offers yoga programs for all levels.

FLOWERS & GARDENS

The Greenwich Department of Parks has a green thumb. The combination of the Department's efforts, together with the talents of many garden club volunteers (who you will often see gardening on many of the town's intersections) make Greenwich incredibly beautiful.

Garden Education Center

Montgomery Pinetum, Bible Street, Cos Cob, 869.9242

The Center's horticulture buildings provide classrooms and workrooms for a variety of programs and lectures. Founded in 1957, the center is not only a strong educational facility, but also provides a good framework for new residents to make friends.

Hours: Closed during the summer. Open September 1 to Memorial Day; weekdays, 9 am - 3:30 pm; in October and December, also Saturday, 10 am - 3 pm.

Greenwich Orchids

106 Mason Street, 661.5544

Grown in a local greenhouse, the orchids are exquisite. They have many varieties, some with unusual colors. They also make lovely flower arrangements.

Hours: Monday - Saturday, 9 am - 6 pm.

Greenwich Fruit and Produce

340 Greenwich Avenue, 869.7903

Although this is primarily a fruit and vegetable shop, we like treating ourselves to their bouquets of lovely, inexpensive, fresh flowers. They always have a nice selection on the street just outside their shop.

Hours: Monday - Saturday, 8 am - 7 pm; Sunday, 9 am -o 6 pm.

Ivy Urn

115 Mason Street (Village Square), 661.5287

A gift shop with attractive ornaments for gardeners.

Hours: Monday - Saturday, 10 am - 5 pm.

Kenneth Lynch & Sons

84 Danbury Road, Wilton, CT, 203.762.8363

If you are looking for an elaborate fountain, pretty garden bench, statuary, topiary, weathervane or sundial, this will be paradise for you. The Lynch family has been crafting garden ornaments for over sixty years. Ornaments are made to order. Their extensive catalog is available for $10. Hours: Weekdays, 8 am - 5 pm.

Directions: Merritt Parkway N to exit 39 (Norwalk), N on Rte 7.

FLOWERS & GARDENS

McArdle-MacMillen Florist & Garden Center

48 Arch Street, 661.5600, 800.581.5558
www.connmart.com/mcardle
Many pretty dinner tables are adorned with their arrangements. A good place to buy flowers (they have a large selection), corsages and plants. Come early on weekends during the garden season, as it is always busy —or place an order on their web site.
Hours: Closed Sunday; Monday - Saturday, 8 am - 5:30 pm.

New York Botanical Gardens

Bronx, NY, 718.817.8705   www.nybg.org
Greenwich garden enthusiasts know their way to the NY Botanical Gardens. The gardens have recently undergone a $25 million renovation and are considered the best in the country.
Hours: Open all year, Tuesday - Sunday, 10 am - 6 pm.
Wednesdays are free.
Directions: (30 minutes) Merritt/Hutchinson Pkw S to exit 15; Cross County Pkw W to exit 6; Bronx River Pkw S to exit 8W (Mosholu Pkw); at second light, L into Garden.

Old Greenwich Flower Shop

232 Sound Beach Avenue, Old Greenwich, 637.0492
Treat yourself to a weekend bouquet—flowers are half price on Friday.
Hours: Monday - Saturday, 9 am - 5 pm.

Sam Bridge Nursery & Greenhouse

437 North Street, 869.3418
www.sambridge.com
A family-run operation that has been welcoming Greenwich residents to their greenhouses since 1930. Many of the more than 50,000 plants available are grown in their own greenhouses. They offer classes on topics such as perennial gardening and pruning. You can select live or cut Christmas trees, which they will deliver to you when you are ready.
Hours: Closed Sunday; Monday - Saturday, 8:30 am - 5 pm.

Secret Garden

28 Sherwood Place, 869.6246
Tucked away behind the Greenwich Women's Exchange, this small store is indeed a secret place. They have unique garden ornaments and a selection of small antiques. Hours: Monday - Saturday, 10 am - 4 pm; during the summer, Saturday hours may vary.

FLOWERS & GARDENS

GARDEN CLUBS

Byram Garden Club
Byram Schubert Library
21 Mead Avenue, Byram
Margaret Wiener, Co-President - 531.7120
Betty McKenna, Co-President - 532.1688

Friends of Binney Park
92 Wesskum Wood Road, Old Greenwich
Robert E. Horton III - 637.8334
Contact: Linda Butler - 637.3558

Garden Club of Old Greenwich
11 Somerset Lane, Riverside
Marcia Livingston, President - 637.9708

Green Fingers Garden Club
PO Box 4655, Greenwich 06830
Robin Browning, President - 661.2670

Greenwich Daffodil Society
38 Perkins Road
Nancy B. Mott, President - 661.6142

Greenwich Garden Club
PO Box 4896, Greenwich 06831
Valerie Stauffer, President - 869.7451

Greenwich Green & Clean
Yantoro Community Center, 113 Pemberwick Road, 629.8439 or 531.0006
Mary G. Hull, Executive Director

Greenwich Woman's Club Gardeners
89 Maple Avenue, 869.2046
Jane Boutelle, President - 869.7341

FLOWERS & GARDENS

GARDEN CLUBS

Hortulus
PO Box 4666, Greenwich, CT 06830
Karen Tell, President
Contact: Letitia Potter - 869.6069

Junior League of Greenwich
Sustainer's Garden Club
Junior League of Greenwich
48 Maple Avenue, 869.1979
Emily Toohey, President - 661.7988

Knollwood Garden Club
170 Clapboard Ridge Road
Paula Burton, President - 869.1315

Riverside Garden Club
PO Box 11
Riverside 06878-0011
Terry Lubman, President - 637.8221
Contact: Joan Denne, Membership Chairman - 637.1350

FOOD STORES

BREAD/BAKERIES

Black Forest
52 Lewis Street, 629.9330
German-style bakery. Don't miss the Black Forest Cake and Chocolate Mousse Bombe.
Try Bread Ventures' chocolate-cherry bread on the weekend.
Hours: Tuesday - Saturday, 7:30 am - 6 pm; Sunday, 8 am - 1 pm.

(The) Kneaded Bread
181 North Main Street, Port Chester, NY, 914.937.9489
Their freshly baked bread—all kinds— is delicious. Have a sandwich when you visit, but be sure to take home their Cinnamon Swirl. It makes great French toast.
Hours: Tuesday - Friday, 7 am - 6 pm; Saturday, 8 am - 4 pm; Sunday, 8 am - 1 pm.

Arnold Bakery Outlet
10 Hamilton Avenue, Byram (between I-95 exits 2 and 3), 531.4770
That good smell wafting onto I-95 just before Greenwich comes from the Arnold Bakery. Their bread is available at local grocery stores, but for a wide selection of bread at bargain prices visit the factory outlet shop.
Hours: Monday - Wednesday, 8 am - 6 pm; Thursday - Friday, 6 am - 6 pm; Saturday, 8 am - 6 pm; Sunday, 10 am - 5 pm.

St. Moritz
383 Greenwich Avenue, 869.2818
Luscious, rich pastries and cakes. Be sure to try the Sarah Bernhardt cookies.
Hours: Monday - Saturday, 7 am - 6 pm; Sunday, 8 am - 1 pm.

Sweet Lisa's Exquisite Cakes
3 Field Road, Cos Cob, 869.9545
Wonderful cakes and party pastries.
Hours: Tuesday - Saturday, 10 am - 6 pm.

FOOD STORES

BREAD/BAKERIES

(The) Upper Crust & Bagel Company

197 Sound Beach Avenue, Old Greenwich, 698.0079
Good place to sit down and chat. Great bagels and sandwiches.
Hours: Weekdays, 6 am - 4 pm; weekends, 7 am - 4 pm.

Versailles

315 Greenwich Avenue, 661.6634
We love their operas and eclairs.
Hours: Weekdays, 7:30 am to 9:30 pm (Friday until 10 pm);
Saturday, 8 am - 10 pm; Sunday, 8 am - 8 pm.

CHOCOLATES

Darlene's Heavenly Chocolates

535 East Putnam Avenue, Cos Cob, 622.7077
Our favorite chocolate shop in town. Not only are the chocolates delicious, Darlene always makes you feel glad you shopped there. Ask her
about special chocolate deliveries.
Hours: Monday - Saturday, 10:30 am to 6 pm; Expanded holiday hours.

Two other chocolate stores with excellent selections are:
Bernard Chocolates, 16 Greenwich Avenue, 552.9180
Leonidas, 49 Greenwich Avenue, 661.7934

FOOD STORES

COFFEE SHOPS

Arcadia Coffee Co.

20 Arcadia Road, Old Greenwich, 637.8766
Good coffee and sandwiches in a friendly setting. Nice historic building.
Hours: Weekdays, 6:30 am - 6 pm; weekends, 7:30 am - 6 pm.

Dunkin' Donuts

375 East Putnam & 271 West Putnam Avenue
We are addicted to their coffee.
Hours: every day, 5:30 am - 10 pm.

Starbucks

301 Greenwich Avenue, 661.3042
60 East Putnam Avenue, 629.0432
1253 East Putnam Avenue, Riverside, 698.1790
Need we say more?
Hours: Monday - Saturday, 6 am - 10 pm (Friday & Saturday to 11 pm);
Sunday, 7 am - 10 pm.

Coffee Tree

50 Greenwich Avenue, 622.6566
22 Railroad Avenue, 629.2230
Indulge in a treat with their gourmet coffee.
Hours: Weekdays, 6:45 am - 6 pm; Saturday, 7 am - 6 pm;
Sunday, 7:30 am - 4 pm.

FOOD STORES

DELICATESSENS

Alpen Pantry

23 Arcadia Road, Old Greenwich, 637.3818

Nice take-out sandwich selection. Order a cheese ball or cheese dip for a party. Amazing sandwiches!

Hours: Monday - Saturday, 9 am - 5 pm.

Apache Place

7 Apache Place, Riverside, 637.3232

www.apacheplace.com

Where is Apache Place you say? This well-liked, but off the beaten path, delicatessen is just one street in from the intersection of Sheephill Road and the Post Road and well worth finding. The Chef-Owner is Dale Ritchey, a graduate of the Culinary Institute of America. He makes an assortment of interesting and well-priced items not normally found in a deli. Hours: Monday - Thursday, 6 am - 4 pm; Friday - Saturday, 7 am - 3 pm. Most Sundays they are closed.

Aux Délices

1075 East Putnam Avenue, Riverside, 698.1066

Getting more popular all the time as a place for a delicious late lunch.

Hours: Every day, 7:30 am - 6:30 pm, (Sunday until 2:30 pm).

Fresh Fields

90 East Putnam Avenue, 661.0631

www.wholefoods.com

This mostly organic grocery store has expanded their selection enormously. When you want the best fresh foods you have to stop here. The deli has become first class.

Garden Caterers

235 East Putnam Avenue, Cos Cob, 861.0099

185 Sound Beach Avenue, Old Greenwich, 698.2900

177 Hamilton Avenue, Byram, 552.1780

If you like fried chicken, don't miss this take-out.

Hours: Weekdays, 5 am - 7 pm; Saturday, 6 am - 4 pm.

FOOD STORES

DELICATESSENS

Garelick & Herbs

48 West Putnam Avenue, 661.7373

A sophisticated deli with a second location in Westport. It has a wide selection of ready-to-serve dishes. Primarily a take-out store, although there are places to sit for the lucky few that get there first.

Hours: Weekdays, 7 am - 8 pm; Saturday, 8 am - 7 pm; Sunday, 9 am - 5 pm.

Gourmet Galley

100 Greenwich Avenue, 869.9618

A good place to revive and rest from Avenue shopping.

Hours: Monday - Saturday, 7 am - 4 pm.

Hayday

1050 East Putnam Avenue, Riverside, 637.7600

A sophisticated, gourmet country shop for fruits, vegetables and treats. Hayday carries hundreds of imported and American cheeses. Don't go in hungry.

Hours: Monday - Saturday, 8 am - 8 pm; Sunday, 8 am - 7 pm.

Katzenberg's Express

342 Greenwich Avenue, 625.0103

A new deli with a wide selection of sandwiches. Primarily take-out, but there are a few places to sit.

Hours: Monday - Thursday, 8 am - 6 pm; Friday & Saturday, 9 am - 10 pm; Sunday 10 am - 4 pm.

Paesano's Deli

146 Mason Street, 625.0040

Open Weekdays for breakfast. Fast friendly service. Limited seating.

Hours: Monday - Saturday, 7 am - 5 pm.

Village Deli

3 West Elm Street, 622.6644

Charmingly decorated, tasty deli with space to sit down and enjoy your meal. A good bet for breakfast.

Hours: Monday - Saturday, 7 am - 7 pm; Sunday, 10 am - 4 pm.

FOOD STORES

FISH

Bon Ton
343 Greenwich Avenue, 869.0576
A reliable stand-by.
Hours: Monday - Saturday, 7 am - 6 pm.

Fjord Fisheries Market
137 River Road, Cos Cob, 661.5006
www.fjordcatering.com
Fresh fish and friendly service.
Hours: Monday - Saturday, 8 am - 7 pm.

Lobster Bin
204 Field Point Road, 661.6559
Just off Railroad Avenue. Plenty of fresh fish as well as parking.
Hours: Monday - Saturday, 8 am - 6 pm; Sunday, 9 am - 1 pm.

FOOD STORES

FRUITS & VEGETABLES

Cos Cob Farmers Market

61-63 East Putnam Avenue, Cos Cob, 629.2267
Fresh fruit, vegetables and flowers at very reasonable prices.
Hours: Weekdays, 8 am - 7 pm; Saturday, 8 am - 6 pm; closed Sunday.

Farmer's Market

604 North Main Street, Port Chester, NY, 914.935.1075
When you are looking for fresh fruit and vegetables at off hours, this store located next to Carvel in the circle between Greenwich and Port Chester is a good bet. In addition their prices are very reasonable.
Hours: Monday - Saturday, 8 am - 7 pm; Sunday, 9 am - 6 pm.

Greenwich Fruit & Produce

340 Greenwich Avenue, 869.7903
The best quality and selection of fruits and vegetables.
Hours: Monday - Saturday, 8 am - 7 pm; Sunday, 9 am - 6 pm.

Greenwich Farmer's Market

Held Saturdays 9:30 am - 1:30 pm from May 17 to late October, in the Greenwich Train Station parking lot (across from the Boys and Girls Club). In its third year and growing rapidly, the market - which operates rain or shine - has fresh produce from local farmers as well as baked goods. It is totally delightful. Don't miss it.

Hayday

Their fruits and vegetables are always attractively displayed as well as delicious. See store details in the FOOD STORES, DELICATESSENS section.

Port Chester Farmer's Market

Held Fridays 9 am - 2:30 pm from late June to the middle of November, at the Marina (one block behind Main Street). Similar in size and quality to the Greenwich Farmer's Market, but with different farmers.
Directions: US 1 S to Port Chester, L to Adee Street.

FRUITS & VEGETABLES

Purdy's Farm & Nursery

Upper King Street (1353 King Street), Greenwich, 531.9815
Greenwich used to have a lot of local farms. Most have disappeared,
but Greenwich insiders keep Purdy's going strong. How can you resist
very fresh from-the-farm produce at reasonable prices, sold by a friendly
owner. In the fall, their pumpkins and cider are worth the trip.
Hours: Open every day, 9 am - 5 pm, sometimes later.

Pick-Your-Own

Picking your own fruit and vegetables has become a popular pastime in
Connecticut. There are nine farms in Fairfield County offering urbanites
the opportunity to pick their own products.
For more detailed information go to www.state.ct.us/doag
Some you might consider are:

Silverman's Farm

Easton, CT, 203.261.3306

Peaches in July, apples in August. Three-acre animal farm for youngsters.

White Silo Farm

Sherman, CT, 860.355.0271

Strawberries, asparagus, raspberries, blackberries and rhubarb.

FOOD STORES

GROCERY STORES

Food Emporium
160 West Putnam Avenue, 622.0374
www.foodemporium.com
A good general purpose grocery. It stays open late, even on weekends.
Hours: Weekdays, open 24 hours-a-day; Saturday, 7 am - midnight;
Sunday, 7 am - 9 pm.

Food Mart
120 Post Road, Cos Cob, 629.2100
Family-owned grocery - helpful and friendly. It's a neighborhood meeting spot.
Hours: Monday - Thursday, 7 am - 7 pm; Friday, 7 am - 8 pm;
Saturday, 7 am - 6 pm; Sunday, 8 am - 5 pm.

Fresh Fields
90 East Putnam Avenue, 661.0631
www.wholefoods.com
This mostly organic grocery store has expanded their selection enormously. When you want the best fresh foods you have to stop here. The deli has become first class.

Fuji Mart
1212 East Putnam Avenue, Old Greenwich, 203.698.2107
An authentic Japanese grocery. Buy a bag of frozen gyoza.
Hours: Tuesday - Friday, 10:30 am - 6 pm; Sunday, 10 am - 6 pm.

Grand Union
11 Glen Ridge Road, Glenville, 531.0541
161 West Putnam Avenue, Greenwich, 625.0622
A general purpose grocery with a wide selection of produce, bakery and delicatessen items.
Hours: The Greenwich store is open seven days a week, 24 hours a day, except Sunday when it closes at 11 pm. The Glenville store is open Monday to Saturday, 7 am - 11 pm and on Sunday until 9 pm.

FOOD STORES

GROCERY STORES

Harrington's of Vermont
83 Railroad Avenue, 661.4479
www.HarringtonHam.com
If you need a ham for a party, this is the place. Try one of their ham sandwiches and you will know what we mean.
Hours: Monday - Saturday, 9:30 am - 5:30 pm; Sunday, 11 am - 4 pm.

Hayday
1050 East Putnam Avenue, Riverside, 637.7600
A sophisticated, gourmet country shop for fruits, vegetables and treats. Hayday carries hundreds of imported and American cheeses. Don't go in hungry.
Hours: Monday - Saturday, 8 am - 8 pm; Sunday, 8 am - 7 pm.

Stew Leonard's
100 Westport Avenue, Norwalk, 203.847.7213
www.stew-leonards.com
Famous throughout the metropolitan area - worth the trip.
Bring your children.
Hours: Every day, 7 am - 11 pm.
Directions: I-95 N to exit 16; L on East; R on Westport (6th light).

FOOD STORES

ICE CREAM

Carvel
604 North Main Street, Port Chester, NY, 914.939.1487
Located just on the border of Greenwich and Port Chester on US 1, this standby is open seven days a week. If you like hot fudge sundaes the way we do, Wednesday is your day. You can get two for the price of one.
Hours: Sunday - Thursday, 10 am - 10 pm; Friday and Saturday, 10 am - 11 pm.

Dr. Mike's
158 Greenwood Avenue, Bethel, CT, 203.792.4388
This ice cream, often rated as the best in Connecticut, is far away for a guide about Greenwich. Once you have tasted it, you too, may forgive its geographical distance.
Hours: Every day, noon - 11 pm.

Häagen-Dazs
374A Greenwich Avenue, 629.8000
It's a toss-up between a hot fudge sundae or a chocolate-laced cone filled with creamy dulce de leche. Hours: Every day, 11 am - 11 pm.

Longford's Ice Cream
4 Elm Place, Rye, NY, 914. 967.3797
Longford's ice cream factory is on Wilkins Street in Port Chester. Many clubs and quality restaurants, in and around Greenwich, are supplied by Longford's. Fortunately, Longford has one ice cream parlor just a short distance away in Rye. Fill your freezer with ice cream, ice cream pies and sorbets. We haven't tasted a flavor we didn't like.
Hours: every day, noon - 10 pm.

Meli-Melo
362 Greenwich Avenue, 629.6153
On the Isle Saint Louis in Paris, Parisians line the street waiting for a chance to buy a fresh fruit sorbet. Parisians would love Meli-Melo's sherbets.
Hours: every day, 11 am - 10 pm.

FOOD STORES

ICE CREAM

Sweet Ashley's

248 East Avenue, East Norwalk, 203.866.7740

If your are in SoNo and hungry for ice cream, this shop in East Norwalk has a long list of homemade flavors at very reasonable prices.

Hours: Weekdays, 11 am - 10 pm; weekends, 11 am - 10:30 pm.

Zoom

Grigg Street, 869.3125

Formerly the Juice Shop, they have expanded their offerings to include wraps and salads along with their juice blends and smoothies. The smoothies are good, but the wraps are just as indifferent as the service.

Hours: Monday - Saturday, 9:30 am - 5 pm.

FOOD STORES
MEATS

Food Mart
26 Arcadia Road, Old Greenwich, 637.1701
120 Post Road, Cos Cob, 629.2100
The courteous and helpful staff in both store's meat departments are happy to take orders by phone, or, if you drop off your order before you shop it will be ready by the time you are finished.
Hours: Monday - Thursday, 7 am - 7 pm; Friday, 7 am - 8 pm; Saturday, 7 am - 6 pm; Sunday, 8 am - 5 pm.

Harrington's of Vermont
The source for superb smoked ham and bacon. See store details in FOOD STORES, GROCERY STORES.

Hayday
Try their delicious homemade sausage.
See store details in FOOD STORES, GROCERY STORES.

Manero's Meat Shop
559 Steamboat Road, 622.9684
www.maneros-greenwichct.com
You can still ask the butcher for your favorite cuts. Phone orders are welcome. Many of the best barbecues in town start here.
Hours: Weekdays, 9 am - 7 pm; Saturday 9 am - 9 pm; Sunday, 9 am - 5:30 pm.

FOOD STORES
WINE

Horseneck Liquors
25 East Putnam Avenue, 869.8944
An excellent selection of wines from California and all over the world. Friendly, good advice. They will deliver and, if needed, gift-wrap for you.
Hours: Monday - Saturday, 9 am - 8 pm.

Var Max Liquor Pantry
16 Putnam Avenue, Port Chester, NY, 914.937.4930
They also have a large selection and are often less expensive. Nice descriptions on their wine specials.
Hours: Monday - Saturday, 9 am - 9 pm (Friday & Saturday until 10).

Wine World on Elm
39 East Elm Street, 869.6008,5067
The wine selection is somewhat smaller than the other two, but the service and help can't be beaten. If you are intimidated by choosing the right wine, this is your store.
Hours: Monday - Saturday, 9 am - 7 pm.

GAMBLING

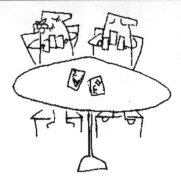

Gambling has come to Connecticut and our two casinos are closer and more attractive than those in Atlantic City, NJ. The casinos are very close to each other.

Foxwoods Resort Casino

800.369.9663

www.foxwoods.com

Just seven miles from Mystic, CT, this resort is owned by the Mashantucket Pequot Tribal Nations. It is the largest hotel complex in the Northeast. The 312-room Grand Pequot Tower is very comfortable, and - in addition to an array of restaurants, entertainment and, of course, gaming tables - there is a golf club.

Directions: I-95 N to exit 92, West on Rte 2. About 2.5 hours from Greenwich.

Mohegan Sun

860.204.8000

www.MoheganSun.com

www.sunint.com

Somewhat smaller than Foxwoods, this casino still has over 192 gaming tables and 3,000 slot machines. The casino is owned by the Mohegan Nation and Sun International. The Mohegan Sun complex reflects the culture and history of the Mohegan Nation. Many people prefer its Native American theme decoration.

Directions: 95 N to exit 76, 395 N to exit 79 A, Rte. 2A less than 2 miles to Mohegan Sun Boulevard. About 2 hours from Greenwich.

GROOMING

BARBERS

Benford Barber Shop

154 Prospect Street, 661.7383

This out-of-the-way shop is used by many of Greenwich's prominent residents. Haircuts are by appointment only.

Hours: Wednesday - Saturday, 8 am - 5 pm.

Off-Center Barber Shop

259 Sound Beach Avenue, Old Greenwich, 637.1161

An Old Greenwich institution. Kids love haircuts in the Jeep.

Hours: Monday and Tuesday, 8 am - 5 pm; closed Wednesday; Thursday, 8 am - 7:30 pm; Friday 8 am - 5 pm;
Saturday, 8 am - 5 pm (summer until 2 pm).

Subway Barber Shop

315 Greenwich Avenue, 869.3263

They cater to children.

Hours: Monday - Saturday (closed Wednesday), 8 am - 5 pm.

DAY SPAS

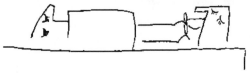

(The) Greenhouse Spa

44-48 West Putnam Avenue, 622.0300

Enjoy treatments in a quiet, private setting. Full-service menu for men and women includes facials, massages, body treatments, hair removal, make-up and more.

Hours: Monday - Wednesday, 9 am - 5 pm; Thursday, 9 am - 7 pm; Friday & Saturday, 8 am - 5 pm.

Harmony

270 Mason Street, 861.7338.

Considered a "real find", this tiny day spa is just the place for an excellent facial, waxing or a relaxing Reiki treatment.

Hours: Monday & Saturday, 11 am - 5 pm; Tuesday - Friday, 8:30 am - 6 pm.

Noelle Spa for Beauty and Wellness

1100 High Ridge Road, Stamford, Ct, 322.3445

Complete day spa with a great variety of services from hair care to facials, massages and nails.

Hours: Monday, 8:15 am - 5:30 pm; Tuesday & Thursday, 8:15 am - 8 pm; Wednesday, 8:15 am - 5:30 pm; Friday, 8:15 am - 6 pm; Saturday, 8:15 am - 5 pm; Sunday, 9:30 am - 6 pm.

Directions: Merritt Parkway to exit 35 (High Ridge Road). Take a right off of the exit. Noelle is immediately on the right.

GROOMING

HAIR SALONS

Carlo and Company Salon
Presently in the Outdoor Traders building at 79 East Putnam Avenue, but moving to 70 East Putnam Avenue (Fresh Fields shopping center), 869.2300
Long established in Greenwich, you will enjoy the friendly, attentive atmosphere as well as their expert haircuts, coloring and styling.

De Berardinis
124 Greenwich Avenue, 622.4247
A comfortable, full-service salon with talented stylists and colorists.
Hours: Monday - Saturday, 9 am to 6 pm (Tuesday & Thursday until 8 pm).

Enzo Ricco Bene Salon
1800 E. Putnam Avenue(at the Hyatt), Old Greenwich, 698.4141
This attractive salon located off the lobby of the Hyatt Regency Hotel offers a pleasant and talented staff of colorists and stylists. For easiest access use the free valet parking.
Hours: Monday & Saturday, 8 am - 5 pm ; Tuesday, 8 am - 7 pm; Wednesday & Friday, 8 am - 6 pm; Thursday, 8 am - 8 pm.

Hopscotch
144 Mason Street, 661.0107
Caters to a fashionable clientele. People come from New York City to go here.
Hours: Monday - Saturday, 8:30 am - 5 pm (Saturday to 4:30).

Lane's Hair Stylists
18 Greenwich Avenue, 622.9566
Old-fashioned beauty shop, serving men, women and children.
Good place for a haircut. No appointments.
Hours: Monday - Saturday, 9 am - 5 pm
(Thursday & Friday, until 8 pm).

Visible Changes
204 Sound Beach Avenue, Old Greenwich, 637.9154, 8467
If you've seen a great haircut - it's likely to have been cut here.
Hours: Tuesday - Saturday, 9 am - 6 pm
(Tuesday & Thursday, until 8 pm).

Nails by Empy
138 Hamilton Avenue, 661-6625
By appointment.
Hours: Weekdays, 9 am - 6 pm; Saturday 9 am - 4 pm.

Nails R Us
1 Havemeyer Lane, Old Greenwich, 698.3320
By appointment or walk-in.
Hours: Monday - Saturday, 9:30 am - 7 pm; Sunday, 10 am - 5:30 pm.

Tiffany Nails
349 Greenwich Avenue, 661.3838
Walk-ins only.
Hours: Monday - Saturday, 9:30 am - 7 pm; Sunday 10 am - 5:30 pm.

HEALTH

PRODUCTS

Fresh Fields

90 East Putnam Avenue, 661.0631

www.wholefoods.com

Since the take over by Whole Foods, this mostly organic grocery store has expanded their selection enormously. When you want the best fresh foods you have to stop here. The deli has become first class. The vitamin and herbal portion of the store is also very complete.

Greenwich Healthmart

30 Greenwich Avenue, 869.9658

A well-stocked health product store, including some foods and a great variety of vitamins and homeopathic remedies. Their cheerful service makes everyone feel well. Be sure to ask for their excellent newsletter.
Hours: Monday - Sunday, 8:30 am - 5:30 pm (Sunday until 5 pm).

Neal's Yard (Natural Remedies)

79 East Putnam Avenue, 629.0885

An attractive shop stocking natural skin and hair care products. They have an extensive range of herbs, essential oils and homeopathic remedies. Treat yourself to this shop.
Hours: Monday - Wednesday, 10 am - 5:30 pm;
Thursday, 10 am - 8 pm; Friday and Saturday, 10 am - 5:30 pm.

(The) Vitamin Shoppe

Shopping Center, 535 Post Road, Port Chester, NY, 914.939.5189

www.vitaminshoppe.com

A national chain with a good web site. They have a large selection of products.
Hours: Monday - Saturday, 9 am - 9 pm; Sunday, 11 am - 6 pm.

HEALTH

MEDICAL CARE

IN AN EMERGENCY, DIAL 911

Burke Rehabilitation Hospital
785 Mamaroneck Avenue, White Plains, NY 914.597.2500
www.burke.org
A nearby 60-acre private, not-for-profit, facility specializing in inpatient and outpatient multi-disciplinary physical rehabilitation and research. They have a national reputation for their tailored programs to lessen disability and dependence resulting from disease or injury.

Convenient Medical Care
1200 East Putnam Avenue, Old Greenwich, 698.1419
Walk-in clinic. Quick and efficient for minor injuries and ailments.

Copeland Optometrists
203 South Ridge Street, Rye Brook, NY, 914.939.0830
For years, they were just over the border in Port Chester, but recently they moved another 5 minutes away to Rye Brook. Nevertheless we followed them because of their reliable, caring service. Owned and operated by the Copeland Family, you can count on a good eye examination, the correct prescription and a set of fashionable glasses or contact lens at a reasonable price.
Hours: Weekdays, 9 am - 6 pm (Wednesday until 1 pm, Thursday until 9 pm); Saturday, 9 am - 5 pm.
Directions: Rte 1 S through Main St, R on Westchester, L on Bowman, L on South Ridge.

Dr. Norman Emerson, Dr. Stuart Sklar
15 North Main Street, Port Chester, NY, 914.939.0982
These personable optometrists and their pleasant staff offer complete family eye care, including a comprehensive eye exam. They are especially good at finding the right contact lenses for hard-to-fit customers. They have a full lab on premises, as well as a large selection of quality eyeglass frames.
Hours: Monday, Tuesday, Friday, 9 am - 5 pm; Thursday, 9 am - 8 pm; Saturday, 9 am - 4 pm. Closed Wednesday and Sunday.
Directions: Route 1 S through Port Chester (Main Street).

HEALTH

MEDICAL CARE

Greenwich Emergency Medical Service (GEMS)

637.7505 (general information)

GEMS has six ambulances, 11 paramedics and 12 full time EMTs. GEMS also provides programs in CPR and basic first-aid.

Greenwich Hospital

5 Perryridge Road, 863.3000

www.greenhosp.chime.org

Greenwich Hospital is a 160-bed, nonprofit, community teaching hospital, affiliated with Yale-New Haven Hospital. The Hospital has just finished a new, 350,000-square-foot facility that will serve as the model for advanced health care. The rooms in this new area are carefully designed to make the patient feel comfortable. As a result, many feel it's more like staying at a fine hotel than a hospital. Even the intensive care unit has woodland views and amazing amenities. Word is spreading fast that this is the most comfortable place to have your baby. Greenwich Hospital has a wonderful **emergency room: 863.3637.** For wellness questions, call Greenwich Health at Greenwich Hospital, ext. 4444.

Physician Referral Service

863.3627

Sponsored by Greenwich Hospital, this service is available weekdays between 8:30 am and 4:30 pm. They will find the doctor with the qualifi cations you are looking for and will even make your first appointment.

Tel-Med

863.3799

Sponsored by Greenwich Health at Greenwich Hospital, Tel-Med is an automated, free 24-hour talking library of medical and health-related information on tape. For general information, call and listen to tape 429 or call 863-4444 and ask for a complete brochure. When you call, ask about their screening, education and support programs.

HEALTH

MEDICAL CLAIMS

National Medical Claims Service
363.0140
They have moved to Stamford, but are still a Greenwich family business. They are one of the few companies in the country that will take on the whole process of filing and collecting medical claims for you.

PHARMACIES

CVS 24-Hour Pharmacy
698.4006
Thru-Way Shopping Center, 1239 East Putnam Avenue, Old Greenwich

Finch Pharmacy
3 Riversville Road, Glenville, 531.8494
Friendly pharmacy in the heart of Glenville.
Hours: Weekdays, 8 am - 6 pm; Saturday, 9 am - 6 pm. Closed Sunday.

Grannick's Pharmacy & Medical Supply Company
277 Greenwich Avenue, 869.3492
They know and care about their customers. A good place to rent or buy medical equipment. Call for their delivery policy.
Hours: Monday - Saturday, 8:30 am - 7 pm (Saturday until 6 pm).

Kerr's Village Pharmacy
212 Sound Beach Avenue, Old Greenwich, 637.0593
A friendly local pharmacy with senior discounts and prescription delivery.
Hours: Weekdays, 8 am - 6:30 pm; Saturday, 8:30 am - 6 pm.

HEALTH

VOLUNTEER OPPORTUNITIES

See also CLUBS/ORGANIZATIONS

American Red Cross
Greenwich Chapter
231 East Putnam Avenue, 869.8444
Rosemary Calderato, Director
Contact: Sarah Mobilia, Director of Communication

Greenwich Hospital Auxiliary
Greenwich Hospital
5 Perryridge Road
863.3222 - auxiliary office
863.3335 - Medicare Assistance
Suzanne Rand, President
Contact: Marguerite Heithaus, Director of Volunteer Services - 863.3221

Volunteer Center
62 Palmer's Hill Road, Stamford, CT, 348-7714
A nonprofit organization which will help you find a good place to volunteer your talents.

HOME

DRY CLEANING

Berger Cleaners
282 Mason Street, 869.7650
A good choice for your curtains and draperies.
Hours: Monday - Friday, 7 am - 6 pm; Saturday, 8 am - 3 pm.

Cleaner Option Dry Cleaners
1081 East Putnam Avenue, 637.1710
A perfect choice for your everyday dry cleaning and laundry. Excellent service at good prices. Free pick-up and delivery.
Hours: No real storefront hours, just leave a message on their answering machine.

Thomas Dry Cleaning and Chinese Hand Laundry
68 Lewis Street, 869.9420
A good choice for fine linens and table cloths.
Hours: Weekdays, 7:30 am - 7 pm; Saturday, 7:30 - 6 pm.

Triple S Carpet and Drapery Cleaners
400 West Main Street (Post Road), Stamford, CT, 327.7471
They do a great job cleaning and/or repairing rugs.
Hours: Weekdays, 8 am - 5:30 pm; Saturday, 8 am - 1:30 pm.

HOME

HARDWARE & DECORATING

See also COOKING/COOKING SUPPLIES
HOME/HOUSEWARES & FURNITURE
For framing see CULTURE/ART

Feinsod

268 Sound Beach Avenue, Old Greenwich, 637.3641
www.servistar.com
A friendly, well-stocked hardware store run by people who take customer service that extra step. They even repair storm windows and screens.
Hours: Monday - Saturday, 8 am - 5:30 pm; Sunday, 10 am - 4 pm.

Greenwich Tile and Marble

388 West Putnam Avenue, 869.1709
Very friendly and helpful staff with a large selection of tiles at good prices. Many lovely Greenwich homes have benefitted from their expertise.
Hours: Weekdays, 9 am - 5 pm; Saturday, 10 am - 4 pm.

Greenwich Hardware

195 Greenwich Avenue, 869.6750
Anyone moving into town will find this one of their most valuable resources. A great place to call when you have forgotten something - they will deliver it to you.
Greenwich Hardware has a 10,000 sq. ft store on Banksville Home Center Complex. A great resource for back country residents: 914-234-2000.
Hours: Monday - Saturday, 8 am - 5:30 pm; Sunday, 9 am - 5 pm.

Home Depot

600 Connecticut Avenue, Norwalk, CT, 203.854.9111
150 Midland Avenue, Port Chester, NY, 914.690.9755
www.homedepot.com
They have 40,000 brand names to choose from.
Hours: Monday - Saturday, 6 am - 11 pm; Sunday, 7 am - 6 pm.
Directions to the Norwalk store:
I-95 N to exit 13, R on US 1 (Connecticut Avenue).

HOME

HARDWARE & DECORATING

McDermott Paint & Wallpaper

35 Spring Street, 622.699.0845

If you are planning to do any of your own home painting, you can count on good advice and products from this long-time Greenwich shop. If you are trying to match a color, take a sample and they can duplicate it with their computer.

Hours: Monday - Saturday, 7:30 am - 5 pm.

Reo Appliances

233 East Avenue, East Norwalk, CT, 203.838.7925

Large selection of major appliances at competitive prices. Lots of personal service.

Hours: Monday - Saturday, 9 am - 5 pm; Thursday, 9 am - 7:30 pm. Closed Sunday.

Directions: I-95 N to exit 16, South on East Avenue

Super Handy Hardware

1 Riversville Road, Glenville Center, 531.5599

A good old-fashioned hardware store with most everything you would need for light and heavy-duty home projects.

Hours: Monday - Saturday, 8 am - 5 pm; Sunday, 9 am - 1 pm.

HOME

HOUSEWARES & FURNITURE

For Garden Furniture see: FLOWERS & GARDENS.
For picture frames, see: CULTURE/ART
For discount furniture see: SHOPPING/MALLS & OUTLETS
For children's furniture, see: CHILDREN/SHOPS

Amish Outdoor Living
346 Ethan Allen Highway (Rte 7), Ridgefield, CT, 203.431.9888
Amish craftsmen from around the country supply this shop. Indoor and outdoor tables and chairs are handcrafted and are of fine quality. Sue Knight, the manager, cares about the people who make it and the people who buy it. Your children will love the outdoor playhouses and you will like the reasonable prices and look of the sturdy children's furniture.
Hours: Summer hours, Monday - Saturday, 9 am to 5 pm; Sunday, noon to 5 pm; Closed Wednesdays. Call for winter hours.
Directions: Merritt Parkway N to exit 39 (or I-95 N to exit 15) (Norwalk), N about 13 miles on Route 7.

Fashion Light Center
168 West Putnam Avenue, 869.3098
A handy local resource for bulbs, lampshades, lamps, chandeliers and repairs.
Hours: Monday - Saturday, 9 am to 5:30 pm.

Go to Your Room
234 Mill Street, Byram, 532.9701
Children's rooms do not have to be boring. Fernando Martinez, an Argentine furniture designer, creates colorful, whimsical furniture to make any child smile.
Hours: Monday - Saturday, 10:30 am - 5 pm.

HOME

HOUSEWARES & FURNITURE

Housewarmings
235 Sound Beach Avenue, 637.5106
Unique home furnishings and decorative accessories.
Hours: Weekdays, 10 am - 6 pm; Saturday, 10 am - 5 pm.

Klaff's
28 Washington Street, South Norwalk, CT, 800.552.3371
A tremendous selection of indoor and outdoor lighting fixtures as well as a huge selection of door hardware, bathroom fixtures, and kitchen cabinets.
Hours: Monday - Wednesday, 9 am - 5:30 pm; Thursday - Saturday, 9 am - 8 pm.
Directions: I-95 N, exit 14, R on West Avenue, left at fork onto Main Street, R onto Washington.

(The) Light Touch
12 Lewis Street, 629.2255
When you are looking for a lamp or lamp shade with character, be sure to stop in here.
Hours: Monday - Saturday, 10 am - 5:30 pm.

Lillian August
289 Greenwich Avenue, 629.1539
Outlet store: 85 Water Street, South Norwalk, CT, 203.838.8026.
Sofas, chairs and desks designed by Lillian August.
Hours: Monday - Wednesday, 10 am - 6 pm;
Thursday - Saturday, 10 am - 7 pm; Sunday, noon - 5 pm.

Pier One Imports
225 Greenwich Avenue, 622.4010
Affordable chain carrying everything for the home, from table linens to wicker furniture and throw pillows.
Hours: Weekdays, 10 am - 8 pm; Saturday, 10 am - 7 pm;
Sunday, 10 am - 6 pm.

HOME

HOUSEWARES & FURNITURE

Restoration Hardware
239 Greenwich Avenue, 552.1040
A very upscale, trendy, combination decorative hardware and home furniture store. It is just fun to walk through.
Hours: Monday - Saturday, 9 am to 8 pm (Thursday until 9 pm); Sunday, 11 am - 6 pm.

Simon Pearce
325 Greenwich Avenue, 861.0780
Beautiful handblown glass, pottery, lamps and furniture. Very reasonable prices for the quality.
Hours: Monday - Saturday, 10 am to 6 pm; Sunday, noon to 5 pm.

HOME

MOVING

Alexander Services
Call Shawn Alexander at 888.656.6838, 203.324.4012.
They are the mover of choice for many antique shops.

Callahan Brothers
133 Post Road, Cos Cob, 869.2239
They are the local agent for North American Van Lines and have been a fixture in Greenwich for many years. When you need to move across the country or across the world, give them a call.

Joe Mancuso Moving
Joe Mancuso, 914.937.2178
An excellent resource when you are making a local move.

Young Man with Van
Contact: Oliver Wright, 203.866.3608, 203.760.0156
Oliver is a good resource for moving small items.

HOME

RECYCLING

Blue Bins

Recycling is now mandated by the state, but it is interesting to note that thanks to Mariette Badger and other volunteers, Greenwich recycling has been organized for over twenty-five years. Our recycling program saves the town money and protects the environment. Each week at a designated day and time, the town picks up recyclables and brings them to the Holly Hill Transfer Station. To get your blue bin(s) and recycling details, call 622.0550.

Hazardous Waste

Whenever you wish to dispose of items such as bug spray, engine oil, old paint cans or other items which are not part of the normal recycling program, call 869.6910, 622.7838 or 622.7740 for specific information.

Holly Hill Resource Recovery Facility (aka *The Dump*)
Holly Hill Lane, 622.0550

Greenwich has one of the world's best dumps. You have to see it to believe it. On any given day, you may see BMWs and Mercedes dropping off items. The "in" decal for your car is a dump permit.

Permit applications are available at the Holly Hill entry gate. To get one of these valuable permits, you must show proof of residency, as well as valid vehicle registration and insurance.

Leaf Collection

Town leaf collection is limited to areas zoned one-half acre or less. Most residents with one or more acres compost on their own property. For a schedule of leaf collection, call 622.7718, or watch for the schedule printed by the *Greenwich Time* in the fall.

Refuse Collectors

Garbage collection is done by independent contractors. New residents may call the Greenwich Independent Refuse Collectors Association at 622.0050 to find out which collector services their home.

HOME

SERVICES

Unwelcome Visitors: To rid yourself of furry or feathery visitors see ANIMALS, WILDLIFE & ANIMAL RESCUE.
Ordering In: See section under RESTAURANTS.

Berman Newspaper Delivery
323.5955

Depending upon where you live, Berman will deliver to your home between 5 and 6 am, where you want it, all of the major papers including: the *New York Times*, *Financial Times* and *USA Today*. The local papers come out too late for this delivery, so unless you want these papers a day late, you should contact them directly: *Greenwich Time*, 625.4400; *Greenwich Post*, 861.9191.

Dark House Service
622.8000

If residents notify the police that they will be away for an extended period of time, Greenwich police will patrol the area with an extra-cautious eye. You can also hire an off-duty police officer to personally check your home each day when you are away.

Deliver Ease of Greenwich
622.3040

For $5 for every 15 minutes of travel time, this reliable service will pamper your every need. They promptly deliver to or pick up from your door just about anything you can imagine: aspirin from your drugstore, poster board for a project, food from your favorite restaurant, forgotten dry cleaning, a late video, or just a cup of Dunkin' Donut's coffee. Why not send a balloon to cheer up someone at the hospital? Hours: every day, 8 am - 10 pm.

Jason, The Handyman, Inc.
625.0411

If you need a mirror hung, gutters installed or cleaned, walls painted, tile re-grouted, or an electrical outlet installed, call Jason Wahlberg. Reasonably priced and offers senior discounts. If he can't do it, he'll recommend someone who can.

HOME
SERVICES

Kennedy Security Services
58 East Elm Street, 661.6814
If you wish extra security while you are away from home, Kennedy Security has been serving Greenwich residents for over 40 years.

Locks and Keys
Charles Stuttig, 158 Greenwich Avenue, 869.6260
A fixture in Greenwich for many years, they provide a wide variety of locks and safes. Whether you have an emergency or just need a key replaced, they can be counted on and trusted.
Hours: Weekdays, 7:30 am to 5:30 pm; Saturday, 8 am to 3 pm.

HOME
UTILITIES

Greenwich Telephone System

Greenwich is on the border between Bell Atlantic (formerly NYNEX) and SNET coverage areas. Old Greenwich exchanges (637 & 698) are covered by SNET. From there you can dial many Connecticut 203 numbers directly. The rest of Greenwich is controlled by Bell Atlantic. This means that many numbers outside of Greenwich require you to dial 1-203 first.

Most Stamford numbers do not require the 203 prefix, but information for Stamford requires you to dial 203.555.1212. Greenwich information can be accessed by dialing 411. We have tried to organize the numbers in this guide to make it clear when you have to dial 203 (if you are in the Bell Atlantic coverage area) or when you can simply dial the local number.

Bell Atlantic: Greenwich, Byram, Cos Cob & Riverside

869.5222 (new service)
661.5444 (repairs), 625.9800 (customer service)
www.bellatlantic.com

SNET: Old Greenwich exchanges 637 & 698

From SNET coverage area, dial 811; from out-of-state, 800.453.SNET (new service); 420.3131 (repairs) or 611
www.snet.com

Connecticut-American Water Company

869.5200 (office)
661.7200 (emergency)
800.292.2928 (customer service)

Connecticut Natural Gas

869.6900 (customer service)
869.6913 (repair & emergency)

Northeast Utilities/Connecticut Light & Power

800.286.2000 www.nu.com
Your local power company.
For customer service and emergencies, call 800.286.5000.

HOME

WHERE TO GET THINGS REPAIRED

For Lock and Key repairs see HOME, SERVICES.

Carollines Studio

24 Byfield Lane, 661.6340 or 2267

Carol O'Neil is a master gilder with over 25 years experience. She specializes in the restoration of fine furniture, and decorative and painted pieces, including mirrors and frames. Hours by appointment.

Dean's China & Glass Restoration

131 Elmwood Drive, Cheshire CT, 800.669.1327, 203.271.3659

Their name says it all. Send them a photo of your broken or chipped piece and they will give you an estimate. If you can't drive to the studio, they have drop-off places in Old Greenwich (Feinsod's Hardware on Sound Beach Avenue) and Port Chester.

Greenwich Metal Finishing

67 Church Street, 629.8479

If you have an ailing silver piece or chandelier, you may want to visit these metal artisans. They polish, replate, refinish and even fabricate metal items. They will completely refinish and rewire your chandelier. Hours: Closed Monday; Open Tuesday - Friday, 9:30 am - 5 pm; Saturday, 9:30 am - 2 pm.

Kiev USA

248 Mill Street, Byram, 531.0900

How lucky we are to have an in-town shop which can repair cameras such as Nikon, Zeiss and Leica. They also sell reconditioned cameras. Hours: Weekdays, 9:30 am - 5:30 pm; Saturday, 10 am - 5 pm (closed on Saturday during the summer).

HOME

WHERE TO GET THINGS REPAIRED

Nimble Thimble

19 Putnam Avenue, Port Chester, NY, 914.934.2934

The resource for home sewing needs. Lots of fabrics, notions, and quilting supplies and sewing machines. This is the place to have your sewing machine repaired.

Hours: Monday - Saturday, 10 am - 5 pm.

Occhicone

42 North Main Street, Port Chester, NY, 914.937.6327

Expert repairs, by Italian craftsmen, for high-quality leather items, such as handbags, briefcases, leather apparel, suitcases and shoes. They can make just about anything look new.

Hours: Monday - Saturday, 8 am - 5:30 pm. Closed Sunday

Raphael's Furniture Restoration

655 Atlantic Street, Stamford, CT, 348.3079

They will repair and restore just about any piece of furniture, but they specialize in the restoration of eighteenth and nineteenth century antiques.

Hours: Summer, Tuesday - Thursday, 8 am - 5 pm; Friday, 8 am - 3 pm; Saturday, 8 am - noon. Hours Labor Day to Memorial Day: Tuesday - Friday, 8 am - 5 pm; Saturday, 8 am - noon.

Directions: I-95 North to Exit 7 (Greenwich Avenue), straight to 4th light, R on Atlantic, 5th building on the R.

Tablescraps

Cheshire, CT, 800.801.4084

www.tabletopdesigns.com

If you are missing a piece of china, crystal or silver from your collection, this is a good place to find a replacement. Call, visit their web site or email them at lenox@ntplx.net.

If for some reason Tablescraps can't help you, try these out-of-the-area replacement services:

China Traders, 800.579.1803

Clintsman International, 800.781.8900

Pattern Finders, 516.928.5158

Replacements Ltd, 800.737.5223

WHERE TO GET THINGS REPAIRED

Village Clock Shop

1074 Post Road, Darien, CT, 203.655.2100
They sell exquisite clocks, and repair clocks worthy of their service.
Hours: Tuesday - Saturday, 10 am - 5 pm.
Directions: I-95 N to exit 11, L on US 1.

Wood Den

266 Selleck Street, Stamford, CT, 324.6957
Wood and metal furniture stripping. Chair caning and furniture repairs.
Hours: Monday, 8 am - noon; Tuesday, Wednesday & Friday, 9 am to 5 pm; Thursday, 8 am to 8 pm; Saturday, 9 am to 1 pm.
Directions: I-95 N to exit 6, straight to 2nd light, R on West to Selleck.

HOTSPOTS

SUMMER

See also SINGLES

Crabshell

46 Southfield Avenue, Stamford, CT, 967.7229

www.mv.com/users/lindaknight/crabshell/

At Stamford Landing, near Dolphin Cove. A seafood restaurant and meeting ground for thirty to fifty year-olds. During the summer the restaurant expands onto a huge outdoor deck which can accommodate over 200.

Attire: Casual.

Hours: Open every day; lunch, noon - 3 pm; dinner, 5 pm - 11 pm; Bar open to 1:30 am or later.

Directions: I-95 N to exit 7, R on Southfield.

Inn at Long Shore/Splash Restaurant

Westport, CT, 203.454.7798

The food at Splash is phenomenal, just like Baang, its Greenwich sister restaurant. The lobster sushi is to die for. Located in a town park, the Inn has a great outdoor terrace right along the water with a bar and good live music. It's a great place to watch the sunset. The bar is open late.

Attire: Shorts and sun dresses. Upgrade if you'll be eating at Splash.

Hours: Dinner, 5:30 pm - 10 pm (Saturday & Sunday open until 11 pm).

Directions: I-95 N to exit 17, L on Riverside Ave, R onto bridge, R at first light after bridge.

Viva Zapata

530 Riverside Avenue, Westport, CT, 203.227.8226

A full menu of good Mexican food and great Margaritas. Nice outdoor terrace under a pergola of flowering vines. No reservations. Bar open until 1 am.

Attire: Jeans/nice casual. Poncho not required.

Hours: Monday - Saturday, 5 pm - 10:30 pm (Saturday until 11:30 pm).

Directions: I-95 N to exit 17.

NOTE: If hours or directions are not listed here, you will find them under RESTAURANTS, DINING OUT.

Bank Street Brewing Company

65 Bank Street, Stamford, CT, 325.2739

Fun atmosphere and good "bar food" such as quesidillas and chicken fingers. If beer is not your thing, it's ok. They have a full bar which is open until late.

Attire: Funky, casual.

Hours: 5:30 pm - 10 pm (weekends open until 11 pm).

Directions: I-95 N to exit 8, L on Atlantic (park on Bell or Main Street).

Boxing Cat Grill

1392 East Putnam Avenue, Old Greenwich, 698.1995

An active, after-work scene with a light bar menu.

A singles place for ages 30 to 50+. Live bands Thursday, Friday, and Sunday evenings.

Attire: Dress to impress.

Dome

253 Greenwich Avenue, 661.3443

The "hottest of the hot." Attracts the "in-crowd" from surrounding towns and New York City! Have a burger at the bar or try the delicious bib and pear salad.

Attire: DKNY or Calvin Klein.

Elm Street Oyster House

11 West Elm Street, 629.5795

A great place to meet after work and to stay for dinner.

Wonderful raw bar.

Attire: Casual, but nice.

MacKenzie's Grill Room

148 Sound Beach Avenue, 698.0223

The perfect place to watch the game. Sit at a bar table and try the nachos, skins or wings. One of the few places that serves food all day.

Attire: Whatever you have on.

Next Door Cafe

1990 West Main Street, Stamford, CT, 316.8101

Regular bar with a good crowd. Fun event nights. Attire: Go as you are.
Hours: Wednesday - Thursday, 4 pm - 1 am;
Friday - Sunday, 4 pm - 2 am.
Directions: I 95N to exit 6; L at light; L at second light.

Shenanigans

Main Street, South Norwalk, CT, 203.853.0142

Fun Reggae bar - not a food place. Great live bands and dancing.
Attire: Totally casual - jeans.
Hours: Wednesday - Thursday, 8 pm - 1 am;
Friday - Sunday, 8 pm - 2 am.
Directions: I-95 to exit 14, R toward SONO.

Sixty-Four Greenwich Avenue

64 Greenwich Avenue, 861.6400

A slightly dressier meeting spot for after work or after dinner. Nice selection of complimentary cheeses at the bar.
Attire: Khakis and loafers.

Tucson

130 East Putnam Avenue, 661.2483

All ages come to listen to live jazz on Wednesdays and weekends at this happening bar with Southwestern flair. Good spicy appetizers to share.
Attire: Blue jeans and boots.

HOTELS & INNS

Cos Cob Inn
50 River Road, Cos Cob, 661.5845
Charmingly redecorated, 1870 Federal bed-and-breakfast. Many of the
fourteen rooms have scenic views of the Mianus River; each has its own
bath. Continental breakfast, no restaurant.

Harbor House Inn
165 Shore Road, Old Greenwich, 637.0145   www.hhinn.com
This 100-year-old Victorian mansion has always served as an inn. Guests
are corporate clients, people relocating and out-of-town visitors. The
twenty-three room bed-and-breakfast is within walking distance of the
beach. No restaurant.

Homestead Inn
420 Field Point Road, 869.7500 www.inns.com
Expensive country inn, with twenty-two lovely rooms/suites and wonderful food. A great choice.

Hyatt Regency
1800 East Putnam Avenue, Old Greenwich, 637.1234
www.Hyatt.com/pages/g/gwicha.html
This 374-room luxury hotel has an elegant interior with excellent food.
Greenwich residents often check into this hotel for a weekend of pam-
pering. The hotel also has a very nice health club open to Greenwich
residents on an annual membership basis.

Rye Town Hilton
699 Westchester Avenue, Rye Brook, NY, 914.939.6300
www.hilton.com/hotels/RYEHIHH/
Situated on 45 acres just next to Greenwich. A lovely hotel with a very
good restaurant. It hosts many conventions.
Directions: I-95 S to exit 21, 287 W to exit 10, at second light, R on
Westchester Ave.

HOTELS & INNS

Stanton House Inn

76 North Maple Avenue, 869.2110 www.inns.com
Located in Central Greenwich, within walking distance of the shops and restaurants, this turn-of-the-century home, converted into a twenty-four room bed-and-breakfast, is a welcoming first-stop for many new residents. No restaurant.

Stamford Marriott

234 Tressor Blvd, Stamford, CT, 203.357.9555
www.marriotthotels.com/STFCT
Recently renovated 506-room hotel, 6 suites.
Directions: I-95 N exit 8, L on Atlantic, R on Tressor.

Stamford Suites

720 Bedford Street, Stamford, CT, 369.7300
www.stamfordsuites.com
An extended-stay hotel with furnished suites for nightly or longer term residence. Each unit contains a bedroom, living room, bathroom and a full-size kitchen. Renovated in 1998.
Directions: I-95 N, exit 8, L on Atlantic (becomes Bedford).

HOTELS & INNS
WORTH A VISIT

Connecticut River Valley Inns

The Connecticut River Valley, www.rotr.com, has outstanding inns in interesting towns to visit, particularly: Chester, Clinton, Deep River, Essex, and Old Lyme. The towns are just what you would expect quaint New England towns to look like. In addition they are loaded with antique shops, art galleries and interesting activities such as the Essex Steam Train (described under Family Outings), the beach in Old Lyme and the Camelot dinner, Long Island or Murder Mystery dinner cruises, Rte.9, exit 7 in Hadden, 860.345.8591. Excellent restaurants also abound in the area. The **Restaurant Du Village** is located in Chester at 59 Main Street, 860.526.2528. This restaurant is one of the best French restaurants in the entire state. You should also try what many consider the best pizza in Connecticut, served at **Alforno**, 1654 Boston Post Road, Brian Alden Shopping Plaza, Old Saybrook, open daily from 4:30 pm to 10 pm, 860.399.4166. Another great place for lunch or Sunday brunch is the **Water's Edge** at 1525 Post Road (I-95 exit 65) in Westbrook, 860.399.5901. Ask for a table on the water. You will also want to try these two Old Lyme Inns for a meal: the **Old Lyme Inn**, 85 Lyme Street, Old Lyme, 800.434.5352, and the **Bee and Thistle Inn**, 100 Lyme Street, (Rte.1, I-95 exit 70), Old Lyme, 860.434.1667. Both inns, particularly the Bee and Thistle, have received many awards for excellent dining. In the area, there is a large shopping mall (Clinton Crossing—see description under Outlets)at I-95 exit 63 and another large mall in Westbrook at exit 65. The state's two casinos, Foxwoods (I-95 exit 92) and Mohegan Sun (I-95 exit 76) are within striking distance (see directions under Gambling).

Copper Beach Inn

46 Main Street, Ivoryton, CT

www.CopperBeechInn.com

860.767.0330, 888.809.2056

Gracious inn with 13 guest rooms and excellent food in a charming New England town. High on our list, this inn fits the perfect image of what a New England Inn should be. The inn is best suited for adults unless the children have very nice manners. Rooms range from $125 to $175 per night. January through March, the dining room is closed Tuesday as well as Monday evening.

Directions: I-95 N to Exit 69, Rte 9 N to exit 3, L (west) 1.75 miles.

Inn at Chester

318 West Main Street (Rte. 148), Chester, CT, 860.526.1307

www.InnAtChester.com

The inn is relatively large with 42 rooms. It is open every day for lunch and` dinner and serves very good food in attractive surroundings.

Directions: I-95 N to Exit 69, Rt. 9 North to exit 6 (Chester), L off ramp. The Inn is 3.2 miles on the right.

INFORMATION SOURCES

Access
977.7176
Free, 24-hour news, information and entertainment service provided by
the *Greenwich Time.*
>Weather, enter 1200
>Entertainment, enter 7100.

Community Answers
101 West Putnam Avenue, 622.7979
www.greenwich.lib.ct.us
Funded by the United Way and private donations, this volunteer group
is located in the Greenwich Library. Ask them anything about Greenwich—all calls are confidential. You can also find information on their
web site.

Community Calendar:
Community Answers provides a Community Calendar of all town events.
It comes out every three months. Be sure to call and ask for it.

Useful Article Reprints:
Stop by and pick up articles which might be helpful, such as: *Finding
Senior Services in Greenwich; Newcomers Guide to Town Government;
Thrift Shops;Childcare and Parenting Services.*
Hours: Weekdays, 9 am - 5 pm.

The Greenwich Bank & Trust Company

115 East Putnam Avenue, 618.8912

1103 East Putnam, Riverside, 698.4030

For as long as we can remember, Greenwich residents have preferred to work with in-town banks. Friendly hellos and loans from bankers who know and work in the community are a much more civilized way to bank than dealing anonymously with a big, inflexible institution. Greenwich is fortunate to have a hometown bank. Drop in and say hello.

Hours: Monday - Thursday, 8:30 am - 4 pm; Friday 8:30 am - 5 pm; Saturday 9 am - 1 pm.

NEWS

MAGAZINES

Avenue News
375 Greenwich Avenue, 629.2429
A popular shop with magazines on every topic.
Hours: Sunday - Thursday, 5:30 am - 9 pm; Friday & Saturday until 10 pm.

Connecticut Family
203.625.9825 www.ctfamily.com
A must for anyone with young children. A monthly magazine with good reviews of children's activities in the Connecticut area.

Connecticut Magazine
800.974.2001 x 313 www.connecticutmag.com
This comprehensive magazine always has well-researched articles on the best of Connecticut.

Fairfield County Magazine
203.291.6936 www.fcmag.com
A new magazine focusing on living and working in Fairfield County. Crisp articles on our county's pleasures and issues.

Greenwich Magazine
869.0009
Sophisticated articles on topics of interest for everyone. A valuable source of information about Greenwich and Greenwich residents.

Inside FC/ Greenwich Lifestyles
203.849.3281
A free monthly publication - 26,000 are sent out each issue. A good way to keep current on design and style in and around Greenwich.

Ronnie's News
26 West Putnam Avenue, 661.5464
Hours: Weekdays, 6 am - 6 pm; Weekends, 6am - noon.

Zyns News
354 Greenwich Avenue, 661.5168
This store boasts the largest selection of magazines and newspapers in Fairfield County. It certainly seems that way.
Hours: Monday - Saturday, 6 am - 9 pm; Sunday, 6 am - 6 pm.

NEWS

NEWSPAPERS

See HOME, SERVICES for newspaper delivery information.

Fairfield County Business Journal

914.694.3600 www.businessjrnls.com

This weekly newspaper tracks trends and developments that impact local businesses. If you are thinking of opening a business or simply want to know the commercial news, this paper is just the ticket.

Greenwich Post

861.9191

The Post, published weekly, concentrates primarily on editorials from its staff and outside writers.

Greenwich Time

625.4400 www.GreenwichTime.com

If we were entering a national competition for the best daily local newspaper, *Greenwich Time* would win the top award. Joseph Pisani's editorials stimulate thought about important town topics. The *Letters from Readers* section is a good barometer of town concerns.

Guide to Arts and Entertainment in Fairfield CT

324.9799

Published as a separate weekly paper by the *Greenwich Time*, it has movie reviews and a good calendar of weekend shows and special events around the area.

Marks Brothers Stationers

42 Greenwich Avenue, 869.2409

A Greenwich landmark shop. Stop in to get your favorite newspaper or a new Mont Blanc fountain pen.

TeenSpeak

42 Greenwich Avenue, 622.0232, Fax: 869.9044

This newspaper by and for teenagers was founded by Greenwich resident Debra Mamorsky. It is operated and published by The Institute for Young Journalists, a nonprofit organization that also brings prominent media people to Greenwich to help educate young journalists. It is published quarterly and is available at Marks Brothers.

NEWS

RADIO & TELEVISION

Bloomberg News - AM 1130
www.bloomberg.com/wbbr
Good national and international news. Best for financial news.

Connecticut Television
www.cpbi.org
Connecticut Public Television has Connecticut-based documentaries as well as sports coverage of Connecticut teams.

Channel 27 is our local community access station. It broadcasts "Greenwich Weekly Video Magazine" Wednesdays at 10:30 pm and Fridays at 9:30 am.

Channel 70 is the Connecticut government access station.

Continuous news, weather and traffic reports.
CBS - AM 880   www.NewsRadio88.com
WINS - AM 1010   www.1010wins.com

Greenwich Radio
1490 Dayton Avenue, 869.1490   www.wgcham.com
Greenwich Radio has been so successful that they had to buy a second station to cover a wider area. Greenwich Radio now broadcasts simultaneously on WGCH - 1490 am & on WVIP - 1310 am. Tune in between 6 am and 10 am for an update on Greenwich happenings, as well as public notices such as school closings and information. Their interviews with Greenwich people making the news are essential to understanding town issues.

Public Radio
Connecticut Public Radio - FM 88.5   www.cpbi.org/radio
National Public Radio - AM 820   www.npr.org
Best in-depth coverage of national and international events.

NUMBERS YOU SHOULD KNOW

Anderson Associates
629.4519
info@Anderson-Real-Estate.com   www.GreenwichRealtors.com
If you don't know where to turn, call us.

Bell Atlantic
www.BellAtlantic.com
869.5222 (new service)
661.5444 (repairs)
625.9800 (customer service)

Cablevision of Connecticut
348.9211, 203.846.4700

Connecticut-American Water Company
869.5200 (office)
661.7200 (emergency)
800.292.2928 (customer service)

Connecticut Natural Gas
869.6900 (customer service)
869.6913 (repair & emergency)

Connecticut Vacation Planning Guide
800.282.6863 www.ctbound.org
You might also try Coastal Fairfield County Tourist Information
at 800.866.7925 or 203.854.7825.

Federal Express
800.238.5355, 800.GO.FEDEX, www.fedex.com

Greenwich Fire Department
911 Emergency
622.3950 (non-emergency)

Greenwich Hospital
863.3000

NUMBERS YOU SHOULD KNOW

Greenwich Police
911 Emergency
622.8000 (complaints and information)
www.GreenwichPolice.com

Greenwich Police/Ambulance
911 Emergency
622.8000 (non-emergency)

Greenwich Public Schools
625.7400, www.greenwich.k12.ct.us

Northeast Utilities/Connecticut Light & Power
www.nu.com
800.286.2000, 800.286.5000

Poison Control Center
800.343.2722

SNET
811 (from SNET coverage area)
800.453.SNET (from outside SNET coverage area)
420-3131 (repairs) or 611

Town Hall
622.7700 (all departments)

USE - Senior Center Job Placement Service
629.8031
Utilize Senior Energy, a volunteer activity run by Grace Knapp, is open weekdays, 9:30 am to 12:30 pm. It is a good resource for everything from painters to babysitters.

PARKS & RECREATION

BEACHES

Open only to Greenwich residents and their guests. Summer and longer-term renters are considered residents. You must have a beach pass before entering the beach. Passes are strictly enforced. Apply early and be sure to have it when you enter.

Beach Card Office
622.7817
Call for information about beach passes.
You will need a utility bill as proof of residency and a photo ID.

Byram Beach
531.8938
This beach on Byram Shore Road has a swimming pool, three tennis courts, picnic area and playground.

Ferry Information
661.5957
The ferry service from the Arch Street dock to Great Captain Island or Island Beach varies according to the tides. Service begins in the middle of June and lasts until September.

Great Captain's Island
622.7814
Take a ferry from the Arch Street dock to this 17-acre island with beach and picnic area. There is only one ferry in the morning and one in the afternoon. Captain's Island is rustic with no concession stand, so bring a picnic lunch. Camp sites available with permits. For camping reservations, call 622.7824.

Greenwich Point (Tod's Point)
Entrance at the south end of Shore Road in Old Greenwich. This 147-acre beach, with concession stand, has jogging, hiking and biking trails, lots of picnic facilities and wind surfing.

Island Beach (Little Captain's Island)
661.5957
Take a ferry from the Arch Street dock to this 4-acre island with beaches, picnic area and concession stand.

PARKS & RECREATION

CIVIC CENTERS

The Civic centers are the sites for many sporting events and public events such as antique shows. Call for their latest catalog of events.

Eastern Greenwich Civic Center

90 Harding Road, Old Greenwich, 637.4583

Also called: Greenwich Civic Center or Old Greenwich-Riverside Civic Center.

Western Greenwich Civic Center

449 Pemberwick Road, Glenville, 622.7821

PARKS & RECREATION

PARKS & NATURE PRESERVES

Greenwich, in addition to its beaches and 32 miles of coastline, has 8,000 acres of protected land, with over 1,000 acres of town parks. The parks and nature preserves listed below are some of the more popular of the twenty parks in Greenwich. Call Greenwich Department of Parks & Recreation (622.7830) for a complete list and directions.

Audubon Center

613 Riversville Road, 869.5272
240 acres with well-kept trails, a great place to walk.

Babcock Preserve

North Street, 622.7824
297 acres located two miles north of the Merritt Parkway. Well-marked running, hiking, and cross-country ski trails.

Binney Park

Sound Beach Avenue, Old Greenwich
Four tennis courts, playground, fields, pond skating. A favorite place for wedding photos.

Bruce Park

Bruce Park Drive and Indian Field Road
Athletic fields, bowling green, fitness trail, picnic area, tennis courts and playground.

Mianus River Park

Cognewaugh Road, 622.7814
215 acres owned by Greenwich and Stamford. Trout fishing. Wooded hills and steep cliffs with miles of hiking trails. Take Valley Road to Cognewaugh, the entrance is on Cognewaugh Road about three miles on the right (there is no sign).

PHOTOGRAPHY

CAMERAS & FILM

35 mm
31 East Elm Street, 629.3566
Extremely competent staff. Leave your film here—you will like the results. There is an after-hours drop off at the front door.
Hours: Weekdays, 8:30 am to 6 pm; Saturday, 10 am to 3 pm.

Images
202 Sound Beach Avenue, Old Greenwich, 637.4193
A high percentage of Old Greenwich residents trust their film to this shop. Among the many things they do in addition to framing are: restore damaged photographs by removing scratches, tears and stains; enhance photographs to reduce red-eye or correct color and brightness; and, of course, enlarge, crop or add a border. No negative is required.
Hours: Monday - Saturday, 9 am to 6 pm. Winter hours may vary.

Kiev USA
248 Mill Street, Byram, 531.0900   www.Kievusa.com
How lucky we are to have an in-town shop which can repair cameras such as Nikon, Zeiss and Leica. They also sell reconditioned cameras.
Hours: Weekdays, 9:30 am to 5:30 pm; Saturday, 10 am to 5 pm (closed on Saturday during the summer).

Ritz Camera Centers
82 Greenwich Avenue, Greenwich, 869.0673
www.ritzcamera.com
Part of a large chain of camera stores. They have an extensive selection of cameras and batteries for watches as well as cameras. They do one-hour photo developing.
Hours: Weekdays, 8:30 am to 6:30 pm; Saturday, 10 am to 5 pm.

PHOTOGRAPHY

PHOTOGRAPHERS

Gretchen Tatge
100 Hendrie Avenue, Riverside, 637.9929
Gretchen is an artist with her camera. She photographs many of the events in town.

Kathleen DiGiovanna
64 West Brother Drive, 869.5432
A freelance photographer specializing in weddings and special events. You can depend on her to capture the spirit of the occasion.

Studio A
418 East Putnam Avenue, Cos Cob, 661.3393
You will like Andres and Fred's wedding, family and children's portraits. They do still photography, video and digital photography.

PASSPORT PHOTOGRAPHY

For information on how to get a passport see TRAVEL, PASSPORT.

Kinkos
48 West Putnam Avenue, 863.0099
When you need a passport photograph quickly.
Hours: Open 24 hours a day, every day.

POST OFFICES & ZIP CODES

There are six post offices and five zip codes in town. The window service hours are different for each office. Mail for Greenwich zip codes is usually sent to Stamford to be sorted. The only post office with bins for all Greenwich zip codes is in Old Greenwich.

Greenwich Avenue Post Office [Zip: 06830]
310 Greenwich Avenue, 869.3737
Hours: Weekdays, 8:30 am to 5 pm;
      Saturday, 8 am to 2 pm.

Greenwich Post Office [Zip: 06831]
29 Valley Drive, 625.3168
Hours: Weekdays, 8:30 am to 5:30 pm;
      Saturday, 8:30 am to 2 pm.

Glenville Post Office [Zip: 06831]
25 Glen Ridge Plaza, 531.8744
Hours: Weekdays, 8:30 am to 4:30 pm;
      Saturday, 8:30 am to noon.

Cos Cob Post Office [Zip: 06807]
152 East Putnam Avenue, 869.1470
Hours: Weekdays, 8:30 am to 5 pm;
      Saturday, 8:30 am to 12:30 pm.

Riverside Post Office [Zip: 06878]
1273 East Putnam Avenue, 637.9332
Hours: Weekdays, 7:30 am to 5 pm;
      Saturday, 8 am to 1 pm.

Old Greenwich Post Office [Zip: 06870]
36 Arcadia Road, 637.1405
Hours: Weekdays, 8 am to 5 pm;
      Saturday, 9 am to 1 pm.

REAL ESTATE

Buyer Agency

On June 1, 1997, Connecticut mandated that realtors represent either the buyer or the seller, but not both (unless dual or designated agency is disclosed and agreed to by both parties) in the same transaction.

Buyers like being represented by their own realtor because their realtor can now tell them what they think a house is worth and provide excellent guidance through the real estate process. This extra protection costs the buyer nothing because the buyer's realtor is still paid by the seller. In the first meeting, the buyer signs a representation agreement with their realtor much the way a seller signs a listing agreement with their realtor.

Greenwich Multiple Listing Service

Greenwich has an outstanding organization devoted to local real estate. This service is funded by the realtors in town and is extremely helpful to homeowners, buyers and realtors. Member Realtors follow a strict code of ethics. Greenwich properties are valuable and unique. It is important to understand how Greenwich real estate works.

When many other towns gave up their local boards, Greenwich did not. When other towns opted to list all of their properties on national web sites, Greenwich did not. In Greenwich all properties - with rare exceptions - are multiple-listed with the Greenwich "MLS". To buy property in Greenwich, you need to select a realtor you like and trust—and you will have access through your realtor to the entire market.

REAL ESTATE

AGENCIES

Anderson Associates
164 Mason Street, 629.4519, 800.223.4519; fax: 629.4786
www.GreenwichRealtors.com
Anderson Associates are Greenwich real estate specialists.
We all live, as well as work, in Greenwich. We spend our full time on Greenwich real estate. You can depend on us to represent your best interests. Our knowledge of Greenwich and our real estate expertise will make your real estate transaction rewarding and stress-free. As you can see from the introduction, we originally wrote the book you are reading to help our buyers feel immediately at home in this wonderful community.

"Whether you are buying or selling, you will love working with Anderson Associates. Their website is second to none—just what you'd expect from a company as customer driven as they are. I found information on renovating my house, my children found statistics for school projects, and there are pictures of lots of Greenwich houses for sale. Highly recommended."
Melanie Kuperberg

MORTGAGE BROKERS

Strategy Mortgage Corp.
15 Neil Lane, Riverside, 637.3333. 800.707.0000; Fax: 698.2222
Call Lucy Krasnor, Vice President Loan Origination.
Strategy is located in Greenwich. They started in 1994 and originated over $42 million in their first year. Strategy now represents fifty-eight of the most aggressive national and regional lenders and generates over $400 million a year in mortgage loans. They work hard to find the best loans for their clients, and best of all, they are available from 8 am to 10 pm every day.

RELIGION

HOUSES OF WORSHIP

The *Greenwich Post* publishes its *"Faith Forum"* each week on Friday, with listings of places of worship and their pertinent information. Each week the *Greenwich Time* publishes Jewish services in the Thursday issue and church services in the Saturday issue. These are the best places to find updated information and times of services.

Albertson Memorial Church
293 Sound Beach Avenue, Old Greenwich, 637.4615

Anglican Church of the Advent
606 Riversville Road, 329.9885, 622.6511
At North Greenwich Congregational Church or 16 Lexington Avenue.

Annunciation Greek Orthodox Church
1230 Newfield Avenue, Stamford, CT, 322.2093

Bethel African Methodist Episcopal Church
42 Lake Avenue, 661.3099

Bethel Tabernacle
United Pentecostal Church
Meets at Greenwich YMCA, 50 East Putnam Avenue, 357.8249

Christ Church of Greenwich
254 East Putnam Avenue, 869.6600

Church of the New Covenant
289 Delavan Avenue, 324.5797
Services held at Byram Archibald Neighborhood Center.

Diamond Hill United Methodist Church
521 East Putnam Avenue, 869.2395

Dingletown Community Church
Stanwich Road and Barnstable Lane, 629.5923

First Baptist Church
10 Northfield Street, 869.7988

RELIGION

HOUSES OF WORSHIP

First Church of Christ, Scientist
11 Park Place, 869.1555
Reading Room, 333 Greenwich Avenue, 869.2503

First Church of Round Hill
464 Round Hill Road, 629.3876

First Congregational Church
108 Sound Beach Avenue, Old Greenwich, 637.1791

First Lutheran Church
38 Field Point Road, 869.0032

First Presbyterian Church
18 Lafayette Place, 869.8686

First United Methodist Church
59 East Putnam Avenue, 629.9584

Grace Church of Greenwich
PO Box 1673, Greenwich, CT 06836, 861.7555
Meets at Women's Club of Greenwich, 89 Maple Avenue.

Greek Orthodox Church of the Archangels
1527 Bedford Street, Stamford, CT, 348.4216

Greenwich Baptist Church
10 Indian Rock Lane, 869.2437

Greenwich Congregation of Jehovah's Witnesses
471 Stanwich Road, 661.1244

Greenwich Reform Synagogue
257 Stanwich Road, 629.0018

Harvest Time Assembly of God
449 Pemberwick Road
Western Civic Center, Glenville, 531.7778

RELIGION

HOUSES OF WORSHIP

Japanese Gospel Church
St. Paul Evangelical Lutheran Church
286 Delavan Avenue, 531.6450

Long Ridge Congregational Church
455 Old Long Ridge Road, Stamford, CT, 322.6975

North Greenwich Congregational Church
606 Riversville Road, 869.7763

Presbyterian Church of Old Greenwich
38 West End Avenue, Old Greenwich, 637.3669

Round Hill Community Church
395 Round Hill Road, 869.1091

Sacred Heart Roman Catholic Church
95 Henry Street, Byram, 531.8730

St. Agnes Roman Catholic Church
247 Stanwich Road, 869.5396

St. Barnabas Episcopal Church
954 Lake Avenue, 661.5526

St. Catherine of Siena Roman Catholic Church
4 Riverside Avenue, 637.3661

St. Mary Roman Catholic Church
178 Greenwich Avenue, 869.9393

St. Michael's Roman Catholic Church
469 North Street, 869.5421

St. Paul Evangelical Lutheran Church
286 Delavan Avenue, 531.8466

RELIGION

HOUSES OF WORSHIP

St. Paul Roman Catholic Church
84 Sherwood Avenue and King Street, 531.8741

St. Paul's Episcopal Church
200 Riverside Avenue, 637.2447

St. Roch Roman Catholic Church
10 St. Roch Avenue, 869.4176

St. Saviour's Episcopal Church
350 Sound Beach Avenue, Old Greenwich, 637.2262

St. Timothy Church
1034 North Street, Banksville, NY, 661.5196

Second Congregational Church
139 East Putnam Avenue, 869.9311

Stanwich Congregational Church
237 Taconic Road, 661.4420

Stamford-Greenwich Religious Society of Friends
572 Roxbury Road, Stamford, CT, 869.0445

Temple Shalom
300 East Putnam Avenue, 869.7191

RELIGION

ORGANIZATIONS

Church Women United of Greenwich
5 Somerset Lane, Riverside
Alice Dais, President - 637.3473
Contact: Kate Bryner, Publicity - 869.6261

Council of Churches and Synagogues
628 Main Street, Stamford, CT, 348.2800
Rev. James Carter, Executive Director

Hadassah, Greenwich Chapter
Temple Sholom, 300 East Putnam Avenue
Alma Rutgers, President - 531.1385
Contact: Natalie Garr, Membership, Vice President - 532.0490

UJA Federation of Greenwich
One Holly Hill Lane, Greenwich 06830-6080, 622.1434
Pamela Zue, President

RESTAURANTS

How Restaurants are Selected

We do not accept advertisements; restaurants are included strictly on merit. Restaurants are visited anonymously several times a year. If we have more than one bad meal, we don't include that restaurant. Our reviews are intended to give you our impression of the restaurant's ambiance, service and food. If a negative note is included, it is because we believe the restaurant has potential. If you have positive or negative comments about a restaurant or our review, please call, write or send us an e-mail to: restaurants@GreenwichGuide.com

How the Restaurant Section is organized

We begin with a cross-reference which provides categories (by type of food and by specialty) to help you make your restaurant selection. RESTAURANTS contains two sections: Dining Out and Ordering In.

Reservations

In most restaurants, reservations are a must. This is especially true if you are going out Friday or Saturday evening.

Restaurants Outside of Greenwich

We include restaurants outside of Greenwich when they are worth the trip. Close to Greenwich are two restaurant areas that draw large Greenwich crowds: Port Chester, NY and SONO (South Norwalk) just off exit 14 of I-95. Very much like SOHO (South of Houston) in Manhattan, SONO contains a mixture of art shops and trendy restaurants, as well as the area's only art theater (SONO Cinema).

Restaurant Design

Although a few restaurants such as Dome, Le Figaro and Sixty-Four Greenwich Avenue are exceptions, many restaurants are moving towards Minimalist Modern. Unfortunately, these trendy restaurants accentuate a problem common to many restaurants—overpowering noise that drowns out conversation. Restaurants should be a place for relaxation, good food, and good company. In some restaurants, the noise level is so high that you can't enjoy your company.

Hours

Establishments change their hours as business dictates. Many change their hours for winter and summer, and during holidays. Some chefs even take vacations. Please don't consider our listings definitive.

RESTAURANTS
BY FOOD TYPE

* Our favorite in the category

Asian
Penang Grill
(Separate categories for Chinese, Japanese & Nouvelle Pacific Rim)

Argentine
Cafe Rue

Brazilian
Pantanal

Casual American
Cobble Stone
Colonial Diner
Country Squire
Garden Cafe
Hubba-Hubba
Jimmy's Grill
Katzenberg's
Landmark Diner
MacKenzie's Grill
Mianus River Tavern
Organic Planet
Skylight Cafe
Smokey Joe's *
Sundown Saloon
Thataway Cafe

Chinese
Hunan Cafe
Hunan Gourmet
Panda Pavilion*

Coffee Shops
Reviews of coffee shops are listed in the Coffee Shop category under Food Stores.

Contemporary
Boxing Cat Grill
Cobble Creek Cafe
Dome
Inn at Pound Ridge
Mediterraneo
River Cat Grill
Roger Sherman Inn
Sage
Silvermine Tavern
Sixty-Four Greenwich Avenue
Sky Top Restaurant
Vivo
Wildfire

Cuban
Habana

Delicatessens with seating space
Reviews for delicatessens without seating space are listed in the Delicatessen section of Food Stores.
Arcuris
Aux Delices
Katzenberg's
Garelick & Herbs *
Gourmet Gallery
Village Deli

Diners
Colonial Diner
Landmark Diner *

French
Aux Delices
(Le) Chateau
Cote d'Azur
(La) Cremaillere
(Le) Figaro
(Thomas Henkelmann at the) Homestead
Jean Louis*
Meli-Melo
Mirage Cafe
(La) Panetiere
Stonehenge Inn
Versailles

RESTAURANTS
BY FOOD TYPE

Greek
Famous Pizza &
    Souvlaki *
Viscardi's Colonial
    Inn

Indian
Chola
Dawat*
Tandoori

Irish
Tigin

Italian
Applausi Osteria
Centro
Inferno
Moreno
Pasta Vera
Piero's
That Little Italian
    Restaurant
Terra
Valbella *

Japanese
Abis
Fuji-Mart Ramen
Kagetsu *
Kazu
Maya of Japan

Mexican
Fonda La Paloma

New American
Rebecca's *
Xaviar's

Nouvelle Pacific Rim
Baang Cafe *
Splash Cafe

Pizza
Arcuris
Famous Pizza &
    Souvlaki
Inferno
Paradisio
Pizza Express
Pizza Factory
Pizza Glenville
Pizza Hut
Pizza Post
Planet Pizza

Seafood
Elm Street Oyster *
Paradise Bar & Grill
Pearl of the Atlantic
Rowayton Seafood
Sono Seaport Seafood
Splash
Winfields at the Hyatt

Southwestern
Boxcar Cantina *
Smokey Joe's Bar-B-Q
Sundown Saloon
Tucson

Spanish
Barcelona *
Sevilla
Meson Galecia

Steak
Manero's
Maya of Japan
Morton's of Chicago *
Porterhouse
Smokey Joe's Bar-B-Q
Willett House

Thai
Mhai Thai

Vegetarian
Chola
Organic Planet

RESTAURANTS
BY SPECIALTY

Best Food
Thomas Henkelmann
   Homestead Inn *
Jean Louis
(La) Panetiere
Rebecca's
Xaviar's

Breakfast
Aux Delices
Cafe Rue
Colonial Diner
Famous Pizza and
   Souvlaki
Homestead Inn
Katzenberg's
Landmark Diner *
Meli-Melo
Sky Top
Versailles
Village Deli & Cafe
Winfields

Brunch on Sunday
Boxing Cat Grill
Dome
Hunan Cafe
Inn at Pound Ridge
Rebecca's
Roger Sherman Inn
Silvermine Tavern
Winfields *

Dinner, Late Night
Barcelona
Mirage Cafe *
Cobble Stone
Colonial Diner
Fuji-Mart
Hubba-Hubba
Mianus River Tavern
Penang
Sevilla
Thataway Cafe
Vivo

Dinner, Less Expensive
For something more special than pizza or deli takeout, try these:
Boxcar Cantina
Cafe Rue
Centro
Cobble Stone
Colonial Diner
Famous Pizza and
   Souvlaki
Garden Cafe
Hubba-Hubba
Hunan Cafe
Hunan Gourmet
Katzenberg's
Landmark Diner
MacKenzie's Grill
Meli-Melo *
Mianus River Tavern
Organic Planet
Panda Pavilion
Pasta Vera
Piero's
River Cat Grill
Sono Seaport Seafood
Smokey Joe's Bar-B-Q
Sundown Saloon
Tandoori
That Little Italian
Tigin
Viscardi's Colonial

RESTAURANTS
BY SPECIALTY

Family Restaurants

Abis
Boxcar Cantina
Centro
Famous Pizza and
    Souvlaki
Hunan Gourmet
Katzenberg's
Landmark Diner
Maneros *
Maya of Japan
Organic Planet
Panda Pavilion
Paradise Bar & Grill
Pearl of the Atlantic
Rowayton Seafood
Silvermine Tavern
Smokey Joe's Bar-B-Q
SoNo Seaport
    Seafood
Sundown Saloon
Thataway Cafe
That Little Italian
Viscardi's Colonial

Hot Spots

*Listed in their own
section*

Healthy Meals

*The following
restaurants were
eertified by the
Greenwich Healthy
Living 2000 Task
Force at the Green-
wich Hospital Center
for Wellness and
Preventive Medicine.*

(Le) Figaro
Garden Cafe
Jean Louis
(La) Panatiere
Rebecca's
Restaurant Sixty-Four
Winfields at the Hyatt

Lunch, For Ladies Who...

Baang
Figaro *
Jean-Louis
Mediterraneo
Rebecca's
Terra

Lunch, Late

Boxing Cat *
Colonial Diner
Dome
Elm Street Oyster
Fonda La Paloma
Garden Cafe
Katzenberg's
Landmark Diner
Pasta Vera
Sixty-Four *
Sevilla

Lunch, Quick Sit-Down

Aux Delices
Colonial Diner
Garelick & Herbs
Katzenberg's *
Landmark Diner
Meli-Melo *
Skylight Cafe

RESTAURANTS
BY SPECIALTY

Lunch, Run In/ Run out
Apache Place (DELICATESSENS)
Aux Delices
Fresh Fields - sushi or deli takeouts
  (GROCERY STORES)
Garelick & Herbs
Harrington's - ham sandwich
  (FOOD STORES / MEATS)
Hay Day (FOOD STORES)
Jimmy's Grill
Katzenberg's Express
Manero's - steak sandwich
Tandoori - box lunch
Zoom (SMOOTHIES)

Open on Most Major Holidays
Abis
Cafe Rue
Cobble Creek Cafe
Cobble Stone
Colonial Diner
Dawat
Hunan Cafe
Hunan Gourmet
MacKenzie's Grill
Mhai Thai
Pasta Vera
Sevilla
Sky Top
Sundown

RESTAURANTS
BY AREA

Banksville, NY
(La) Cremaillere

Byram
Famous Pizza &
  Souvlaki
That Little Italian
  Restaurant

Cos Cob
Fonda La Paloma
Landmark Diner
Mianus River Tavern
Pizza Post
Sevilla

Glenville
Centro Ristorante
Pizza Glenville
Pizza Hut
Rebecca's

Central Greenwich
Abis
Boxcar Cantina
Cafe Rue
Chola
Colonial Diner
Dome
Elm Street Oyster
Garden Cafe
Thomas Henkelmann
  Homestead Inn
Hunan Gourmet
Jean-Louis
Jimmy's Grill
Kagetsu
Katzenberg's
Manero's
Maya of Japan
Mediterraneo
Meli-Melo
Mhai Thai
Moreno Ristorante
Organic Planet
Panda Pavilion
Paradiso
Pasta Vera
Penang Grill
Pizza Express
Planet Pizza

Sage
Sixty-Four Greenwich
Skylight Cafe (YWCA)
Sundown Saloon
Terra
Thataway Cafe
Tucson
Versailles
Village Deli & Cafe
Vivo
Wildfire

New Canaan, CT
Roger Sherman Inn

Norwalk, CT
Barcelona
Cote D'Azur
Habana
Kazu
Mason Galicia
Porter House
Silvermine Tavern
Sono Seaport Seafood

RESTAURANTS

BY AREA

Old Greenwich
Applausi Osteria
Arcuris
Boxing Cat Grill
Hunan Cafe
MacKenzie's Grill
Viscardi's Colonial
Winfields

Port Chester, NY
Mirage Cafe
Pantanal
Pearl of the Atlantic
Piero's
Tandoori
Willett House

Purchase, NY
Cobble Creek Cafe
Cobble Stone

Riverside
Aux Delices
Baang
Fuji-Mart Ramen
Valbella

Rowayton, CT
River Cat Grill
Rowayton Seafood

Stamford, CT
Hubba-Hubba
Morton's of Chicago
Paradise Bar/Grill
Smokey Joe's Bar-B-Q
Tigin

White Plains, NY
Dawat
Sky Top Restaurant

Worth the Trip but more than 30 Minutes away
(See also Inns Worth a Trip)
(Le) Chateau,
    Salem, NY
Inn at Pound Ridge,
    Pound Ridge, NY
(La) Panetiere,
    Rye, NY
Splash,
    Westport, CT
Stonehenge Inn,
    Ridgefield, CT
Xaviar's,
    Piermont, NY

RESTAURANTS

DINING OUT

Abis

381 Greenwich Avenue, 862.9100

A full menu with lots of choices. We like them best for their Japanese noodle dishes such as udon or soba. If you have a large party, consider ordering shabu-shabu.

Hours: Lunch, Weekdays, 11:30 am - 2:30 pm, Saturday, noon - 2:30 pm; Sunday, 11:30 am - 2:30 pm; Dinner, Weekdays, 5:30 pm - 9:30 pm (Friday until 10:30 pm); Saturday, 5 pm - 10:30 pm; Sunday, 5 pm - 9:30 pm. Closed Thanksgiving, but open most holidays, including Christmas and New Year's. Reservations accepted.

Main course price range: Lunch, $8 - $12; Dinner, $15 - $20.
Major credit cards accepted.

Applausi Osteria

199 Sound Beach Avenue, Old Greenwich, 637.4447

Since its opening in 1993, Applausi has become a favorite in Old Greenwich. Its informal atmosphere and good Italian dishes, such as Osso Bucco and their homemade pastas, explain its popularity.

Hours: Lunch, Weekdays, noon - 2:30 pm; Dinner, Monday - Thursday, 5 pm - 10 pm; Friday & Saturday, 5 pm - 11 pm.

Closed Thanksgiving, Easter, New Year's, July 4, Labor Day, Memorial Day and Sunday.

Reservations accepted.

Main course price range: Lunch, $25 per person; Dinner, $35 per person. Major credit cards accepted.

Arcuris

178 Sound Beach Avenue, Old Greenwich, 637.1085
226 East Putnam Avenue, Cos Cob, 869.6999
Popular for their pizza and take-out sandwiches. They deliver.
Hours: Weekdays, phone orders from 11 am - 9:45 pm;
Friday and Saturday until 10:15 pm.
Closed most major holidays.

Aux Delices

1075 East Putnam Avenue, Riverside, 698.1066
www.AuxDelicesFoods.com
This tiny shop, with its fourteen seats, provides gourmet eat-in or carryout Provencal French food. The shop is owned and run by Debra Ponzek, named Chef of the Year by the Chefs of America Association in 1990. Perfect for a quick, superb breakfast or lunch or dinner take-out. Try their veal burgers, osso bucco, scones, croissants or chocolate mousse cake.
Hours: Monday - Saturday, 7:30 am - 6:30 pm; Sunday 7:30 am - 2 pm.
Closed Thanksgiving, Christmas, New Year's. No reservations.
Main course price range: Breakfast, $4 - $7; Lunch, $10 - $15; Dinner, $12 - $25. Major credit cards accepted.

Baang Cafe

1191 East Putnam Avenue, Riverside, 637.2114
Interesting drinks and Pan Asian cuisine in a fun atmosphere. Lively, noisy atmosphere and creative combinations of food. Try the Baang chicken salad, lobster Indochine or Szechuan beef. Outdoor dining in the summer.
Hours: Lunch, Friday, from 11:30 am - 2:30 pm; Dinner, Monday - Thursday, 6 pm - 10 pm; Friday & Saturday, 6 pm - 11 pm; Sunday 5 pm - 10 pm. Closed Thanksgiving and Christmas.
Reservations are only accepted for parties of six or more, so arrive early, especially on Friday and Saturday nights.
Main course price range: Dinner, $21 - $32. Major credit cards accepted.

RESTAURANTS

DINING OUT

Barcelona

63 North Main Street, South Norwalk, CT, 203.899.0088
www.CulinaryMenus.com

An authentic tapas restaurant near SONO theaters. Makes for a fun date. The bar is loud and lively. For a quieter spot, dine on the patio. We love all of the tapas - our favorites were: eggplant rollatini, empanadas of spiced beef and polenta with mushrooms. The chocolate indulgence with coconut ice cream is scrumptious.

Hours: Lunch, Tuesday - Friday, noon - 2:30 pm; Dinner every night, 5 pm - 10 pm; tapas only from 10 pm to closing.

Closed Christmas Day, New Year's and Thanksgiving.

Reservations are accepted. On Friday and Saturday nights reservations are only accepted for dining before 7 pm.

Main course price range: Lunch, $9 - $12; Dinner, $16 - $22; Tapas, $3.50 - $8. Major credit cards accepted.

Directions: I-95 North, Exit 14, R at stop sign, L at 2nd traffic light into Sono Plaza.

Boxcar Cantina

44 Old Field Point Road, 661.4774

Popular, informal, and child-friendly, this restaurant is an incredible hit in town. It is conceived as a homage to all of the wonderful honky-tonk Route 66 cantinas of the Southwest, serving a mix of Mexican and Southwestern food. We are hooked on their posole soup, fajitas and salmon burritos. You should also consider the carne avocado burrito, cod cakes or Southwest chopped salad. Choose from an original menu of home-made margaritas.

Hours: Lunch, Weekdays, 11:30 am - 3 pm; Dinner, Monday -Thursday, 5:30 pm - 9:30 pm; Friday & Saturday, 4:30 pm - 10:30 pm; Sunday, 4:30 pm - 9 pm. Closed Christmas, July 4th, and New Year's.

Reservations are accepted only for large parties. On Friday and Saturday nights, be sure to arrive early.

Main course price range: Dinner, $8 - $16. Major credit cards accepted.

RESTAURANTS

DINING OUT

Boxing Cat Grill

1392 East Putnam Avenue, Old Greenwich, 698.1995

Its creative American food has kept this restaurant popular for over ten years. It is a place to see and be seen. The good food and varied menu make this a perfect choice when you have guests and you don't know their tastes. Boxing Cat features live music Thursday nights. An evening hot spot.

Hours: Lunch, Weekdays, 11:30 am - 3 pm; Dinner, Weekdays, 5:30 pm - 10 pm (10:30 on Friday); Saturday, 5:30 pm - 10:30 pm (no lunch); Sunday, noon - 9:30 pm. Closed Thanksgiving and Christmas.

Main course price range: $9 - 25.

Cafe Rue

95 Railroad Avenue, 629.1056

The fare in this charming little restaurant resembles food from a Buenos Aires bistro, with a strong emphasis on Argentine beef. It is a convenient place for a light meal before or after a movie. If you call in advance, they will even buy theater tickets for you. When in doubt, try their lomito sandwich and french fries.

Hours: Breakfast, Friday & Saturday, 8:30 am - 10:30 am; Lunch & dinner, every day, 11 am - 10 pm. Open Christmas and New Year's, closed Thanksgiving. Reservations accepted.

Main course price range: Lunch, $5 - $15, Dinner $5 - $19.

Major credit cards accepted.

Centro Ristorante

328 Pemberwick Road, Glenville, 531.5514

Relaxed atmosphere —just right when you hunger for homemade pastas and a good glass of wine from their extensive list. Try the outdoor patio and order their ravioli or carpaccio San Marco. Some of our friends go just for the desserts.

Hours: Lunch, Monday - Saturday, 11:30 am - 3 pm; Lite fare, Monday - Saturday, 3 pm - 5:30 pm; Dinner, Monday - Thursday, 5:30 pm - 10 pm, Friday & Saturday, 5:30 pm - 11 pm, Sunday 5 pm - 9:30 pm. Closed July 4th, Memorial Day, Labor Day, Thanksgiving, Christmas Eve and Christmas. Reservations accepted.

Main course price range: Lunch, $8 - $9, Dinner $8 - $14. Major credit cards accepted.

RESTAURANTS

DINING OUT

(Le) Chateau

Junction of Routes 35 and 123, Salem, NY, 914.533.6631
www.ezpages.com/lechateau
About thirty minutes from Greenwich, on the grounds of the 1907 J.P. Morgan estate. It is a spacious, romantic and rather elaborate background for a large party or just a night out with friends. The food is classic French. Be sure to order their lobster and seafood ragout and chocolate souffle.
Hours: Tuesday - Sunday, dinner, 5:30 pm - 9 pm. Closed Monday.
Be sure to make a reservation in advance.
Main course price range: $20 - $33. Major credit cards accepted.
Directions: Merritt Pkw N to exit 38, 123 N, R on Rte 35.

Chola

107-109 Greenwich Avenue, 869.0700
www.FineIndianDining.com
This restaurant, hidden away upstairs next to the back of CVS, has good food and a staff eager to please. Entrees are from areas all over India, including a large selection of vegetarian dishes. We particularly liked the baingan bhartha and aloo gobi palak.
Hours: Lunch, every day from noon to 2:30 pm; Dinner every day from 5 pm - 10 pm.
Main course price range: Lunch $8 - $10; Dinner, $10 - $20.
Major credit cards accepted.

Cobble Creek Cafe

586 Anderson Hill Road, Purchase, NY, 914.761.0050
A charming, romantic setting with excellent contemporary American food. Try the sauteed foie gras, sweet potato ravioli, swordfish or tuna. This out-of-the-way restaurant is high on our list!
Hours: Lunch, Weekdays, 11:30 am - 3 pm; Dinner, Sunday - Thursday, 5:30 pm - 9 pm, Friday & Saturday, 5:30 pm - 11 pm. Open most major holidays. Reservations are recommended.
Main course price range: Lunch, $8 - $16; Dinner, $14 - $23. Major credit cards accepted.
Directions: King Street to Anderson Hill Road, on the left, just past SUNY Purchase.

DINING OUT

Cobble Stone

Anderson Hill Road, Purchase, NY, 914.253.9678

Open since 1933. Informal pub-style restaurant, with college-student atmosphere. Try the onion soup, Maryland crab cakes, pink vodka pasta or one of their many hamburgers. Try the Toll House dessert.

Hours: Sunday brunch, 11:30 am - 3 pm; Lunch, Monday - Friday, 11:30 am - 5 pm; Dinner, 5 pm - 10 pm. Late-night drinks and light meals, 10 am - 12 am. Open on major holidays. Reservations accepted.

Main course price range: Brunch, $4 - $11; Lunch, $4 - $10; Dinner, $5.25 - $15; Late night, $4 - $12. Major credit cards accepted.

Directions: King Street to Anderson Hill Road, just past SUNY Purchase on the left.

Colonial Diner (a/k/a Greenwich Diner)

69 East Putnam Avenue, 661.9067

A friendly landmark diner that has been open since 1923. Nick, the friendly owner, has operated the restaurant for fifteen years. He keeps prices low and serves large portions. This is what a diner is supposed to be. When in doubt, try their Greek salad. Popular late-night meeting place for Greenwich High School students.

Hours: Open 24 hours a day, every day, even holidays.

No reservations.

Main course price range: Breakfast, $2 - $5; Lunch, $4 - $7; Dinner, $8 to $15. Major credit cards accepted.

Cote D'Azur

86 Washington Street (Water & North Main), South Norwalk, CT, 203.855.8900

A bistro for the French or a Francophile, it has charm, energy and delicious food. The fish soup was every bit as good as our favorite in San Tropez. Make a reservation and be prepared for a wait on weekends.

Hours: Lunch, Tuesday - Saturday, noon - 3 pm; Dinner, Tuesday - Saturday, 6 pm - 9 pm (Saturday until 10 or 11 pm); Closed Sunday, Monday, Christmas, New Year's, and July 4th.

Main course price range: Lunch $7 - $12; Dinner, $14 - $24. Specials may cost more. Reservations accepted. Major credit cards accepted.

Directions: I-95 N, exit 14, R on West Avenue, left at fork onto Main Street, 2nd light L onto Washington.

RESTAURANTS

DINING OUT

(La) Cremaillere

46 Bedford/Banksville Road, Banksville, NY, 914.234.9647

Fine wines with traditional French food in a dressy, romantic setting with pretentious service. There is a lot of tradition here. Many Greenwich couples become engaged in this restaurant.

Hours: Lunch, Thursday - Saturday, noon - 2:30; Dinner, Tuesday - Saturday, 6 pm - 9:30 pm; Sunday, 1 pm - 8 pm. Closed Christmas and New Year's.

Main course price range: Lunch is prix-fixed at $33; Dinner, $20 - $36.

Directions: Four miles N of the Merritt on North Street.

Dawat

230 East Post Road, White Plains, NY, 914.428.4411

This is the sister to the famed Manhattan top-rated Indian restaurant. Order the assorted appetizers to begin and follow it with the gosht chennai as your entre. Don't forget to order sweet lassi to drink. This is by far our favorite Indian restaurant.

Hours: Lunch, noon - 2:45 pm every day; Dinner, Monday - Thursday, 5:30 pm - 10:15 pm; Friday and Saturday, 5:30 pm - 10:45 pm; Sunday, 5 pm - 9:45 pm. Closed Thanksgiving, open most other holidays. Reservations accepted.

Main course price range: Buffet lunch, $9.95; Dinner, $8 - $21.

Major credit cards accepted.

Directions: 287 West, exit 6, left at first light; left onto 22 South, 1 mile (sign for South Broadway and E. Post Road), bear right onto E. Post Road.

RESTAURANTS

DINING OUT

Dome
253 Greenwich Avenue, 661.3443
Dennis Ossorio has created another winning restaurant. The contemporary American menu is eclectic and always terrific. Food is served in an equally interesting atmosphere. The restaurant—with its high, vaulted ceiling—was originally built for a bank. The atmosphere is relaxed, and somewhat noisy, but quiet seating is available. It is a weekend evening hot spot. Also fun for a weekend jazz brunch. Newcomers should try the shrimp ala plancha, lacquered tuna or the hanger steak.
Hours: Lunch, every day from 11:30 am - 3 pm (in addition, brunch is served on Saturday & Sunday); Dinner, every day from 5:30 pm - 10 pm, Friday and Saturday, until 11 pm. Closed Christmas, Thanksgiving and Labor Day. Be sure to make reservations in advance.
Main course price range: Brunch, $7 - $13; Lunch, $9 - $16; Dinner, $15 - $24. Major credit cards accepted.

Elm Street Oyster House
11 West Elm Street, 629.5795
Good raw bar and chowders—our friends agree it is the best seafood in Greenwich and we have yet to be disappointed. You will like the creative recipes and yummy desserts. Try their seared tuna and oriental vegetable salad. The pan-fried oysters are great for an appetizer. An evening hot spot.
Hours: Monday - Thursday, 11:30 am - 10 pm; Friday & Saturday, 11:30 am - 11 pm; Sunday, 5 pm - 9 pm. Closed New Year's, Christmas and Thanksgiving. No reservations, so for dinner arrive before 7 pm or after 9 pm for your best chance to get quick seating.
Main course price range: $20 - $25. Major credit cards accepted.

Famous Pizza & Souvlaki Restaurant
10 North Water Street, Byram, 531.6887
A friendly, owner-run restaurant. Delicious Greek sandwiches and thin-crust pizza are the hallmark of this Byram restaurant. Don't miss the gyro sandwich, chicken souvlaki or the baklava. A perfect lunch or late-night snack for the casual diner.
Hours: Open every day: Breakfast, 7 am - 11:30 pm; Lunch/dinner, noon - 10 pm. Closed Christmas, Easter and New Year's.
Reservations accepted.
Main course price range: Breakfast, $4 - $6; Lunch & dinner, $10 - $14. Major credit cards accepted.

DINING OUT

(Le) Figaro

327 Greenwich Avenue, 622.0018

Le Figaro calls itself a Paris bistro and nothing could be more descriptive. From the moment you enter you feel like you are in France, albeit in a rather elegant bistro. The service is very friendly and at the pace you would expect in France. We particularly enjoy the Mediterranean salad with sesame tuna.

Hours: Lunch, Monday - Sunday, noon - 2:30 pm; Dinner, Monday - Friday, 5:30 pm - 9:30 pm; Saturday & Sunday, 5:30 pm - 10 pm. Closed Christmas and New Year's. Reservations highly recommended.

Main course price range: $16 - $28. Major credit cards accepted.

Fonda La Paloma

531 Post Road, Cos Cob, 661.9395

For years this has been our town's traditional Mexican (not "Tex-Mex") restaurant, complete with strolling mariachi band.

Hours: Lunch, Weekdays, 11:30 am - 3 pm; Dinner, Monday -Thursday, 5 pm - 10 pm; Friday, 5 pm - 11 pm; Sunday, 4:30 pm - 11 pm. Closed Thanksgiving, Labor Day, July 4th, and New Year's.

Reservations recommended. On weekends, reservations are necessary.

Main course price range: Lunch, $5 - $13; Dinner, $9 - $23.

Major credit cards accepted.

Fuji-Mart Ramen Stand

1212 East Putnam Avenue, Riverside

In the parking lot of the Fuji-Mart (Japanese grocery store), an enterprising group has transplanted a typical Japanese noodle shop to Greenwich. Enjoy big bowls of Ramen noodles served under a tent.

Hours: From April until about October, they are usually open Thursday through Sunday, from 7 pm - 11 pm.

RESTAURANTS

DINING OUT

Garden Cafe/Coffee Shop

At the Greenwich Hospital, 5 Perryridge Road, 863.3228

Newly redecorated, serving healthy American food. This coffee shop with its friendly staff is a pleasant meeting spot for lunches even when you are not visiting a friend in the hospital.

Hours: Weekdays, 9:30 am - 3:30 pm.

Main course price range: Prices vary; daily specials.

Garelick & Herbs

48 West Putnam Avenue, 661.7373

A sophisticated deli with a second location in Westport. It has a wide selection of ready-to-serve dishes. Everything is first-rate. They also have special take out menus for major holidays such as their Thanksgiving feast. Primarily a take-out store, although there are places to sit for the lucky few who get there first.

Hours: Weekdays, 7 am - 8 pm; Saturday, 8 am - 7 pm; Sunday, 9 am - 5 pm.

Gourmet Galley

100 Greenwich Avenue, 869.9618

A good place at the top of Greenwich Avenue to revive and rest from shopping.

Hours: Monday - Saturday, 7 am - 4 pm.

Habana

70 North Main Street, South Norwalk, CT, 203.852.9790

Enjoy the atmosphere and music, while dining on excellent contemporary Cuban cuisine. Be sure to try the spring rolls, Tuna citrones or plantain-coated sea bass. Don't forget to have some red sangria or Chilean merlot to go with your meal.

Hours: Open for dinner every night from 5 pm - 10 pm; on Friday and Saturday until 11 pm. Closed Thanksgiving & Christmas.

Reservations are necessary.

Main course price range: $19 - $24; all credit cards accepted.

Directions: I-95 North, Exit 14, R at stop sign, L at 2nd traffic light into Sono Plaza.

(Thomas Henkelmann at the) Homestead Inn
420 Field Point Road, 869.7500

Nestled in Belle Haven, in a lovely, formal inn with antiques and a garden setting, with contemporary French food. The owner and chef, Thomas Henkelmann, is regarded as one of the best chefs in the USA. Hours: Breakfast every day from 7 am - 9:30 am; Sunday - Friday, Lunch, noon - 2:30 pm; Dinner every day, 6 pm - 9:30 pm; Closed Labor Day, Memorial Day, July 4th, and the first two weeks in March. Closed Sundays from mid-July through August.
Main course price range: Lunch, $19 - $23; Dinner, $27 - $36.
Reservations accepted, preferably well in advance.
Major credit cards accepted.

Hubba-Hubba
189 Bedford Street, Stamford, CT, 359.1718

We are not sure one would drive to Stamford just to eat here, although we do sometimes crave their hot chili. If you are shopping or going to the movies in Stamford and you want a quick snack, this is the place. Try their burgers, steak wedge with hot chili or chili cheese fries.
Hours: Weekdays, 9 - 1 am; weekends, 9 am - 3 am.

Hunan Cafe
1233 East Putnam Avenue, Old Greenwich, 637.4341

Often chosen to cater special events for the Chinese American Association of Fairfield County, you can't go wrong whatever you select. Serves a delicious dim sum on Sundays.
Hours: every day, 11:30 am - 10 pm. Reservations accepted.
Main course price range: Lunch, $6; Dinner, $12.
Major credit cards accepted.

RESTAURANTS

DINING OUT

Hunan Gourmet

68 East Putnam Avenue, 869.1940

A Chinese restaurant with white tablecloths and an elegant flair. Count on good food served without much spice. The staff is especially nice to children, making it a popular family place. Free delivery with a minimum purchase of $20 or more.

Hours: Monday - Thursday, 11:30 am - 10 pm; Friday, 11:30 am - 11 pm; Saturday, noon - 11 pm; Sunday, noon - 10 pm. (Lunch is served every day until 3 pm). Reservations accepted.

Main course price range: Lunch, $7 - $8; Dinner, $10 - $28.

Major credit cards accepted.

Inferno

99 Railroad Avenue, 863.9780

An excellent location (like Cafe Rue) across from the train station and the Crown Plaza movie theater. An ultra modern, pricey, upscale pizza parlor (with bar) serving Tuscan-style, thin-crusted pizza cooked in a brick oven as well as a number of Italian pastas and other simple Mediterranean dishes. We like their pizzas but find the other dishes rather bland.

Hours: Lunch, Monday - Saturday, 11: 45 am - 3 pm; Dinner Monday - Thursday, 5 pm - 9:30 pm, Friday and Saturday, 5 pm - 10 pm, Sunday noon -5:30 pm.

Main course price range: Dinner $12 to $26; Lunch is somewhat less.

Large pizzas range from $12 - $18.

Inn at Pound Ridge

258 Westchester Avenue/Route 137, Pound Ridge, NY, 914.764.5779

This historic inn, with its lovely, quiet, country setting, serves elegant, international food. It is perfect for Sunday brunch or celebrations. Although the inn does not have rooms for overnight guests, it has a private dressing/bath suite for brides, hosts and hostesses.

Hours: Sunday brunch, noon - 2:30 pm; Lunch, Weekdays, noon - 2:30 pm; Dinner, 6 pm - 9 pm; Sunday, 5 pm - 9 pm.

Main course price range: $18 - $30; Saturday price fixed at $47.

Major credit cards accepted.

Directions: Merritt Pkw N to exit 35, L on Rte. 137 N (High Ridge), N for 7.5 miles past Rte. 172 on the left.

RESTAURANTS

DINING OUT

Jean-Louis

61 Lewis Street, 622.8450

www.RestaurantJean-Louis.com

Still our very favorite place, this intimate and refined French restaurant has service intended to make you feel special and comfortable. One of the best in Connecticut. You will be delighted with Jean Louis Gerin's new French cuisine. The menu degustation is always a great choice, as is the ostrich.

Hours: Lunch, Weekdays, noon - 2 pm; Dinner, Monday - Saturday, seatings start at 6 pm. Closed Sunday, Thanksgiving and Christmas. Be sure to make reservations.

Main course price range: Lunch, $21 - $29; Dinner, $33 - $36. Major credit cards accepted.

Jimmy's Grill

Parking Lot of Greenwich Town Hall

101 Field Point Road

An outdoor stand (mobile van). They have great chili dogs, Chicken souvlaki and Philly cheese steaks, all for very reasonable prices. When you are in a hurry for lunch, it's a great place to go. They even serve breakfast for people on-the-go.

Hours: Weekdays, 8 am - 2 pm, though these hours seem flexible.

Kagetsu

28 West Putnam Avenue, 622.9264

This attractive restaurant is a favorite of many Japanese residents. We think they make the best sushi in town and are hooked. Try their Futomaki. The atmosphere is usually serene and quiet.

Hours: Lunch, Tuesday - Friday, noon - 2:30 pm; Dinner, Tuesday - Thursday, 5 pm - 9:30 pm; Friday & Saturday, 5 pm - 10 pm; Sunday, 5 pm - 9:30 pm. Closed Monday.

Main course price range: $10.50 - $16.

RESTAURANTS

DINING OUT

Katzenberg's Gourmet Deli

33 Lewis Street, 629.8889

A newcomer in town receiving loud applause. So popular, they have opened a takeout place on Greenwich Avenue (see express address below). They have a large menu and lots of seating space. If you decide to take out, be sure to choose some of their delicious homemade bakery treats.

Hours: Open every day, 9 am - 8 pm; lunch is served until 3:30 pm. Closed Thanksgiving, Christmas and Easter. No reservations.

Main course price range: Lunch/dinner, $4.95 - $15.

Major credit cards accepted.

Katzenberg's Express

342 Greenwich Avenue, 625.0103

A new deli with a wide selection of sandwiches. Primarily takeout, but there are a few places to sit.

Hours: Monday - Thursday, 8 am - 6 pm; Friday and Saturday, 9 am - 10 pm; Sunday 10 am - 4 pm.

Kazu

64 North Main Street, South Norwalk, CT, 203.866.7492

Very near the Sono Theater. Order the movie box. It has a tasty sampling of their Japanese specialties. You will also find their sushi or teriyaki good choices.

Hours: Weekdays, lunch, noon - 2 pm; Dinner, 5:30 pm - 10 pm; Friday & Saturday, 5:30 pm - 11 pm; Sunday, 5 pm - 9:30 pm. Closed Christmas Eve, Christmas and Thanksgiving.

Reservations accepted.

Main course price range: Lunch, $6.75 - $16; Dinner, $13.75 - $22.75.

Major credit cards accepted.

Directions: I-95 North, Exit 14, R at stop sign, L at 2nd traffic light into Sono Plaza.

RESTAURANTS

DINING OUT

Landmark Diner

31 East Putnam Avenue, Cos Cob, 869.0954

Formerly the Country Squire, then Cassi's, it has now been taken over by the owner of the Colonial Diner. Cheers! It serves a wide variety of hearty breakfast and dinner dishes, in a slightly more upscale atmosphere than the Colonial Diner. It has the great prices, large servings and friendly service you expect.

Hours: Sunday - Thursday, 6 am - 11 pm; Friday and Saturday, 6 am - 1 pm. No reservations.

Main course price range: Breakfast, $3 - $7; Lunch, $3 - $11; Dinner, $4 - $16. Major credit cards, except Discover, accepted.

MacKenzie's Grill Room

148 Sound Beach Avenue, Old Greenwich, 698.0223

Casual, friendly restaurant and bar. Try their penne con pollo, Steak au poivre and key lime pie. On weekends, MacKenzie's is a "hot spot" and tends to get crowded and noisy.

Hours: Sunday - Thursday, 11:30 am - 1 am; Friday and Saturday, 11:30 am - 2 am. Open every day, including all holidays.

Main course price range: Lunch, $6.95 - $13.50; Dinner, $8.95 - $20.95. No reservations. Major credit cards accepted.

Manero's

559 Steamboat Road, 869.0049

www.maneros-greenwichct.com

A Greenwich institution, known for their kindness to children. Waiters sing Happy Birthday with gusto. To grow up never having Manero's steak, Gorgonzola salad and garlic bread would be too sad. When you are looking for a quick snack, order their wonderful steak sandwich to go.

Hours: Lunch/dinner, Weekdays, noon - 10 pm; Saturday, noon - 11 pm; Sunday, noon - 9 pm. Closed Thanksgiving and Christmas. It's best to call for reservations, especially in the evening.

Main course price range: Lunch, $8 - $11; Dinner, $16 - $34.

Major credit cards accepted.

RESTAURANTS

DINING OUT

Maya of Japan
4 Lewis Court, 869.4322
Traditional Japanese steak house. Sit around cooktop tables and watch the chef perform. For years this has been a favorite of ours. They also have a good sushi bar.
Hours: Tuesday - Friday, lunch, noon - 2 pm; Dinner, Friday & Saturday, 5 pm - 10:30 pm; Sunday, 5 pm - 9:30 pm; closed Mondays. Closed Thanksgiving, New Year's, July 4th, Halloween and Super Bowl Sunday.
Reservations accepted for parties of six or more.
Main course price range: Lunch, $10 - $13.50; Dinner, $13.50 - $18.
Major credit cards accepted.

Mediterraneo Restaurant
366 Greenwich Avenue, 629.4747
Fun atmosphere and good Mediterranean food. This is still a very happening scene. The terrace provides an interesting perspective on life along Greenwich Avenue. We like their pasta dishes and nice wine selection. The same group owns another Greenwich restaurant, Terra Ristorante Italiano.
Hours: Lunch, Monday - Saturday, noon - 2:30 pm; Dinner, Monday - Saturday, 5:30 pm - 10 pm; Friday & Saturday, 5:30 pm - 10 pm. Closed Sunday, Thanksgiving, Christmas and New Year's.
Reservations are usually required.
Main course price range:$18 - $28. Major credit cards accepted.

Meli-Melo
362 Greenwich Avenue, 629.6153
Tiny jewel of a restaurant with French casual foods such as yummy onion soup and crepes. Our favorite, however, is their croque monsieur. Be sure to have a sampling of their fresh fruit sorbets for dessert. The weekend breakfast menu consists mainly of delicious omelets.
Hours: every day, 11 am - 10 pm. On Saturday and Sunday, they serve breakfast from 9:30. Closed Christmas, New Year's and Thanksgiving.
No reservations.
Main course price range: $4.50 - $10.50. Major credit cards accepted.

RESTAURANTS

DINING OUT

Meson Galicia

10 Wall Street, Norwalk, CT, 203.866.8800

The menu changes frequently, but they always have wonderful seafood selections and desserts. Try their tapas to begin or as your whole meal. You won't be disappointed.

Hours: Lunch, Tuesday - Friday, noon - 2:30 pm; Dinner, Tuesday - Sunday, 6 pm - 9:30 pm; Friday and Saturday until 10:30 pm; Sunday until 8:30 pm. Closed Monday and most holidays. Reservations accepted.

Tapas price range: $18 - $24.

Major credit cards accepted.

Directions: I-95 N to Exit 16, Left off the exit, L on Wall, entrance on Hugh St.

Mhai Thai

280 Railroad Avenue, 625.2602

Very good authentic Thai food. We love their green curries.

Hours: Lunch, Tuesday - Friday, noon - 2 pm; Dinner, Tuesday - Thursday, 5:30 pm - 9:30 pm; Friday & Saturday, 5:30 pm - 10 pm; Sunday, 5:30 pm - 9 pm. Closed Monday, but open most holidays.

Reservations accepted for any size group.

Main course price range: Lunch, $8 - $15; Dinner, $16 - $20.

Major credit cards accepted.

Mianus River Tavern

136 River Road Extension, Cos Cob, 862-0640

On a small street just off of the Post Road, Augie's (since 1898) has been redecorated and turned into a charming restaurant. Although there are a number of entrees, we would suggest you stick to the tavern fare portion of the menu.

Hours: Sunday - Thursday, 11 am - 10 pm; Friday and Saturday, 11 am - 11 pm.

The bar is open later on weekends.

Main course price range: Lunch sandwiches, $6.50 - $7.50; Dinner entrees $14 - $20, Tavern fare $7.50 - $8.50.

RESTAURANTS

DINING OUT

Mirage Cafe

531 North Main Street, Port Chester, NY, 914.937.3497

Funky decor with excellent French-Caribbean food. Their menu changes often. Try the wonderful steak au poivre or steak diable. Their lemon grass shrimp, and Southwestern tuna are also good choices. Their dessert wine, muscat, is to die for!

Hours: Dinner only. Sunday - Tuesday, 6 pm - 11 pm; Wednesday and Thursday, 6 pm - 1 am; Friday & Saturday, 6 pm - 3 am. Closed Mondays in winter, and on most major holidays. Reservations in advance are recommended, especially for weekends.

Main course price range: $13 - $24. Major credit cards accepted.

Moreno Ristorante

554 Old Post Road #3 (just off West Putnam Ave), 661.3200

Tucked away in an off-the-beaten-path location, with valet parking, this is the successor to the Ivy Restaurant. The atmosphere is attractive but noisy. Service and food are still rough but lots of diners are enjoying it and we hope it will succeed.

Hours: Lunch, Monday - Saturday, noon - 3 pm; Dinner, Sunday - Thursday, 5 pm - 9:30 pm; Friday & Saturday, 5 pm - 10:30 pm.
Closed Christmas. Reservations accepted.

Main course price range: Lunch, $16 - $25; Dinner, $20 - $35.
Major credit cards accepted.

Morton's of Chicago

377 North State Street (Swiss Bank Center), Stamford, CT, 324.3939

If the menu presentation doesn't turn you into a vegetarian, you will find the steak as good as it gets. We especially liked the tenderloin brochette with diable sauce and Godiva hot chocolate cake. A popular place for men in suits.

Hours: Dinner, Monday - Saturday, 5 pm - 11 pm; Sunday, 5 pm - 10 pm. Closed Thanksgiving, Christmas, Labor Day, Memorial Day, New Year's and July 4th.

Main course price range: $21 - $31. Major credit cards accepted.

Directions: I-95 N to exit 8, immediate L on Atlantic, immediate L on State.

RESTAURANTS

DINING OUT

Organic Planet
35 Amogerone Crossway, 861.9822
Low-fat, dairy-free, delicious vegetarian cuisine. The service is relaxed, the atmosphere minimal, and the servings healthy and abundant. One to four specials daily.
Hours: Monday, 10 am - 5 pm; Tuesday - Saturday, 10 am - 8 pm; Friday and Saturday until 9 pm. Sunday brunch, 11:30 am - 5 pm. Closed Thanksgiving, July 4th and Christmas.
Main course price range: Kids menu, $4.95 - $7.95; Sunday brunch and regular menu, $7 - $14.
All major credit cards accepted.

(La) Panetiere
530 Milton Road, Rye, NY, 914.967.8140
www.lapanetiere.com
Westchester County's best. Extremely good classic French food only fifteen minutes away. Attractive Provencale dining room. Try their roast noisette of lamb.
Hours: Weekdays, Lunch, noon - 2 pm; Dinner, 6 pm - 9 pm; Saturday seatings at 6 pm and 8:30 pm; Sunday, 1 pm - 3 pm and 5 pm - 8 pm. Advanced reservations recommended, no minimum.
Main course price range: Lunch, $16 - $21; or price fixed at $29; Dinner, $24 - $32. All major credit cards accepted.
Directions: I-95 S to exit 19, R on light to Milton Rd.

Panda Pavilion
137 West Putnam Avenue, 869.1111
We always feel at home at this well-priced Chinese restaurant with friendly service. Try the delicious sesame chicken, spicy broccoli or the house special bean curd. Free delivery for orders of $20 and over.
Hours: Monday - Thursday, 11 am - 10 pm; Friday, 11 am - 11 pm; Saturday, 11:30 am - 11 pm; Sunday, noon - 10 pm. (Lunch is served until 3 pm). Reservations accepted.
Main course price range: Lunch, $5.50 - $6.50; Dinner, $7 - $26.
Major credit cards accepted.

RESTAURANTS

DINING OUT

Pantanal

29 North Main Street, Port Chester, NY, 914.939.6894

The best Brazilian restaurant in the area. Try their speciality meat dish, Rodizia. The trick here is to not eat your weight in their delicious cheese bread (Pao de Queijo) before your meal.

Hours: Lunch, Tuesday - Friday, noon - 3 pm (Closed Monday for lunch); Dinner, Weekdays, 5 pm - 11:30 pm; Lunch/Dinner, Saturday and Sunday, noon - 11:30 pm. Closed Christmas, New Year's, and closes early on Christmas Eve (approximately 8 pm).

Accepts reservations—recommended for weekends.

Main course price range: Weekday specials, lunch, $8.50 - $11.00; Dinner, $13.95 - $19.95. Major credit cards accepted.

Paradise Bar & Grill

78 Southfield Avenue, Stamford, CT, 323.1116, www.paradisebarandgrille.com

Located on the water at the Stamford Landing, near Dolphin Cove. Eating here is like stepping into a tropical island restaurant. In summer you can dine open-air on the boardwalk. Try the many charcoal-broiled fish entrees. The seafood pizzas are also worth trying. Children are welcome.

Hours: Sunday brunch, 11:30 am - 3 pm; Monday, Thursday, Saturday lunch, noon - 5 pm; Monday - Thursday and Sunday, dinner, 5 pm - 9 pm;

Friday and Saturday, open until 10 pm.

Closed Christmas and Thanksgiving. During the winter, closed Monday & Sunday evenings and Saturday lunch. In the summer reservations are accepted for eight or more. In the winter, reservations are limited to two or more.

Main course price range: Lunch, $11 - $13; Dinner, $15 - $25.

Major credit cards accepted.

Directions: I-95 N to exit 7, R on Greenwich Avenue, next light is intersection of Greenwich Avenue/Selleck/Southfield. Stamford Landing is .2 miles on the left.

RESTAURANTS

DINING OUT

Paradiso

356 West Putnam Avenue, 622.8111

It's an old-fashioned Italian eatery. Glenville locals especially like their individual pizzas. The large pizzas can be soggy.

Hours: Monday - Thursday, 11 am - 10 pm; Saturday, 11 am - 11 pm; Sunday, noon - 10 pm. Closed Easter, Christmas, Thanksgiving, July 4th. Reservations accepted.

Main course price range: Lunch, $10 - $15; Dinner, $12 - $17.

Major credit cards accepted.

Pasta Vera

48 Greenwich Avenue, 661.9705

A casual Italian restaurant noted for its homemade pastas. It is usually quiet enough to have a good conversation. It's also a great place for a late lunch. First-time visitors should try their homemade ravioli.

Hours: Monday - Saturday, lunch, 11:30 am - 3 pm; Monday - Thursday, dinner, 5 pm - 10 pm; Friday & Saturday, until 10:30 pm; Sunday, 4 pm - 9 pm. In the winter, their Sunday hours are noon - 9 pm. Open all holidays, with no vacation closings.

Reservations are accepted for parties of six or more.

Main course price range: Lunch, $9 - $11; Dinner, $13 - $18.

Major credit cards accepted.

Pearl of the Atlantic

102 Fox Island Road, Port Chester, NY, 914.939.4277

www.thepearlrestaurant.com

A casual Portuguese restaurant right on the Byram River and just a little difficult to find. Specializes in seafood, particularly lobster dishes. Be sure to order the lobster soup and paella.

Hours: Sunday brunch (November - April), noon - 2:30 pm; Lunch, every day except Tuesday, 11:30 am - 5 pm; Dinner, every day except Tuesday, 5 pm - 10 pm. Open 7 days a week from May 1 to September 30. Closed Tuesdays, Christmas and New Year's. Reservations are recommended on the weekends.

Main course price range: Brunch, $15 - $19; Lunch, $7 - $14; Dinner, $10.95 - $24.95. Children's menu. Major credit cards accepted.

Directions: Rte 1 S through Main Street Port Chester, to Grace Church Street, left onto Fox Island.

DINING OUT

Penang Grill

55 Lewis Street, 861.1988

New to Greenwich and well-received. Casual dining with samplings of spicy Asian foods. Try the spicy mango shrimp, beef satay or curry dishes.

Hours: Monday - Thursday, 11 am - 10 pm; Friday and Saturday, 11 am - 11 pm. Lunch menu is served until 3 pm.

Closed Thanksgiving and Christmas.

Make reservations for parties of three or more.

Main course price range: Lunch, $7 - $8; Dinner, $12 - $20.

Major credit cards accepted.

Piero's

44 South Regent Street, Port Chester, NY, 914.937.2904

Casual, off-the-beaten-path Northern Italian. The friend who introduced us to this small restaurant was concerned that putting it in our guide would make it even harder to get reservations. Once you try the house red wine and veal saltimbocca or scampi, you will understand.

Hours: Tuesday - Friday, Lunch, noon - 2:30 pm; Tuesday - Thursday, Dinner, 5 pm - 9:30 pm; Friday, 5 pm -10:30; Saturday, 1 pm - 10:30 pm; Sunday, 1 pm - 9:30 pm.

Closed Thanksgiving and Christmas. Reservations accepted.

Main course price range: Lunch, $9 - $14; Dinner, $12 - $21.

Visa and MasterCard only.

Directions: Rte 1 S thru Port Chester, R on Westchester, L on South Regent.

Pizza Express

160 Hamilton Ave, 622.1693

A friendly place to call for free delivery. They will fax you their menu.

Hours: Monday - Saturday, 10 am - 10 pm; Sunday, 11 am - 10 pm.

Pizza Factory

380 Greenwich Avenue, 661.5188

We can't agree on the best pizza joint, but Pizza Factory's pizza is always competing for the top of the list. Be sure to try their Gorgonzola salad. They have table service and carry out.

No credit cards, checks or delivery.

Hours: Open every day, 11:30 am - 9 or 9:30 pm.

Pizza Glenville

243 Glenville Road, 532.1691

Most Glenville residents we know love Glenville Pizza and it is one of the few places serving by the slice.

No deliveries. No credit cards, but they will accept a check.

Hours: Monday - Sunday, 10:30 am - 11 pm (Sunday until 10 pm).

Pizza Hut

19 Glenville Road, 531.4411

This is a favorite. We like their pan pizza,

Major credit cards accepted. No deliveries.

Hours: Sunday - Thursday, 11 am - 10 pm (Sunday from noon); Friday & Saturday, 11 am - 11 pm.

Pizza Post

522 East Putnam Avenue, 661.0909

A local favorite.

No deliveries. No credit cards, but they accept checks.

Hours: Monday - Thursday, 11 am - 10 pm; Friday & Saturday, 11 am - 11 pm; Sunday, noon - 10 pm.

Planet Pizza

28 Railroad Avenue, 622.0999

Traditional New York City-style pizzeria in a central Greenwich location next to the theater. Meals run $2 - $15. Try their "Penne Planet." Clean, well-lighted dining area.

Major credit cards accepted. They will deliver.

Hours: Sunday - Thursday, 10 am - 11 pm; Friday & Saturday, 10 am - 12 pm. Closed Christmas, Easter and Thanksgiving.

Porterhouse

124 Washington Street, South Norwalk, CT, 203.855.0441
www.culinarymenus/porterhouse
A little loud and slow, but the great steaks and desserts, served in a warm and friendly atmosphere, will make you a regular. Be sure to try their delightful fresh-brewed tea. The lamb, calamari with chili sauce and flank steaks are all delicious.
Hours: Tuesday - Sunday, dinner, 5 pm - 10 pm; Friday and Saturday, until 11 pm. Closed Monday, Thanksgiving, Easter, Christmas, Christmas Eve and July 4th. No minimum for reservations.
Main course price range: $16 - $35. Major credit cards accepted.
Directions: I-95 N, exit 14, R on West Avenue, left at fork onto Main Street, 2nd light left onto Washington.

Rebecca's

265 Glenville Road, 532.9270
One of the best restaurants in town, serving modern American cuisine in a simple, contemporary setting. Following the trend, there is a large window that allows you to see the kitchen. Although we loved the tuna with mustard, be sure to try their signature dishes: three ravioli appetizer and lobster with lemons (completely out of the shell and easy to eat) for your main course. Other main courses to try are the grilled Dover sole with lemon sauce or the squab with pomegranate sauce.
Hours: Tuesday - Friday, lunch, 11:30 am - 2:30 pm; Tuesday - Thursday, dinner, 5:30 pm - 9:30 pm; Friday & Saturday, 5:30 pm - 10:30 pm; Sunday 5:30 pm - 9:30 pm. Closed Monday, Christmas Eve, Christmas, Thanksgiving, Easter, New Year's Eve and New Year's. Be sure to make a reservation well in advance (a month's notice wouldn't hurt), although you might be able to drop in and eat at the bar.
Main course price range: Dinner, $27 - $38 (Kobe beef runs $75 - $100). Major credit cards accepted.

RESTAURANTS

DINING OUT

River Cat Grill

148 Rowayton Avenue, Rowayton, CT, 203.854.0860

A new restaurant, serving (like their sister restaurant, the Boxing Cat Grill) an eclectic menu with great flavors. We liked their spicy chowder, crispy tuna and Asian duck entrees, as well as their large selection of wines by the glass. The portions are small, so if you are hungry, order a full course meal or more than one main dish per person. The prices reflect this approach. The atmosphere is sophisticated with good service, and you can hear your dinner companions speak.

Hours: Tuesday - Thursday, 11:30 am - 10 pm; Friday, 11:30 am - 11 pm; Saturday, 11:30 am - 3:30 pm & 5:30 pm - 11 pm; Sunday, 11 am - 9:30 pm. The bar stays open to 1:30 am or 2 am.

Closed Mondays, Christmas, Thanksgiving and New Year's.

Dinner reservations on the weekend are a must.

Main course price range: Lunch/dinner, $10 - $13. MasterCard, Visa and American Express accepted.

Directions: I-95 N, exit 12, Rte 136 toward Rowayton.

Roger Sherman Inn

195 Oenoke Ridge Road (Route 124), New Canaan, CT, 203.966.4541 www.rogershermaninn.com

Built in the 1700's, it is one of the oldest inns in Fairfield County. The Swiss owners have also made the inn one of the prettiest. Try their vegetable lasagne, fricassee of lobster and scallops, pepper steak or the chef's signature chicken. Be sure to order the chocolate souffle in advance. It is superb. The inn is well set up for elegant parties and can accommodate groups from 8 to 180 guests. Ask to see a copy of their typical wedding banquet menu.

Hours: Breakfast served only to inn guests. Sunday brunch, 11:30 am - 2 pm (not available January - March); Monday - Saturday, lunch, noon - 2 pm; Monday - Thursday, dinner, 6 pm - 9:30 pm; Friday and Saturday, 6 pm - 10 pm; Sunday, 6 pm - 8 pm.

Make reservations two days in advance.

Main course price range: $32; Saturday night fixed price, $48; Brunch, $28. Major credit cards accepted.

Directions: Merritt N exit 37, L onto Rte 124 N - 2 miles, Rte 124 makes a right at Cherry Street. Next left (light) - on Main continue on 124 for 1 mile. Inn is on the right.

DINING OUT

Rowayton Seafood Company

89 Rowayton Avenue, Norwalk, CT, 203.866.4488

www.RowaytonSeafood.com

Small and popular, informal and relaxed, just what one wants for summer dining. A good place to bring land-locked visitors for lobster and a view of the water. Just in case you don't want lobster, try their seafood stew, grilled tuna or fresh oysters.

Hours: Open every day. Lunch, 11:30 am - 3 pm; a limited menu is sometimes available from 3 pm - 5 pm; Dinner, 5 pm - 11 pm. Closed Christmas, Thanksgiving, New Year's Eve and New Year's. On weekends, be sure to make reservations well in advance.

Main course price range: Lunch, $8 - $20; Dinner, $18 - $24; Lobster by the pound.

Directions: I-95 N, exit 12, Onto Rte 136 - 1.5 miles to stop sign, 500 yards the right.

Sage

363 Greenwich Ave, 622.5138

A pleasant dining experience with attentive waiters and an excellent menu. Our favorites include crab cakes and duck.

Hours: Sunday brunch, 11 am - 3 pm; Weekdays, Lunch, 11:30 am - 2:30 pm; Dinner, Tuesday - Thursday, 6 pm - 9:30 pm; Friday & Saturday, 6 pm - 10 pm; Sunday, 5:30 pm - 9 pm. Closed Thanksgiving, one week between Christmas and New Year's, and one week at the end of August, including Labor Day.

Reservations are recommended for weekends and large parties, preferably two to three days in advance.

Main course price range: Brunch/lunch, $14 - $23; Dinner, $17 - $28. Major credit cards accepted.

RESTAURANTS

DINING OUT

Sevilla

203 East Putnam Avenue (Mill Pond Shopping Center), Cos Cob, 629.9029

Greenwich's first tapas restaurant is an instant hit.

Hours: Monday - Saturday, 11:30 am - 11:30 pm; Sunday, 11:30 am - 9 pm. Lunch menu from 11:30 am - 3 pm; reduced menu from 3 pm - 5 pm; dinner menu, 5 pm - 10 pm.

Reservations accepted for parties of six and up. Can be very crowded for dinner, so come early.

Main course price range: Dinner, Tapas, $5 - $8; Entrees, $15 - $20. Everything is a la carte.

Major credit cards are accepted.

Silvermine Tavern

194 Perry Avenue, Norwalk, CT, 203.847.4558

A 15 - 20 minute drive from Greenwich, this eighteenth century Colonial inn, situated right on the river, is a good choice for Sunday brunch. The reasonably-priced buffet has a selection of dishes to delight every one. We especially enjoyed their french toast, Yogurt with strawberry preserves and their justifiably famous buns. The atmosphere is informal and children are always welcome. The inn is very spacious, but it is also popular, so arrive early. For lunch try their seafood angel hair pasta. For dinner try their herb-crusted rack of lamb.

Hours: Monday - Saturday (closed Tuesday), lunch, noon - 3 pm; Monday - Saturday (closed Tuesday), dinner, 6 pm - 9 pm; Sunday dinner, 3:30 pm - 8:30 pm; Sunday brunch, 11 am - 2:30 pm; late night jazz with appetizers and desserts only, Friday and Saturday, 9 pm - 12 pm. Reservations for brunch are given only for parties of seven or more. Closed Tuesdays & Christmas.

Main course price range: Sunday brunch is $18.50 for adults, $8.75 for children ages 5-10, children under 5 are free; Lunch, $6.50 - $12; Dinner, $15 - $26.

Directions: Merritt Parkway N to Exit 40A, R on Main Street, R on Perry Avenue. R on Silvermine Road.

RESTAURANTS

DINING OUT

Sixty-Four Greenwich Avenue

64 Greenwich Avenue, 861.6400

Fortunately there are still a few restaurants bucking the minimalist decorative trend. We like the tasteful decor and food in this popular New York-style restaurant.

Hours: Weekdays, lunch, noon - 2:30 pm; Monday - Thursday, dinner, 6 pm - 9 pm; Friday, dinner, 6 pm - 10 pm; Saturday, dinner, 6 pm - 11 pm. Closed Sunday, Thanksgiving and Christmas. Reservations accepted.

Main course price range: Lunch, $8 - $15; Dinner, $16 - $30.

Major credit cards accepted.

Skylight Cafe (by Mary & Martha's Catering)

YWCA, 259 East Putnam Avenue, 869.6501

Well-priced, bright and sunny eatery where you can enjoy a continental breakfast, a healthy lunch or just grab a freshly baked muffin. Try their chicken salad sandwich on a spinach tortilla. On many afternoons they serve tea. Call for dates and reservations. Children are always welcome!

Hours: Winter hours, Weekdays, 8:30 am - 5:30 pm; Saturday, 8:30 am - 1 pm; Summer hours start in June, Monday - Thursday, 8:30 am - 4:30 pm; Friday, 8:30 am - 2:30 pm. Closed all major holidays including Christmas through New Year's, and the last week in August.

No credit cards.

Sky Top Restaurant

Westchester County Airport, White Plains, NY, 914.428.0251

We happened to be there just at sunset and we were delighted to find delicious continental food, pleasant service and a pretty view of our local airport.

Hours: Open every day; Breakfast, 5:30 am - 11 am; Sunday brunch, 11 am - 3 pm; Lunch, Monday - Saturday, 11 am - 4 pm; Dinner, Monday - Saturday, 4 pm - 10 pm.

Reservations are accepted.

Main course price range: Sunday brunch, $14; Lunch, $7 - $13; Dinner, $16 - $29.

Major credit cards accepted.

Directions: King Street N to Rye Lake Road.

RESTAURANTS

DINING OUT

Smokey Joe's Bar-B-Q

1308 East Main Street (US-1), Stamford, CT, 406.0605

Formerly Buster's, it still has the best Texas Bar-B-Q this side of Fort Worth. In addition, it is priced inexpensively. Smokey Joe's offers a great variety of meats, gumbos and side dishes, in a cafeteria-style restaurant setting—servings are on paper, not porcelain. The servings are large, especially the Texan size. Order their beef brisket and pulled pork, with a side of collard greens and sweet potato fries.

Hours: Monday - Thursday, 11:30 am - 3 pm, 4:30 pm - 9 pm; Friday and Saturday, 11:30 am - 10 pm; Sunday, 11:30 am - 9 pm. The upstairs bar is open until 1 am.

Main course price range: Sandwiches, $3 - $6; two-meat combos, $9.50 - $12.

Directions: I-95 N to exit 9, R on US 1.

Sono Seaport Seafood

100 Water Street, South Norwalk, CT, 203.854.9483

A very informal spot on the water to have lobster or fish and chips. Bring your children. Nice outside deck with raw bar.

Hours: Open every day. November - April, 11 am - 9 pm; May - October, 11 am - 10 pm. Closed Christmas, New Year's and Thanksgiving.

Reservations accepted for parties of six or more.

Main course price range: $5 - $15. Major credit cards accepted.

Directions: I-95 N, exit 14, follow signs for Maritime Museum, past museum to light, 100 yards on the left.

Splash Cafe - Inn at Long Shore

Westport, 203.454.7798

A Baang relative with the same sort of delicious eclectic Pacific Rim menu. A lovely setting on the water, with a variety of spicy fish entrees.

Hours: Monday - Saturday, lunch, 11:30 am - 2:30 pm; Monday - Friday, dinner, 5:30 pm - 10 pm; Saturday & Sunday, dinner, 5:30 pm - 11 pm; Sunday brunch, 11 am - 3 pm.

Directions: I-95, exit 17, 2 lights to stop sign, L onto Riverside Avenue, R onto Bridge. R at first light after bridge, R at 1st light (look for golf course).

RESTAURANTS

DINING OUT

Stonehenge Inn

Route 7, Ridgefield, CT, 203.438.6511

Well-respected eclectic French food by the former chef of Bertrand's in Greenwich, in an attractive 16-room inn set on ten acres. Order one of the fantastic souffles at the beginning of your meal. If you forget, try the raspberry creme souffle. For the adventurous, the buffalo steak entree is excellent.

Hours: Dinner, Tuesday - Saturday, 6 pm - 9 pm; Sunday, 4 pm - 8 pm; Sunday brunch, noon - 2:30 pm; Closed Mondays. An advance reservation is always a good idea.

Main course price range: Dinner, $18 - $34; Brunch, $30 price fixed. Major credit cards accepted.

Directions: Merritt Parkway N to exit 39B, Take Rte 7N for 13 miles, Inn on the L.

Sundown Saloon

403 Greenwich Avenue, 629.8212

This informal restaurant serves both traditional and imaginative Western food. Try the brisket sandwich and the apple burrito dessert. Be sure to order the lemonade. The friendly staff—and crayons for writing on the tablecloths—makes this a good choice for the whole family.

Hours: Monday - Thursday, 11:30 am - 1 am; Friday & Saturday, 11:30 am - 2 am; Sunday, 11:30 am - 1 am. Open all holidays. Does not accept reservations.

Main course price range: $8 - $17. Major credit cards accepted.

Tandoori (Taste of India)

163 North Main Street, Port Chester, NY, 914.937.2727

It's so nice to have a good Indian restaurant close to Greenwich. Try their fixed-price buffet lunch, weekdays.

Hours: Lunch, Monday - Saturday, noon - 2:30 pm; Dinner, every day from 5:30 - 10 pm; Sunday brunch, noon - 2:30. Closed Thanksgiving and July 4th. Reservations accepted.

Main course price range: Lunch, $9.95; Dinner, $9 - $17; Brunch, $12. Major credit cards accepted.

DINING OUT

Terra Ristorante Italiano

156 Greenwich Avenue, 629.5222

Walking along Greenwich Avenue, it's hard to escape the wonderful smells coming from their wood-burning ovens serving up Northern Italian food. A lively, hip trattoria, with mediocre service. We recommend the Gamberoni appetizer or the chicken, both made in their special oven. If you want to escape the noise, dine on the terrace. Given the choice between Terra and their sister restaurant, Mediterraneo, we would choose Mediterraneo.

Hours: Lunch, Monday - Saturday, noon - 2:30 pm; Dinner, Monday - Saturday, 5:30 pm - 10:30 pm; Sunday dinner, 6 pm - 9:30 pm.

Main course price range: Dinner, $11 - $32. Major credit cards accepted.

That Little Italian Restaurant

228-230 Mill Street, Byram, 531.7500

Tucked away on a small street in the Byram section of Greenwich, this attractive restaurant just keeps getting better. The place to go when you want good pasta without going to a fancy restaurant. In addition, this is one restaurant where you can actually have a conversation.

Hours: Tuesday - Sunday, lunch, 11:30 am - 2:30 pm; Sunday - Thursday, dinner, 5 pm - 9:30 pm; Friday & Saturday, 5 pm - 10:30 pm. Closed Monday, Thanksgiving, Easter, and Christmas. During the summer, they stay open one hour later. They do not accept reservations.

Main course price range: $11 - $19; personal pizzas $9.

Major credit cards accepted.

Thataway Cafe

409 Greenwich Avenue, 622.0947

A casual restaurant situated at the end of the avenue. Try the cajun rock shrimp popcorn, grilled chicken quesadillas, teriyaki marinated skirt steak, chicken fajitas or the cheddar burger; the Oreo decadence dessert is a must. The outdoor patio is the place to be in summertime.

Hours: Monday - Thursday, 11:30 am - 11 pm; Friday & Saturday, 11 am - 12 am; Sunday, 11 am - 11 pm; Sunday brunch, 11 am - 3 pm. Live seasonal entertainment - call for days and times. They do not accept reservations.

Main course price range: $8 - $20. Major credit cards accepted.

DINING OUT

Tigin

175 Bedford Street, Stamford, CT, 353.8444

A pub designed to make you feel you've stepped into Ireland. Hearty food and lots of cozy nooks.

Hours: Monday - Thursday, 11:30 am - 12:30 pm; Friday & Saturday, 11:30 am - 1:30 am. Closed Christmas. Reservations accepted.

Main course price range: Lunch, $6 - $10; Dinner, $8 - $14.

Major credit cards accepted.

Directions: I-95 N, exit 8, left off ramp, go straight, Atlantic turns into Bedford St, Tigin is on the right.

Tucson

130 East Putnam Avenue, 661.2483

Listen to live jazz on Wednesdays and weekends at this happening bar/restaurant with Southwestern flair. Good spicy appetizers to share. A noisy singles place with great margaritas. If you are going there for a meal, try the filet mignon al chipolte or lobster ravioli main courses — and be sure to ask to sit on the terrace.

Hours: Lunch, Monday - Saturday, 11:30 am - 3:30 pm; Dinner, Sunday - Saturday, 5:30 pm - 10:30 pm. Closed Thanksgiving and Christmas. Reservations recommended.

Main course price range: Lunch, $7.50 - $16; Dinner, $11.50 - $23.

Major credit cards accepted.

Valbella

1309 East Putnam Avenue, Riverside, 637.1155

Excellent Italian food, good service and a dressy decor. There is something wonderful on the menu for everyone. Try their cold seafood combo, fettuccini with white truffles or the Dover sole. They have a spectacular wine cellar with 850 wines to choose from. Truly a town favorite and our vote as the best Italian restaurant in town.

Hours: Lunch, Weekdays, noon - 3 pm; Dinner, Monday - Saturday, 5 pm - 10 pm; Friday and Saturday until 11 pm; closed on Sunday and Christmas. Reservations required.

Main course price range: Lunch, $18 - $15; Dinner, $24 - $32.

RESTAURANTS
DINING OUT

Versailles

315 Greenwich Avenue, 661.6634

A very French bistro with excellent pastries. Just the right place to meet a friend for a late lunch. The good food and atmosphere are reminiscent of our Paris favorites.

Hours: Monday - Thursday, 7:30 am - 9:30 pm; Friday, 7:30 am - 10 pm; Saturday, 8 am - 10 pm; Sunday, 8 am - 8 pm. Closed Thanksgiving and Christmas Eve.

Reservations accepted.

Main course price range: Breakfast, $10; Lunch (set course menu), $17, or $6.95 - $12.50; Dinner, $17.50 - $23.50.

Major credit cards accepted.

Village Deli & Cafe

3 West Elm Street, 622.6644

Open since 1991, they serve hearty pancakes and other breakfast and deli fare, in a light, clean and attractive mid-town deli with nice seating space.

Hours: Monday - Saturday, 7 am - 7 pm; Sunday, 10 am - 4 pm.

Reservations can be made for parties of six or more.

All major credit cards accepted except American Express.

Viscardi's Colonial Inn

220 Sound Beach Avenue, Old Greenwich, 637.0367, 637.4634

An institution in Old Greenwich for over 30 years—perfect when you want excellent value and a wholesome meal. The Viscardi family makes this restaurant a warm, friendly place for your family.

Hours: Open every day, Monday - Saturday, 11:30 am - 11 pm; Sunday, noon - 9 pm. Closed Thanksgiving and Christmas. Summer hours vary; it's a good idea to call first.

Reservations accepted.

Main course price range: Lunch, $8 and up; Dinner, $12 and up.

Major credit cards accepted.

RESTAURANTS

DINING OUT

Vivo

21 Field Point Road, 625.0004

Vivo is decorated in a very trendy fashion—waiters in black, dark wood paneled walls and lit by candles. The service, from the valet parking to the food, is friendly and competent. The food selection is limited, but good, with lots of pasta dishes. We like their system of providing specials on a written menu with prices. The dining area around and behind the bar is very, very noisy.

Hours: Lunch, every day from 11:30 am to 2:30 pm; Dinner, every day from 6 am - 10 pm; Late Night menu from 10 pm - midnight; Bar closes at 1 am, Monday - Thursday, 2 am on Friday. (The restaurant just opened at time of review, so hours may change radically).

Reservations accepted for six or more only , so small parties should plan to arrive before 8 pm. No seating until party is complete.

Main course price range: Dinner, $16 - $26; Lunch, $10 - $14.

Major credit cards accepted.

Wildfire

18 West Putnam Avenue, 422.2303

With a manager from Terra and a chef who has worked at Daniel and Bouley in New York city, this American contemporary restaurant could only be great—and it is. Although its selection of entrees is limited, we enjoyed them all. With its excellent food and service, it has the potential of becoming one of Greenwich's best.

Hours: Dinner, Monday - Thursday, 5:30 pm - 10 pm; Friday & Saturday, 5:30 pm - 11 pm.

RESTAURANTS

DINING OUT

Willett House

20 Willet Avenue, Port Chester, NY, 914.939.7500
www.TheWillettHouse.com
A steak house serving good steaks and seafood in a meticulously restored turn-of-the-century granary building. When in doubt, try their porterhouse steak or Maine lobster. Fun atmosphere and good steaks, but pricey.
Hours: Lunch, Weekdays, 11:45 am - 3 pm; Dinner, Monday - Thursday, 3 pm - 10 pm; Friday, 3 pm - 11 pm; Saturday, 4 pm - 11 pm; Sunday, 4 pm - 9 pm. Closed New Year's and Super Bowl Sunday.
Reservations accepted for any size party.
Main course price range: Lunch, $8.50 - $23.50; Dinner, $18.50 - $48.50. Everything is ala carte, so salads and side dishes are extra, making this a good place to go on an expense account.
Major credit cards accepted.

Winfields

Hyatt Regency, 1800 East Putnam Avenue, Old Greenwich, 637.1234
A very interesting restaurant setting in a beautifully converted factory building. Not a typical hotel nor typical hotel fare. The Hyatt demonstrates what good hotel dining can be. The indoor garden with water, flowers and very high ceilings gives the feeling of dining outdoors—even in the middle of the winter. The food is first-rate. We especially like their weekday buffet lunches, Sunday brunch and their Friday night fish buffet.
Hours: Open every day and all holidays. Breakfast, 7 am - 10:30 am; Sunday brunch, 11:30 am - 2:30 pm; Lunch every day except Sunday, 11:30 am - 2:30 pm; Dinner, 5 pm - 10:30 pm.
Reservations are accepted and are a good idea, especially for Sunday brunch or Friday evenings.
Main course price range: Breakfast, $3.30 - $13; Lunch, $10 - $16.50; Dinner, $18.50 - $15; Brunch price fixed at $35 per person, although on important holidays it may be higher.
All credit cards accepted.

DINING OUT

Xaviar's

506 Piermont Avenue, Piermont, NY, 914.359.7007

Rockland County's best. Just twenty-five minutes from Greenwich across the Tappan Zee Bridge. This small romantic, nouvelle American restaurant is one of the best in the area. Piermont has a number of very good art galleries—don't miss the Piermont Flywheel Gallery—so arrive in time to peruse them first.

Hours: Lunch, noon - 2 pm, Friday and Sunday; Dinner, Wednesday - Friday, 6pm - 9pm; Saturday seatings 6 pm and 9:30 pm; Sunday, 5 pm - 8 pm.

Do not even consider going without making reservations well in advance.

Main course price range: Lunch, $28 price fixed; Dinner, price fixed, $55 for 5 courses, $75 tasting menu with 7 courses, $115 tasting menu with wine; Sunday lunch, price fixed, $32.

No credit cards are accepted, only cash or check.

Directions: I-95 S to I-287 W, cross the Tappan Zee Bridge and take first exit for Rte 9W West, left when you see the signs to Piermont, follow the road downhill to the Hudson River and turn right.

Aux Délices
1075 Putnam Avenue, Riverside, 698.1066
See description under RESTAURANTS, DINING OUT.
They have a weekday home delivery service and will deliver your order even when you are not home, packaged to keep the food at the proper temperature. This service is reasonably priced for Riverside and Old Greenwich, expensive elsewhere.
Hours: Monday - Saturday, 9 am - 6:30 pm; Sunday, 9 am - 2 pm.

Butler's Tray
629.8878
Although many restaurants will deliver, the Butler's Tray makes ordering easy and offers food deliveries from a number of our favorite restaurants.
Hours: Weekdays, lunch, 11 am - 2 pm (take-out orders until 1 pm); Sunday - Wednesday, dinner, 5 pm - 9 pm; Thursday - Saturday, dinner, 5 pm - 9:30 pm.

Doorstep Express
Norwalk, CT, 327.6368, 203.831.8333
Doorstep is open every day for lunch and dinner. Dinner orders can be placed from 5 pm - 9 pm. Doorstep can provide delivery from fifty-seven restaurants from Greenwich to Fairfield. Many are different from those available from the Butler's Tray.

CHINESE
Hunan Gourmet
869.1940
Hours: Weekdays, 11:30 am - 10 pm (Friday to 11 pm); Weekends, noon - 10 pm (Saturday to 11 pm).

Panda Pavilion
869.1111
Hours: Weekdays, 11 am - 10 pm (Friday to 11 pm); Saturday, 11:30 am - 11 pm; Sunday, noon - 10 pm.

RESTAURANTS

ORDERING IN

PIZZA

Arcuris
178 Sound Beach Avenue, Old Greenwich, 637.1085
226 East Putnam Avenue, Cos Cob, 869.6999
Hours: Monday - Thursday, phone orders until 9:45 pm.
Friday and Saturday, until 10:15 pm.

Pizza Express
160 Hamilton Avenue, 622.1693
Hours: Monday - Saturday, 10 am - 10 pm; Sunday, 11 am - 10 pm.

Planet Pizza
28 Railroad Avenue, 622.0999
Hours: Monday - Thursday, phone orders until 10:45 pm.
Friday and Saturday until 11:45 pm.

For restaurant descriptions and directions see RESTAURANTS, DINING
OUT.

SCHOOLS

ADULT CONTINUING EDUCATION

There are a great variety of language schools and other continuing education resources in and around the town. The following are some of our favorites. For additional information on art, dance or music instruction, see the appropriate section under CULTURE or contact the Greenwich Arts Council (see CULTURE, ART). For cooking schools, see COOKING. For Sports Instruction, see FITNESS & SPORTS.

Alliance Française
299 Greenwich Avenue, 629.1340
An ideal way to learn or refresh your French.

Allegra Dance Studio
37 West Putnam Avenue, 629.9162
Adult classes in ballroom dancing. Open all year.

Connoisseurs of Dance
Mary and Richard Conseur
596 Stillwater Road, Stamford, CT 06902, 359.0076
If you suddenly need to look confident on the dance floor, give them a call. Discreet private lessons for ballroom or country and western dancing.

Fairfield University
Fairfield, CT, 203.254.4220, 4000, www.fairfield.edu
Fairfield is a major university with a 200-acre campus and great offerings in almost every conceivable subject. Definitely worth a call to get their catalog. They have over 1,000 continuing education students. Directons: I-95N to exit 22; L at 2nd stop sign; R onto Barlow; at light, L onto N. Benson.

SCHOOLS

ADULT CONTINUING EDUCATION

Garden Education Center

Montgomery Pinetum, Bible Street, Cos Cob, 869.9242
The Center's new horticulture buildings provide classrooms and workrooms for a variety of programs and lectures. Founded in 1957, the center is not only a strong educational facility, but also provides a good framework for new residents to make friends. They are closed during the summer.

Greenwich Adult and Continuing Education

625.7474, www.gps.lhric.org
This amazing program offers a wide range of courses taught at the High School, with interesting teachers. It is always priced right. Registration is in January and August/September. Be sure to call for a catalog; you are bound to see several courses you can't resist.

Greenwich Library

101 West Putnam Avenue, 622.7900   www.greenwich.lib.ct.us
The most utilized library in the State of Connecticut. It is also a popular spot for those who want to learn about the Internet. See the complete description of the Library system under GREENWICH, ENJOYING GREENWICH. With its $40 million building development, it can only get more impressive. You can access the library's catalog on the Internet.
Hours: Weekdays, 9 am - 9 pm (June - August until 5 pm);
Saturday, 9 am - 5 pm; Sunday, 1 pm - 5 pm (October through April).
Closed on major holidays.

Manhattanville College

Purchase, NY, 914.694.2200, 800.328.4553
www.mville.edu, asp@mville.edu
A local college with a very attractive campus.
Be sure to check out their course offerings.
Directions: King St. N to Anderson Hill Rd., L onto Rte 120 (Purchase St.).

SCHOOLS

ADULT CONTINUING EDUCATION

Norwalk Community Technical College

Norwalk, CT, 203.857.7080   www.nctc.commnet.edu

A surprisingly large selection (more than 300 courses) of adult education courses on a variety of subjects. Nice, modern facilities. They also offer courses at satellite locations in Stamford, Greenwich & Darien.
Directions: Exit 13 off I-95 N.

Silvermine School of Art

New Canaan, CT, 203.966.6668, 866.0411

Programs for adults and youngsters alike. For art instruction, it can't be beat.
Directions: Merritt Pkw N, exit 38; R onto Rte 123 N; straight until Rte 106 junction; R onto 106 N; at stop sign, R onto Silvermine Rd; one mile on R.

SUNY - Purchase

735 Anderson Hill Road, Purchase, NY, 914.251.6500
www.purchase.edu, conted@purchase.edu

A local college on a beautiful campus. Check out their adult education offerings.
Directions: King St. N to Anderson Hill Rd., R into SUNY.

UCONN Stamford
Connecticut Information Technology Institute

One University Place, Stamford, CT, 800.622.9905
www.citi.uconn.edu

Close by in Stamford is an exciting new facility where the University of Connecticut offers undergraduate programs plus professional and technical continuing education courses.
Directions: I-95 N to exit 7, L on Washington, L on Broad.

SCHOOLS

PRESCHOOL

For early childcare, see CHILDREN, CHILDCARE.

Preschool programs are usually very popular. You should contact the school well in advance to make sure you have reserved a place. Usually programs are half-day until the child is four years old.

Banksville Nursery School

12 Banksville Road, 661.9715

Children, ages 3 - 4. Creative movement classes. Morning and afternoon sessions available. Closed during the summer.

Bridges

Old Greenwich Civic Center, Harding Road, 637.0204

Children, ages 2 - 4. New theme each month. Morning and afternoon sessions.

Brunswick Preschool

Ridgeview Avenue, 625.5800

Boys, ages 4 - 6. Admission to pre-K usually ensures admission to the school. Co-ed summer camp for children ages 4 - 5.

Christ Church Nursery School

254 East Putnam Avenue, 869.5334

Children, ages 2 - 4. Blend of enrichment and free play. Kindergarten alternative, 9 am - 1:30 pm.

Christian Day School

139 East Putnam Avenue, 869.5395

Children, infants - 5 years. All-day, year-round childcare and preschool located in the Second Congregational Church. Stresses cooperation and integration of projects.

SCHOOLS

PRESCHOOL

Convent of the Sacred Heart Early Learning Program
1177 King Street, 531.6500
Girls, ages 3 - 4; Half-day program for 3-year-olds optional; 4-year-olds, full day. Grounded in the Catholic tradition, although 35% of students are not Catholic.

Family Center
40 Arch Street, 869.4848
Children, ages 3 - 4. An all-day, year-round childcare and preschool. 5:30 pm pick-up available. Learn-through-discovery approach.

Giant Steps Head Start at Wilbur Peck Court
629.6286 Ages: 3 - 4

Kids Corner Head Start at Armstrong Court
869.2730 Ages: 3 - 4

First Church Preschool
108 Sound Beach Avenue, Old Greenwich, 637.5430
Children, ages 3 - 4. Hours: 9 am - 11:30 am or 12:30 pm - 3 pm.
Some preference is given to parishioners. Summer camp program for ages 3 - 4.

First Presbyterian Church Preschool
37 Lafayette Place, 869.7782
Children, ages 2½ - 4. Morning and afternoon classes.
Also 2 x 2 program, 2 days per week. Enrichment programs change every 6 - 8 weeks. Art Scampers summer camp for ages 3 - 6.

Greenwich Academy
200 North Maple Avenue, 625.8990
Girls, ages 4 - 5. Morning and afternoon sessions.
Admission to pre-K usually ensures admission to the school.

Greenwich Catholic School
471 North Street, 869.4000
Children, ages 4 - pre-K. Pre-K is a structured program with academics for 4-year-olds. Little Angels is a play group for younger children. Admission to these programs does not ensure admission to the school.

SCHOOLS

PRESCHOOL

Greenwich Country Day
Old Church Road, 622.8529
Starting at age 3. Admission to pre-K usually ensures admission to the school. Summer camp for children ages 4 - 5.

Greenwich Dundee School
55 Florence Road, Riverside, 637.3800
A public school with an integrated program for typically developing children and those with special needs.

Greenwich Kokusai Gakuen
Worldwide Children's Corner
521 East Putnam Avenue, 629.5567, 618.0790
Children, ages 2½ - 5 years. Full-day program.

Greenwich Public Preschool
625.7472
Greenwich runs a preschool for ages 3 - 4 at the Dundee School on Florence Road. Preschool Evaluation Clinic and referral services for children from infancy to age 3. Call 625.7496.

Reform Synagogue Hilltop Preschool
257 Stanwich Road, 629.0018
Children, ages 1 - 4. Jewish traditions stressed. Special program for parents with one and two-year-olds, to introduce them to their first school experience.
Fun-for-Ones for age 1, Mommy-and-Me for age 2.
Half-day preschool classes for ages 2 - 4.

North Greenwich Nursery School
606 Riversville Road, 869.7945
Children, ages 3 - 4. Half-day program with optional extended-day available. Computers integrated into program. US Gymnastic Academy is at the same location and can provide afternoon classes.

Putnam Indian Field School
101 Indian Field Road, 869.0982, 661.4629
Children, ages 2½ - 5. Summer camp program for ages 3 - 5.

SCHOOLS

PRESCHOOL

Round Hill Nursery School
466 Round Hill Road, 869.4910
Children, ages 2 - 4. fifty years of giving children a love of going to school.
Computer training and special teachers for music and art.

St. Catherine's
6 Riverside Avenue, Riverside, 637.9549
Children, ages 2 - 4. Age 2, 1 - 3 pm; ages 3 - 4, 9 am - 12:30 pm.

St. Agnes Preschool
247 Stanwich Road, 869.8388
Children, ages 2 yrs 9 mos - 5. Flexible 3, 4 or 5-day a week programs.
Half-day programs with extended-day options. Summer camp program.

St. Paul's Christian Nursery School
286 Delavan Avenue, 531.5905
Children, ages 3 - 4; 9 am - 11:30 am. Religious values stressed.

St. Paul's Day School
200 Riverside Avenue, Riverside, 637.3503
Children, ages 2 - 5. Nonsectarian, with enrichment program for older children. Summer camp program for ages 3 - 6.

St. Savior's Nursery School
350 Sound Beach Avenue, Old Greenwich, 698.1303
Children, ages 2 yrs 5 mos - 5. Nondenominational.
Summer camp program for ages 3 - 5.

Selma Maisel Nursery School
Temple Sholom, 300 East Putnam Avenue, 622.8121
Children, ages 2 - 5. "Mommy & Me" program for 2 and under.
Programs with Judaic content.

Tiny Tots
97 Riverside Avenue, Riverside, 637.1398
Children, ages 2 - 5. Residential setting. One of the oldest nursery schools in town. Summer camp program for ages 2 - 6.

SCHOOLS

PRESCHOOL

Whitby School
969 Lake Avenue, 869.8464
Children, ages 1 - 5 years. This is the oldest American Montessori school. Summer camp program for ages 2 - 6.

YMCA Rainbow Connection Preschool
40 Gold Street, Byram, 869.3381
Children, ages 2 years 9 months. - 5., 8:30 am - 1:15 pm. Follows public school calendar. Offers enrichment curriculum.

YWCA 1-2-3 Grow/Beginnings
259 East Putnam Avenue, 869.6501 x 221
Children, ages 15 months - 3 years; toddlers, 9 am - 11:30 am; age 2, 9 am - 11:30 am or noon - 2:30 pm.

YWCA Tinker Tots
259 East Putnam Avenue, 869.6501 x 241
Children, ages 2 - 4. Half-day program for age 2; ages 3 - 4, full-day, 7:30 am - 6 pm. Enrichment programs. Summer camp.

SCHOOLS

PRIVATE/PAROCHIAL

Greenwich has an abundance of excellent private schools. Typical annual tuition is $9,000 to $15,000, depending upon the grade. Private schools typically have more applicants than they have spaces. It is prudent to apply early. Private schools often have one or more open houses for parents of prospective attendees. Many offer extended-day programs or early drop-off for their preschoolers.

Brunswick School
100 Maher Avenue, 625.5800
Boys, pre-K (age 4) through 12th grade.

Convent of the Sacred Heart
1177 King Street, 531.6500
Girls, pre-K (age 4) through 12th grade.

Eagle Hill
45 Glenville Road, 622.9240
Co-ed, ages 6 - 16. A school for bright children with learning disabilities. Day and 5-day boarding. Student faculty ratio is 4:1.

Greenwich Academy
200 North Maple Avenue, 625.8900
Girls, pre-K (age 4) through 12th grade.

Greenwich Country Day
Old Church Road, 622-8510
Co-ed, pre-K (age 3) through 9th grade.

Greenwich Catholic School
471 North Street, 869.4000
Co-ed, pre-K (age 4) through 8th grade.

Greenwich Japanese School
270 Lake Avenue, 629.9039
Co-ed, grades 1 - 9.

SCHOOLS

PRIVATE/PAROCHIAL

Stanwich School

257 Stanwich Road, 869.4515

Founded by Patricia Young, the former head of the lower school at Greenwich Academy, our newest school has opened its cheerful classrooms. Plans for additional grades are in place. Co-ed, K to 2.

Whitby

969 Lake Avenue, 869.8464

Co-ed, grades K - 8.

SCHOOLS

PUBLIC SCHOOLS

www.greenwich.k12.ct.us

Greenwich public schools rank among the best in the nation and are consistently ranked the best in Fairfield County. In addition to their other fine programs, Greenwich schools have outstanding ESL (English as a Second Language) programs for all grades K - 12.

The elementary schools serve students in grades K - 5, the middle schools serve students in grades 6 - 8 and the high school serves students grades 9 - 12.

Schools open for students around Labor Day and close in the middle of June.

Board of Education

290 Greenwich Avenue

Call 625.7400 for school district information.

Call 625.7447/6 for brochures and pamphlets.

Before and After-School Child Care Programs

Ten of the elementary schools offer before and after-school programs for enrolled students. These programs are paid for by the parents. These programs are on-site at the elementary schools. Children can usually be dropped off at 7:30 am and must be picked up by 6 pm. There is often a waiting list - apply early. Some of the schools also offer enrichment programs where children can take computer or other classes. Call your elementary school to see what programs they sponsor. For other programs, see CHILDREN, CHILDCARE or SCHOOLS, PRESCHOOL.

Kindergarten

To register for kindergarten, your child must have reached the age of five on or before January 1 of his or her kindergarten year. Parents must provide a birth certificate and proof of residence. Your child must also have a complete physical examination and a record of immunizations.

SCHOOLS

PUBLIC SCHOOLS

School Closings

If schools are closed for snow, or if opening is delayed, listen to Greenwich Radio WGCH (1490) and WSTC (1400). Announcements begin at 6:30 am.

School Bus Information

625.7449

Call for information on school bus pick-up times and locations. If your child is young and other children are not nearby, you can often get the school bus to stop in front of or near your home. Bus service is provided for students who live beyond:

Grades K - 5, one mile from the school;
Grades 6 - 8, one and a half miles from school;
Grades 9 - 12, two miles from school.

Public School Web Site:

www.greenwich.k12.ct.us

SCHOOLS

PUBLIC ELEMENTARY

Cos Cob Elementary School
300 East Putnam Avenue, Cos Cob, 869.4670
Dominic Butera, Principal (490 students, 8:45-3:15)

Glenville Elementary School
33 Riversville Road, 531.9287
Ellen Flanagan, Principal (452 students, 8:30-3:00)

Hamilton Avenue Elementary School
184 Hamilton Avenue, 869.1685
Carol Sarabun, Principal (304 students, 8:15-2:45)

Julian Curtiss Elementary School
180 East Elm Street, 869.1896
Nancy Carbone, Principal (363 students, 8:15-2:45)

New Lebanon Elementary School
25 Mead Avenue, Byram, 531.9139
Connee Sepe, Principal (257 students, 8:15-2:45)

North Mianus Elementary School
309 Palmer Hill Road, Riverside, 637.9730
Frank Arnone, Principal (454 students, 8:45-3:15)

North Street Elementary School
381 North Street, 869.6756
Elisabeth Burfeind, Principal (526 students, 8:45-3:15)

Old Greenwich Elementary School
285 Sound Beach Avenue, Old Greenwich, 637.0150
Marjorie Sherman, Principal (564 students, 8:45-3:15)

Parkway Elementary School
141 Lower Cross Road, 869.7466
Sandra Mond, Principal (427 students, 8:45-3:15)

Riverside Elementary School
90 Hendrie Avenue, Riverside, 637.1440
Elizabeth Ehik, Principal (520 students, 8:45-3:15)

SCHOOLS

PUBLIC HIGH SCHOOL

College Selection Guidance

Mary Leinbach, 531.9434

Mary has helped many public and private Greenwich students select the right college and prepare for college interviews. Her $200 fee goes to the First Congregational Church's College and University Loan Fund and is tax-deductible.

Dundee School

55 Florence Road, Riverside, 637.3800

A public school with an integrated program for typically developing children and those with special needs.

Greenwich High School

10 Hillside Road, 625.8000

Elaine Bessette, Headmistress (1991 students, 7:30-2:15)

PUBLIC MIDDLE SCHOOLS

Central Middle School

9 Indian Rock Lane, 661.8500

James Bulger, Principal (526 students, 7:45-2:35)

Eastern Middle School

51 Hendrie Avenue, Riverside, 637.1744

Benjamin Davenport, Principal (554 students, 7:45-2:35)

Western Middle School

Western Junior Highway, 531.5700

Donald Strange, Principal (516 students, 7:45-2:35)

SENIORS

INTRODUCTION

Seniors in Greenwich typically stay actively involved in the community, often serving on town boards, the RTM, and philanthropic organizations. Many of our volunteer organizations are run by the retired presidents and leaders of major companies. This wealth of talent of our senior leaders is a significant reason Greenwich is America's number one town. Most senior citizens continue living in their own homes by utilizing the many services the town has available.

CLUBS AND ORGANIZATIONS

Glenville Senior Citizens
110 Pilgrim Drive, Byram
Contact: Celine Crothers, 531.6784

Greenwich Old Timers Athletic Association
PO Box 558, Greenwich 06836
Nino Sechi, President - 661.7134
Contact: Jeffrey D. Harris, Secretary - (H)869.8762

Greenwich Seniors Club
Sheila Shea Russo, President - (W)622.1500, (H)531.4345
Contact: Wilma Kasprak, Membership - 531.7753

Retired Men's Association
YMCA
50 East Putnam Avenue
Gene Waggaman, President - 637.9924
Contact: Dom DiMaio, Program Chairman - 661.3833

SENIORS

COMPUTERS & THE INTERNET

Computer Training

The internet and e-mail are sparking a communications revolution among seniors who find it the easiest way to stay connected with their family and interests. In addition to the extensive list of computer courses given by Greenwich Continuing Education, and other resources described in SCHOOLS, ADULT CONTINUING EDUCATION, there are several senior-specific computer programs.

DeCaro Associates

3 Sweet Briar Lane, Cos Cob, 921.4757
Noted Greenwich web site designers, responsible for many of Greenwich's best web sites, help seniors with computer problems at discounted prices.

Norwalk Community-Technical College

Norwalk, CT, 857.7160
This community college allows seniors to audit any course free of charge. For more details on the college see the entry in SCHOOLS, ADULT CONTINUING EDUCATION.

Senior Connections

622.3992
This very popular program—offered at both Brunswick School and Greenwich Academy—is open to Greenwich residents ages 62 and up with little or no familiarity with computers. It features eight 3-hour sessions. Computer coaches are students at the schools.

SeniorNet

622.3990/3992
This program, underwritten by telephone and computer companies, has over 140 locations nationwide. It offers courses at the Greenwich and Stamford Senior Centers.

SENIORS

HOUSING

According to the town's 1998 Plan of Conservation and Development, the Housing Authority has 291 independent living units for seniors with low income and who are over 62. The town also owns Nathaniel Witherell SNF (skilled nursing facility), with 200-beds on Parsonage Road which offers many outstanding programs for its residents. Admission preference is given to Greenwich residents, but because the facility is almost always 100% occupied, it is wise to call 869.4130 for an application well in advance of expected need.

(The) Mews
½ Bolling Place, 869.9448
Assisted living for seniors 55 and over. The Mews is a managed-care residential community in the heart of downtown Greenwich, very close to the town's Senior Center. Rooms and suites are available at affordable rates.

SENIORS

INFORMATION & REFERRAL

For information on medical resources, see the HEALTH section.

Commission on Aging

622.3992

Located in the Senior Center, the Commission on Aging provides information and written materials on a variety of issues of interest to seniors. Commission staff provide information and referral services and locate resources.

Hours: Weekdays, 9 am - 4 pm.

Community Answers

622.7979

This volunteer group will guide you to the right number for your need. See their more complete description under INFORMATION, SOURCES.

Greenwich Hospital

863.4444

Provides health education and disease prevention services.

Infoline

324.1010

A 24-hour confidential information, referral, advocacy and crisis help line. Caseworkers have information about hundreds of services, including health, transportation, housing, safety, employment, support services, counseling, financial/legal services and activities.

Municipal Agent for the Aged

622.3805

Assists seniors in accessing programs, benefits and services.

SENIORS

SERVICES & ACTIVITIES

Call-A-Ride
37 Lafayette Place, 661.6633
Non-profit organization. Residents 60 years or older can call for a ride to anywhere in Greenwich for any purpose. Please give them 24 to 48-hours notice.

Friendly Connections
20 Bridge Street, 661.8841
Family Centers, Inc. provides two Friendly Connections programs:
Telephone Groups
This program brings seniors - or those who have difficulty getting out - together on the telephone for a variety of recreational, support and discussion groups. All groups are conducted over the phone and are facilitated by a moderator. There are more than 50 groups scheduled each month. They are a great way to meet new friends and stay connected.
Telephone Reassurance
Professionally-trained volunteers make daily calls to elderly, homebound or isolated individuals. Telephone Reassurance provides an opportunity to have a friendly chat, stay in-touch and feel safer at home. They can also provide medication reminders and a "safety check," when requested. Calls are made every day from 9 am - 9 pm.

Friendly Visitors
622.6455
This program, run by the Town Department of Social Services, provides trained volunteers to visit seniors.

Jewish Family Services of Greenwich
One Holly Hill Lane, 622.1881
A free service for Greenwich residents over 60 providing grocery shopping for the homebound; also, carpentry, minor plumbing and snow shoveling.

Meals-on-Wheels
869.1312
Non-profit organization prepares and delivers to homes of anyone recovering from illness or an accident, regardless of age.
$7 per day for two meals, one hot and one cold.

SENIORS

SERVICES & ACTIVITIES

Senior Center
299 Greenwich Avenue, 622.3990
Stop in to see the monthly bulletin board of activities. There are a lot of activities going on! Recent listings included: "Qigong" Chinese exercises, chess and bridge instruction, a luncheon cruise, trips to the opera, ice cream socials, painting, shopping center trips and a brown bag auction. Free classes (in conjunction with Greenwich Continuing Education) were being held in line dancing, writing short stories, writing Your memoirs and sewing.
Hours: Weekdays, 9 am - 4 pm.

Supermarketing for Seniors
One Holly Hill Lane, 622.1881
One of the wonderful Jewish Family Service programs to help homebound older residents. They will arrange grocery shopping on a weekly basis, and this kind service is free.

USE - Senior Center Job Placement Service
Job Placement Service, 629.8031
Utilize Senior Energy, a volunteer activity run by Grace Knapp, is open weekdays, 9:30 am - 12:30 pm. It is a good resource for everything from painters to babysitters.

Weekend Lunch Bunch
Greenwich Hospital, 863.3690
Anyone age 55 or older can enjoy a $4 meal in the cafeteria.
Hours: Saturday & Sunday, noon - 2 pm.

YMCA Exercise Programs
50 East Putnam Avenue, 869.1630
The Y offers a number of programs tailored to the needs of seniors, including walking, stretching, resistence training and swimming.

SHOPPING

INTRODUCTION

Greenwich has a wonderful supply of large and small shops, many of which are family businesses with a high level of personal service. Stroll along the major shopping streets and you will find a wealth of fine stores. What follows is a selection of stores we wouldn't want you to miss:

For Repairs, see HOMES, WHERE TO GET THINGS REPAIRED.

For Children's Clothes, see CHILDREN, SHOPS.

For appliances, keys & hardware see HOME, SUPPLIES & STORES.

INDEX

SHOPPING

INDEX

SHOPPING

ANTIQUE & CONSIGNMENT SHOPS

Antique and consignment shops thrive in and around Greenwich. Although many antique shops take consignments, stores that are primarily consignment are often less expensive and they sometimes have outstanding selections. We have included the places we like best, but if you really want to get into the antique scene in a big way you might want to get one or both of the following:

Antiques and the Arts Weekly, Bee Publishing, Newtown, CT, 203.426.8036,
www.thebee.com, info@thebee.com.
A thick newspaper with a treasure trove of articles, advertisements and information on shows, auctions and events in the world of paintings and antiques. Good coverage not only of Connecticut, but of the tri-state area.

Sloan's Green Guide to Antiquing in New England, published by Antique Source, Inc, Belmont, Vermont, 888.875.5999, www.antiquesource.com.
A large book covering over 2,000 antique shops throughout New England & Eastern NY State. It includes a map which highlights the antique shops in Greenwich.

Alexander Services
Call Shawn Alexander at 888.656.6838, 203.324.4012
They are the mover of choice for many antique shops.

Consign It
115 Mason Street, 869.9836
Not a lot of display room, as a result they are often light on furniture. During the summer months, they are able to display a wider variety by using an outdoor tent. A good source for jewelry, silver and china. Fairly priced.
Hours: Monday - Saturday, 10 am - 5 pm. Closed Sunday.

SHOPPING

ANTIQUE & CONSIGNMENT SHOPS

Estate Treasures
1162 East Putnam Avenue, 637.4200
They have a wide selection of jewelry and china and are a good source for silver services and serving pieces. A large number of tables and desks, although some are high quality reproductions (always marked as reproductions).
Hours: Monday - Saturday, 10 am - 5:30 pm; Sunday, noon - 5:30 pm.

Federalist
365 Greenwich Avenue, 625.4727
Not antiques, but only experts would know it. The shop is filled with fine reproductions of 18th century furniture and accessories.
Hours: Monday - Saturday, 10 am - 6 pm; Sunday, noon - 5 pm.

Guild Antiques
384 Greenwich Avenue, 869.0828
Fine quality period American and English furniture.
Hours: Monday - Saturday, 10 am - 5 pm.

Manderly Antiques
134 East Putnam Avenue, 861.1900
Enter the shop from Milbank Avenue, "Mill Post Plaza," where there is easy parking. This shop, with its quality collection of antiques, many with animal motifs, will make you smile—and want to buy.
Hours: Monday - Saturday, 10 am - 5 pm.

Ox Cart
1152 East Putnam Avenue, 637.1620
Vintage and antique furniture and home accessories from India.
Very interesting chests and architectural pieces.
Hours: Monday - Saturday, 10:30 am - 5 pm; Sunday, noon - 5 pm.
Summer hours: Wednesday - Saturday, 10:30 am - 5 pm. Call before you go.

SHOPPING

ANTIQUE & CONSIGNMENT SHOPS

Rose d'or
1076 Post Road, Darien, CT, 203.655.4668
A small, but good collection of consigned items.
Hours: Monday - Saturday, 10 am - 5 pm. Closed Sunday.
Directions: I-95 N to exit 11, L on US 1.

Rue Faubourg St. Honoré
44 West Putnam Avenue, 869.7139
For over 30 years this small shop has supplied antique lighting fixtures and fireplace accessories to Greenwich mansions and vintage homes.
Hours: Monday - Saturday, 9 am - 5 pm. Closed Sunday.

Stamford Antique Mall
Tucked away in converted manufacturing buildings are three collections of antique dealers with enough collectibles and fine antiques to suit just about anyone. Don't go unless you are prepared to buy. With antiques from over 350 dealers, it's hard to imagine anyone not finding something they want. In fact, just around the corner, another 25,000 square feet of space at 21 Harborview Drive has been rented to create another antique center. A great outing for the antique enthusiast.
Hours: Monday - Saturday, 10:30 am - 5:30 pm; Sunday, noon - 5 pm.
Directions: I-95 N to Exit 8, R on Canal (at second light), continue straight or L on Jefferson.
Antique and Artisan Center, 69 Jefferson Street, 327.6022
Look in the Modernism Room and see their collection of 20th Century "antiques-in-the-making."
Hiden Galleries, 481 Canal Street, 323.9090
Stamford Antiques Center, 735 Canal Street, 888.329.3546
Open every day 10:30 am - 5:30 pm

Surry Collectibles
563 Steamboat Road, 869.4193
Next to Manero's Restaurant, they specialize in nostalgia. A good place to find an old Victrola or radio.
Hours: Closed Wednesday; Monday - Saturday, 11 am - 5 pm; Sunday, by appointment.

SHOPPING

ANTIQUE & CONSIGNMENT SHOPS

United House Wrecking
535 Hope Street, Stamford, CT, 348.5371
www.United-Antiques.com
An unusual source for the unusual. Thirty-thousand square feet of inventory with everything from collectibles to antiques to architectural items, to junk. Don't miss it.
Hours: Monday - Saturday, 9:30 am - 5:30 pm; Sunday, noon - 5 pm.
Directions: I-95 N to exit 9, R on Courtland (Rte 106), L on Glenbrook, R on Hope.

Vallin Galleries
516 Danbury Road (Route 7), Wilton, CT, 203.762.7441
Located far from the source of these antiques, is a quaint saltbox filled with a collection of Asian art, some rare, all beautifully displayed.
Hours: Wednesday - Saturday, 10:30 am - 5 pm; Sunday, 1 pm - 5 pm.
Directions: Merritt Pkw. N to exit 39 (Norwalk) or I-95 N to exit 15, Rte 7 N.

Village Clock Shop
1074 Post Road, Darien, CT, 203.655.2100
If you love the gentle sound of a clock ticking, this shop has lovely antiques. They will also repair clocks worthy of their service.
Hours: Tuesday - Saturday, 10 am - 5 pm.
Directions: I-95 to exit 11, L on US 1.

SHOPPING

BOOKS

Barnes & Noble

360 Connecticut Avenue (Grade A Plaza), Norwalk, CT, 203.866.2213

www.bn.com

This is the closest of their super-stores and like all of their stores, stocked with a multitude of volumes on all subjects.

Hours: Monday - Saturday, 9 am - 11 pm; Sunday, 9 am - 9 pm.

Directions: I-95 N to exit 13, R on US 1.

Book Exchange

At the Greenwich Recycling Center, Holly Hill Lane, 622.0550

This is fun you cannot miss. Residents drop off unwanted books. A volunteer "librarian" organizes the books by topic and author. Free books are available on all subjects. Just follow the rules: keep the shelves neat, ten books per family, enjoy your reading!

Donation hours: Monday, Friday & Saturday, 7 am - noon.

Exchange open: Monday through Friday, 7:30 am - 3 pm.

Borders Books

1041 High Ridge Road, Stamford, CT, 968.9700

www.borders.com

When you need to visit a mega-bookstore, this store is nearby. There is a nice coffee shop with good treats.

Hours: Monday - Saturday, 9 am - 11 pm; Sunday, 9 am - 9 pm.

Directions: Merritt Pkw N to exit 35, R on High Ridge.

Diane's Books of Greenwich

8A Grigg Street, 869.1515

A family book store with a faithful following. You will find a wealth of children's books, a good travel book section and, best of all, a knowledgeable, resourceful sales staff.

Hours: Weekdays, 9:30 am - 5 pm; Saturday, 9 am - 4 pm.

July and August, 9:30 am - 5pm.

SHOPPING

BOOKS

Just Books
19 East Putnam Avenue, 869.5023
http://justbooks.org
Just Books is a haven for the sophisticated reader or someone looking for personal service. You can get a book delivered to a friend in Greenwich Hospital. Ask to be on their mailing list. The book reviews are interesting and keep you up-to-date with the literary world. They host many events to meet important authors. Be sure to stop in this charming bookstore.
Hours: Weekdays, 9 am - 5:30 pm; Saturday, 9 am - 5 pm.

Parkers
43 Purchase Street, Rye, NY, 914.921.6400
The ultimate travel store run by Catherine Parker, a helpful and knowledgeable traveler. If you are planning a trip or searching for a gift for a traveler, this store is worth a trip—books on every conceivable destination, travel clocks, travel games, voltage converters, and an interesting selection of picnic and hand-carry luggage.
Hours: Monday - Saturday, 9 am - 6 pm; Sunday, 11 am - 5 pm.
Directions: US 1 South (Boston Post Road West) through Port Chester. Just past the intersections with I-287 & I-95, R on Purdy, L on Purchase.

Waldenbooks
173 Greenwich Avenue, 869.6342
Greenwich's largest book store, very conveniently located.
Hours: Monday - Saturday, 9 am - 6 pm (Thursday - 8 pm); Sunday, 11 am - 5 pm.

Smith College Book Sale
Waveny House, South Avenue, New Canaan, CT
This annual event benefits the Smith College Scholarship Fund and has more than 80,000 well-priced, quality used books including cookbooks, art histories and bound sets to decorate your home. Just a visit to Waveny House is worth the trip. Dealers descend early on the first morning grabbing books which they later resell at a substantial profit. It's fun to arrive early with them, but be prepared for pushy, over-zealous types. On the last day books are free. Don't forget to bring a big book bag.
Look for it around the first week in April.
Directions: Merritt Parkway N to exit 37, L on South.

SHOPPING

CLOTHING & SHOES

On Greenwich Avenue you will find most of the major chain stores including: The Gap, The Limited, Banana Republic, Talbots, Saks, Nine West, and Ann Taylor. However, Greenwich has a wealth of smaller shops many of which are family owned and have been in business for several generations. We encourage you to support these locally owned businesses. These smaller stores, with their blend of ambiance and personal service, are part of what makes Greenwich such a special place to shop.

For Children's clothing see: CHILDREN, SHOPS
For Consignment clothing see: SHOPPING, THRIFT SHOPS
and SHOPPING, CLOTHING CONSIGNMENT SHOPS
For outlets and Malls see: SHOPPING, MALLS & OUTLETS

Chancy D'Elia
244 Greenwich Avenue, 869.0654
One of the oldest stores in Greenwich. For years this friendly staff has been helping local residents find the right moderately-priced apparel.
Hours: Monday - Saturday, 9 am - 5:30 pm.

Dorothy Mann
36 East Putnam Avenue, 622.8588
Sophisticated business, evening and casual clothing. An exceptionally friendly staff to go with their exceptionally good taste.
Hours: Monday - Saturday, 10 am - 6 pm.

Grossmans Shoe Store
88 Greenwich Avenue 869.2123
Their good selection of top of the line shoes has made them a favorite of several generations in Greenwich. Twice a year they have a half-price sale. It is a big draw, so arrive early.
Hours: Monday - Saturday, 9:30 am - 5:30 pm; Sunday, noon - 5 pm.

SHOPPING

CLOTHING & SHOES

Otto's

68 Water Street, South Norwalk, CT, 203.857.4717

Otto Williams was for 24 years the manager of Decker's (a well liked men's discount clothing store, now closed). Happily he is continuing the tradition of great savings on fine men's clothing. This is the place to buy cashmere and wool sweaters.

Hours: Tuesday - Saturday, 10:30 am - 5 pm; Sunday, noon - 5 pm. In the summer and during holidays, hours are usually extended.

Directions: I-95 N to exit 14, R on West, bear left at fork onto North Main, cross intersection with Washington street, L on Haviland.

Parfumerie Douglas

96 Greenwich Avenue, 625.9392

Large selection of brand-name cosmetics, skin-care products and perfumes. The courteous staff is quite willing to help you sample new products or pick out a gift.

Hours: Monday - Saturday, 9 am - 6 pm; Sunday, noon - 5 pm.

Razooks

45 East Putnam Avenue, 661.6603

A friendly, family-owned shop with elegant, traditional designer fashions. They have custom wedding gowns and wonderful choices for the bride's mother.

Hours: Monday - Saturday, 9:30 am - 5:30 pm.

Richards of Greenwich

350 Greenwich Avenue, 622.0551

A Greenwich classic carrying fine quality men's clothing. They intend to add women's clothing when they move across the street.

Hours: Monday - Saturday, 8:30 am - 6 pm.

Saturnia

39 Lewis Street, 625.0390

A favorite of the younger set. A good place to find a cute dress, leather pants or the perfect sweater.

Hours: Monday - Saturday, 9:30 am - 6 pm; Sunday, noon - 4 pm.

SHOPPING

CLOTHING & SHOES

Shoes'n More
251 Greenwich Avenue, 629.2323
Besides the selection of shoes for women and children, they have a large selection of Western boots. They have clothing for women and children.
Hours: Weekdays, 10 am - 8 pm; Saturday, 10 am - 7 pm; Sunday, noon - 7 pm.

Sophia's Great Dames
1 Liberty Way, 869.5990
Wonderful shop for vintage clothing and costume rentals. Fun to visit.
Hours: Monday - Saturday, 10 am - 5:30 pm; open later during holidays.

Sound Beach Sportswear
239 Sound Beach Avenue, Old Greenwich, 637.5557
The sportswear is an interesting mix of casual dressiness. The owners know what Greenwich residents like to wear. They also carry adorable infant and children's wear. Expect a friendly reception in this family-owned business.
Hours: Weekdays, 10 am - 6 pm; Saturday, 10 am - 5 pm.

Tetonia
28 Arcadia Road, Old Greenwich, 698.1240.
Unique clothing, jewelry and gifts in the heart of Old Greenwich.
Hours: Monday - Saturday, 10 am - 5 pm.

Wendy's Closet
375 Greenwich Avenue, 622.7130
A nice mix of trendy casual and business outfits.
Hours: Monday - Saturday, 10 am - 6 pm; Sunday, 1 am - 5 pm.

See also: SHOPPING, THRIFT SHOPS

CLOTHING CONSIGNMENT SHOPS

Act II Consignment Shop

48 Maple Avenue, 869.6359

On the grounds of the Second Congregational Church. Clothing and objects are high quality and very nicely displayed. If you are looking for a bargain, this is not to be missed.

Shop Hours: Tuesday, 1 pm - 5 pm; Wednesday, Thursday and Friday, 10 am - 1:30 pm.

Consignment Hours: Tuesday, 1 am - 4 pm; Thursday, 10 am - 1 pm.

Roundabout

48 West Putnam Avenue, 552.0787

Clothes must be from a well-known designer, in perfect condition, and less than two years old to be consigned. The store also buys show and end-of-season stock from designers.

Hours: Monday - Saturday, 10 am - 5 pm.

SHOPPING

COMPUTERS

CompUSA

US 1, Grade A Plaza, Norwalk, CT, 203.852.7005
20 Tarrytown Road, White Plains, NY, 914.761.5111
For shoppers who know just what they want.
Hours: Monday - Saturday, 10 am - 9 pm; Sunday, noon - 6 pm.
Directions to White Plains: I-95 S to I-287 W, I-287 exit 5, L over hwy, L on Tarrytown (100S/119E).
Directions to Norwalk: I-95 N to exit 13, R on US 1.

Computer Super Center

103 Mason Street, 661.1700
For friendly help and expert advice try the Super Center.
Hours: Monday - Saturday, 10 am - 9 pm; Sunday, noon - 6 pm.

DeCaro Associates

3 Sweet Briar Lane, Cos Cob, 921.4757
Noted Greenwich web site designer.

SHOPPING

ELECTRONICS

Al Franklin's Musical World

163 Greenwich Avenue, 869.1900

www.AlFranklins.com

Although there is a Wiz in Norwalk and a number of Radio Shacks in the area, we keep buying at this local Greenwich store. The sales people are knowledgeable and reliable and the store stands behind the products it sells.

Hours: Monday - Saturday, 9:30 am - 6 pm; Sunday, noon - 5 pm.

Fairfield Audio & Video

229 Greenwich Avenue, 629.8430

A handy place on the Avenue to find small electronic items at good prices.

Hours: Monday - Friday, 9:30 am - 6 pm, Saturday, 9:30 am - 5:30 pm.

Performance Imaging

115 East Putnam Avenue, 862.9600

www.hdtvsystems.com

Wow. If your are considering a home theater, this is a must-see place. Many people can show you pictures of how a theater might look, but here you can sit down in a variety of theaters just as if they were already installed in your home.

Hours: Weekdays, 10 am - 6 pm; Saturday, 10 am - 5 pm; after hours, by appointment.

Radio Shack

1265 East Putnam Avenue (Riverside Shopping Center), 637.5608

www.RadioShack.com

Although there are several locations in Greenwich and Port Chester, we like this one best. It's easy to park and up-to-date. If you need a telephone or telephone supplies, a strange battery, or you are not sure where to find some piece of electronic equipment, they will probably have it here.

Hours: Weekdays, 9 am - 9 pm; Saturday, 9 am - 7 pm;
Sunday, 11 am - 5 pm.

SHOPPING

GIFT SHOPS

Gift Shop - at Bruce Museum

1 Museum Drive, 869.0376   www.brucemuseum.com

Cynthia Richardson has created an attractive, high-quality store filled with unique gifts from around the world. She coordinates the merchandise in the store to complement the Museum's current exhibits. The majority of the items in the store are selected for their educational value. The selection of books is excellent. Be sure to attend their holiday gift bazaar.

Hours: Tuesday - Saturday, 10 am - 5 pm; Sunday, 1 am - 4:30 pm. Closed Mondays.

Gift Shop - at Christ Church

254 East Putnam Avenue, 869.9030

This is the "in" place to go when you need a special gift with meaning. Marijane Marks and her helpful staff have a fine selection of books, gifts, jewelry and greeting cards. During holidays, gifts cascade out of the shop, making the store a joy to visit.

Hours: Monday, Saturday & Sunday 10 am - 1 pm;
Tuesday - Friday, 10 am - 5 pm; Summer, the hours may vary.
Closed on Saturdays in July and August.

Gift Shop - at Greenwich Hospital

5 Perryridge Road, 869.3371   www.greenhosp.chime.org

If you need a present for a patient, they have a wide array of gifts, including pretty planters and beautiful nightgowns. The items selected by the volunteer staff have made this shop a place to go whether or not you are visiting in the hospital. Selections are well-priced and tax free. All profits go the hospital.

Hours: Weekdays, 9:30 am - 8 pm; Saturday, 11 am - 6 pm;
Sunday, noon - 6 pm.

Goldenberry

215 East Putnam Avenue (Mill Pond Shopping Center), 863.9522
www.goldenberry.com

Traditional teas, never out of fashion, are more popular than ever in Greenwich. This English importer can supply all of your tea party needs. Put together a gift basket from their selection of English teas, marmalades and biscuits.

Hours: Weekdays, 10 am - 5:30 pm; Saturday, 10 am - 5 pm.

SHOPPING

GIFT SHOPS

Hoagland's of Greenwich
175 Greenwich Avenue, 869.2127
A first-class gift shop. Many famous, and not-so-famous, Greenwich brides and grooms have registered here.
Hours: Monday - Saturday, 9 am - 5:30 pm.

Inspirations
73 Greenwich Avenue, 629.8473
Located upstairs near the top of the Avenue. Gloria Aslanian has gifts and books that appeal to the Catholic, Jewish and Protestant faiths. If you are looking for a religious CD or children's game, she has a wide selection.
Hours: Tuesday - Saturday, 10:30 am - 5 pm; summer hours may vary.

Quelques Choses
259 Sound Beach Avenue, Old Greenwich, 637.5655
Tiny shop brimming with unique gifts.
Hours: Monday - Saturday, 10 am - 5 pm.

Michelangelo of Greenwich
353 Greenwich Avenue, 661.8540, 800.677.4490
Wide selection of clocks, crystal, pewter, brass and silver which can be engraved for personal or corporate gifts. They have produced awards for the Super Bowl and the Pebble Beach Golf Tournament.
Hours: Weekdays, 10 am - 5:30 pm; Saturday until 5 pm.

Parfumerie Douglas
96 Greenwich Avenue, 625.9392
Large selection of brand-name cosmetics, skin-care products and perfumes. The courteous staff is quite willing to help you sample new products or pick out a gift.
Hours: Monday - Saturday, 9 am - 6 pm; Sunday, noon - 5 pm.

WH Smith Gift Shop - at Hyatt Regency
1800 East Putnam Avenue, Old Greenwich, 637.1234
When we need a gift with "Greenwich" on it, we dash to this shop.
Hours: Every day, 7 am - 11 pm.

SHOPPING
HOME OFFICE

For computers or other hardware, see SHOPPING, COMPUTERS or SHOPPING, ELECTRONICS.

Kinko's
48 West Putnam Avenue, 863.0099
www.kinkos.com
A little expensive, but a great resource for copies to meet a deadline.
Hours: Open 24 hours a day, 7 days a week.

Marks Brothers Stationers
42 Greenwich Avenue, 869.2409
A Greenwich landmark shop with great customer service. Stop in to get your favorite newspaper or a new Mont Blanc fountain pen or anything in between. They are a complete office outfitter for supplies, equipment and furniture.
Hours: Opens every day at 6:30 am; Monday until 5:45 pm; Tuesday - Friday until 7 pm; Saturday until 5 pm; Sunday until 3 pm.

Staples
1297 East Putnam Avenue, 698.9011
Yes, they have staples, too.
Hours: Weekdays, 7 am - 10 pm; Saturday, 9 am - 9 pm; Sunday, 10 am - 7 pm.

Zip Quality Printing
37 West Putnam Avenue, 661.0289
Our favorite place for larger volume printing. They are very careful and easy to work with. Their low prices don't hurt, either.
Hours: Weekdays, 8:30 am - 5:30 pm.

SHOPPING

JEWELRY

Betteridge Jewelers

117 Greenwich Avenue, 869.0124

A long-established family business, good inventory, very trustworthy. They are known for their fine jewelry. Also a good place to buy Tiffany, Rolex and other brand names.

Hours: Tuesday - Saturday, 9 am - 5 pm.

Carolee Jewelry

19 East Elm Street, 629.1515

Classy costume jewelry. Pearls are her signature. She bought Jackie Kennedy's pearls.

Hours: Monday - Saturday, 10 am - 5:30 pm.

Consign It

115 Mason Street, 869.9836

A good source for pre-owned jewelry, silver and china. Fairly priced. If you have jewelry you'd like to consign, this is the place.

Hours: Monday - Saturday, 10 am - 5 pm. Closed Sunday.

George Bennett Jewelers

38 West Putnam Avenue, 869.1271

Another long established, very trustworthy family business. George provides superb customer service.

Hours: Tuesday - Saturday, 9 am - 6 pm.

Penny Weights

124 Elm Street, New Caanan 966.7739

This is a great place to find an inexpensive piece of jewelry for a teenager. Most of the jewelry is silver. The sales staff is friendly and helpful. The prices are terrific.

Hours: Open Tuesday - Saturday, 10 am - 5 pm; Sunday, 12 pm - 5 pm. Closed Mondays.

Steven B. Fox

8 Lewis Street, 629.3303

A full service fine jewelry store that has a good selection of antique jewelry. They also make estate purchases.

Hours: Monday - Saturday, 9:30 am - 5 pm; Closed Sundays.

SHOPPING
MALLS & OUTLETS

Greenwich has not allowed malls or superstores to be built in the town. Superstores can be found in nearby Stamford, Norwalk and White Plains. Outlet shopping centers are short trips away. Dedicated shoppers know that items on sale at local stores can often be as good or better bargains than those found in outlet centers.

Clinton Crossing Premium Outlets
Route 81, Clinton, CT, 860.664.0700   www.chelseagca.com
The largest outlet center in Connecticut, they have seventy upscale stores. If you have time, have dinner at the nearby Inn at Chester, 318 West Main Street (Rts 145 & 81), Chester, CT, 860.526.9541 or at the top-rated French Restaurant Du Village, 59 Main Street (at Maple Street), Chester, CT, 860.526.5301.
Summer Hours: Monday - Saturday, 10 am - 9 pm; Sunday, 10 am - 8 pm. Winter Hours: Sunday - Wednesday, 10 am - 6 pm; Thursday - Saturday, 10 am - 9 pm.
Directions: I-95 N exit 63.

Exposures Catalog Outlet
87 Water Street (Sono Square), South Norwalk, CT, 203.866.5259
Excellent prices on their decorative accessories and pretty frames.
Hours: Monday - Saturday, 10 am - 5:30 pm.
Directions: I-95 N to exit 14, R on West, bear left at fork onto North Main, cross intersection with Washington street, L on Haviland, R on South Water.

SHOPPING

MALLS & OUTLETS

Liberty Village

1 Church Street, Flemington, New Jersey, 908.782.8550
www.chelseagca.com
Shop until you drop. There are more than 120 outlet stores in a number of outlet centers in Flemington. Sixty of the shops are in Liberty Village.
Hours: Sunday - Wednesday, 10 am - 6 pm; Thursday - Saturday, 10 am - 9 pm.
Directions: I-95 to I-287 W to I-287 S to Rte 202 W.

Lillian August Home Outlet Store

85 Water Street (Sono Square), South Norwalk, CT, 203.838.8026
Sofas, chairs and desks designed by Lillian August.
Hours: Monday - Wednesday, 10 am - 6 pm; Thursday - Saturday, 10 am - 7 pm; Sunday, noon - 5 pm.
Directions: I-95 N to exit 14, R on West, bear left at fork onto North Main, cross intersection with Washington street, L on Haviland, R on South Water.

J.M. McLaughlin Company Store

68 Water Street, South Norwalk, CT, 203.838.8427
Next to Otto's men's discount store, this fashionable women's store has their outlet. An excellent resource for the fashionable business woman.
Hours: Monday - Saturday, 10 am - 5 pm; Sunday, noon - 5 pm.
Directions: I-95 N to exit 14, R on West, bear left at fork onto North Main, cross intersection with Washington street, L on Haviland.

Stamford Town Center

Stamford, CT, 324.0935
A large, attractive mall with plenty of brand-name shops. Macy's (964.1500) and Filene's (357.7373) are the anchor stores.
Hours: Weekdays, 10 am - 9 pm; Saturday, 10 am - 6 pm; Sunday, noon - 6 pm.
Directions: I-95 N to exit 8, L on Atlantic, R on Tresser, L onto ramp.

SHOPPING

MALLS & OUTLETS

Westbrook Factory Stores
Westbrook, CT, 860.399.8656
www.charter-oak.com/westbrook
Just barely smaller than Clinton Crossing and only a few miles away. If you are in the area, you should stop by.
Hours: Monday - Saturday, 10 am - 9 pm; Sunday, 11 am - 6 pm.
Directions: I-95 N to exit 65, L on Flat Rock Place.

Westchester Mall
White Plains, NY, 914.683.8600
An even larger mall than the Town Center, good place to go if you want to spend some time in Tiffany (914.686.5100). Primarily upscale shopping. Neiman Marcus (914.428.2000) and Nordstrom (914.946.1122) are the anchor stores.
Hours: Monday - Saturday, 10 am - 9 pm; Sunday, 11 am - 6 pm.
Store hours may vary.
Directions: I-95 S to I-287 W, exit 8 (Westchester Avenue), L on Bloomingdale or on Paulding.

Woodbury Commons
Harriman, NY, 914.928.4000
A huge outlet location with over 220 stores, including Burberrys, Mark Cross and Brooks Brothers. Definitely worth the 60-minute drive.
Hours: Monday - Saturday, 10 am - 9 pm; Sunday, 10 am - 8 pm.
Directions: Take I-95 to I-287 W across the Tappan Zee Bridge and follow I-87 N to exit 16. You can't miss it.

SHOPPING

MUSIC

Al Franklin's Musical World
163 Greenwich Avenue, 869.1900
www.alfranklins.com
A wonderful selection of CDs for all tastes with a special emphasis on classical music. Large number of listening stations. Good audio department with excellent service. Rated best CD store by *Fairfield Weekly*.
Hours: Monday - Saturday, 9:30 am to 6 pm; Sunday, noon to 5 pm.

Sam Goody
145 Greenwich Avenue, 862.9630
www.samGoody.com
A chain store with a good selection of tapes and CDs, a pleasant staff and great hours. Good music web site.
Hours: Monday - Saturday, 9 am to 9 pm; Sunday, 11 am to 6 pm.

SEWING

Nimble Thimble
19 Putnam Avenue, Port Chester, NY, 914.934.2934
The resource for home sewing needs. Lots of fabrics, notions, and quilting supplies and sewing machines. This is the place to have your sewing machine repaired.
Hours: Monday - Saturday, 10 am to 5 pm.

Village Ewe
244 Sound Beach Avenue, Old Greenwich, 637.3953
Beware of stopping here unless you are ready to get hooked on needlepoint. Individual lessons for beginners can be arranged. Group classes are offered in the fall and spring.
Hours: Weekdays, 10 am to 5:30 pm; Saturday, 10 am to 4 pm, (August, 10 am to 1 pm).

SHOPPING

SIDEWALK SALES

Greenwich residents eagerly await summer sidewalk sales. Expect a good time with bargains galore. Don't forget to go inside the stores, they are also full of incredible buys during these sales. Both are held mid-July on Thursday, Friday and Saturday in central Greenwich and Old Greenwich.

STATIONERY

Marks Brothers Stationers

42 Greenwich Avenue, 869.2409

A Greenwich landmark shop with great customer service. Stop in to get your favorite newspaper or a new Mont Blanc fountain pen or anything in between.

Hours: Opens every day at 6:30 am; Monday until 5:45 pm;
Tuesday - Friday until 7 pm; Saturday until 5 pm; Sunday until 3 pm.

Papery

268 Greenwich Avenue, 869.1888 www.thepapery.com

A great selection of high-end greeting cards, as well as a variety of other stationary items. They also sell Madame Alexander dolls.

Hours: Monday - Wednesday, 9:30 am - 6 pm; Thursday - Saturday, 9:30 am - 8 pm; Sunday, noon - 5 pm.

Saint Clair

23 Lewis Street, 661.2927

Going to Cartier's for fine stationery is not necessary if you live in Greenwich. This shop is THE place for invitations and elegant stationery. Stop in and see the range of things they can do.

Hours: Tuesday - Saturday, 9:30 am - 5:30 pm. Closed Sunday and Monday.

TAG SALES

The Friday and weekend *Greenwich Time* newspaper lists tag sale locations. A popular Greenwich weekend pastime.

Greenwich Radio, 869.1490 has a Saturday morning trading post from 8 am - 9 am. A free way to find items or to buy or sell. They will also announce your tag sale.

SHOPPING

THRIFT SHOPS

Donating your unwanted good items to these thrift shops is a practical way to help our neighbors in need. Proceeds from these shops, which are often run by volunteers, go to helping others. So donate with a happy heart and take a moment to explore the shops for a treasure ... they can be found!
See also: CLOTHING and CONSIGNMENT SHOPS

(The) Attic
464 Round Hill Road at The First Church of Round Hill, 629.3876
Back country bargain shopping which benefits The Round Hill Volunteer Fire Company and other charities.
Hours: Tuesday, 10 am - 12:30 pm.

ELDC (Early Learning Development Center)
522 East Putnam Avenue, Cos Cob, 869.0464
Generous donors seem to always leave small items and fine clothing. When one of our editors broke his arm, he needed to cut his jacket sleeve open to accomodate the cast. At ELDC he found a handsome Brooks Brothers blazer for $10. He liked it so much that even after the cast was removed, he had the sleeve repaired. He continues to wear it. A recent find: Wedgewood vase.
Hours: Monday - Saturday, 9:30 am - 4:30 pm; donations, 10 am - 3 pm.

Goodwill Industries of Western CT, Inc.
At the Greenwich Recycling Center, Holly Hill Lane, 203.576.0000
800.423.9787   www.goodwillwct.com
A large trailer with a friendly person ready to receive your donations is conveniently parked just inside our town "dump." Goodwill needs clothing, shoes, toys, tools, kitchenware, linens and small appliances in "saleable" condition. This is recycling in the true sense of the word.
Hours: Weekdays, 7:30 am - 3 pm.

Hospital Thrift Shop
29 B Sherwood Place, 869.6124
Larger furniture items plus clothing and books are welcome here. Our finds: an old steamer trunk; and a lovely white Laura Ashley graduation dress for $45!
Hours: Weekdays, 8:30 am - 4:30 pm; Saturday, 8:30 am - 1 pm.
Closed Sunday.

THRIFT SHOPS

Merry-Go-Round

38 Arch Street, 869.5912, 869.3115
Clothing and small objects are all neatly displayed.
Our finds: two pretty framed watercolors, and a tennis skirt for $3.
Hours: Weekdays, 10 am - 3 pm; Saturday, 10 am - 2 pm;
Closed July and August.

Neighbor-to-Neighbor

Christ Church, 622.9208
This volunteer organization is greatly respected and appreciated in our Greenwich community. They have helped so many people in such a sensitive way. Donations of food, warm coats and clothing (in good condition) are always needed. The shop is restricted to people identified by our social service agencies as "in need" and the selections made in the nicely organized shop are free.
Hours: Weekdays, 9 am - 12:30 pm.

Rummage Room

191 Sound Beach Avenue, Old Greenwich, 637.1875
Notice the artistic window displays of this gem of a shop manned by cheerful volunteers. The shop is filled with clothing for young and old and interesting bric-a-brac. Our finds: a Marissa Christina sweater and a lace tablecloth.
Shop Hours: Weekdays 10 am - 5 pm; Saturdays, 10 am - 1 pm.
Donation Hours: Monday - Thursday, 9 am - 5 pm;
Fridays, 9 am - 1 pm; Saturdays, 10 am - 1 pm.
Closed on Sundays and for the month of August.

Salvation Army

800.897.8188 (truck pick-up); 800.958.7825
Stamford Thrift Shop, 914.975.7630
A marvelous service is available for picking up furniture for donation. Every time we have called, a courteous, strong man has arrived promptly to take items destined to help people serviced by this most worthy organization. Two to four days notice is appreciated for pick-ups. A bin for donations (of clothing only) is located inside our Recycling Center on Holly Hill Lane.
Dispatcher Hours: Monday - Saturday, 7:30 am - 4 pm.

SINGLES

In addition to HOT SPOTS, which often have a mixture of singles and couples, the following are specifically for singles.

Capers Professionals

PO Box 2126, Westport, CT, 06880, 203.221.2209
A Greenwich-based, for-profit singles club, created by Jim Godbout. It conducts respected, upscale, dressy singles events all over lower Fairfield County for ages 30 to 50+. Even when held in towns such as Westport, a great many of the attendees are from Greenwich.

Cotton Club

Christ Church, 245 East Putnam Avenue, 869.6600
Contact Jay Kane Co-President, 661.9478 or
Diane Wilcox Co-President, 334.6220
A social club, with approximately 350 members, for singles of all faiths, ages 35 and up. Members participate in a variety of activities, from hiking and tennis to attending the theater and polo matches. Be sure to get their newsletter.

Fridays-in-the-Round

Bruce Museum, One Museum Drive, 869.0376 x 328 or 329, York Baker
From September to July, the Bruce Museum is a gathering place for local singles, 25 to 45+, to meet, and to enjoy entertainment and the museum. The gatherings are usually the second or third Friday of the month, from 6:30 pm - 9:30 pm.

Singles Under Sail

Contact: Charlie Fisher, 838.1367
Social events for singles who love sailing. Meetings are held on the first and third Thursday during the summer at the Norwalk Motor Inn.

Ski Bears of Connecticut

11 Wall Street (entrance in rear), Norwalk CT, 203.454.6498
www.skibears.org
A ski and social club for singles and married adults. Membership is open to anyone over 21. Emphasis is on outdoor activities.

SINGLES

Sound Sailing Club

37 Fieldstone Drive, Hartsdale, NY, 212.479.7767
Contact Joan Marnara, Rear Commodore 718.792.6981
A non-profit organization for singles ages 30 to 60 who enjoy sailing.
Monthly weekend get-acquainted parties in Fairfield and Westchester
counties, as well as NYC.

Tri-County Talls of NY & CT

Box 736, Bedford Hills, NY, 914.422.5664
A nonprofit social club for tall singles. It sponsors social events for
people over 21 years. Men must be at least 6' 2", women 5' 10".

Westport Singles

Unitarian Church, Westport, CT, (203.227.8173: Recording)
(203.227.1537: Administrative Office)
A nonprofit singles group, with about 800 members, sponsoring programs at various locations in Fairfield County. Ask for their newsletter.

TEENS/YOUNG ADULTS

See also: Teen Speak under NEWS/NEWSPAPERS

Ambassadors in Leotards

Contact: Felicity Foote, 869.9373

For twenty-four years, Felicity, director of the Greenwich Ballet Workshop, has taken a group of accomplished 14-to-18-year-old dancers to Europe to dance for charitable events. Auditions are required.

Arch Street

100 Arch Street, 629.5744

Founded in 1991, Arch Street (also known as the Greenwich Teen Center, Inc.) is a refurbished warehouse right on the harbor. Whether at the dance floor and bandstand or the upstairs snack shop with booths, Arch Street provides teens with the opportunity to be together in a healthy environment. Arch Street is more than just a place to hang out, the Center provides everything from college application advice and counseling help, to opportunities for teens to participate in community service projects or to learn leadership. Although there is an adult board, the teens run Arch Street through the teen board. This board has sixty members, from 9th to 12th grades, and has representatives from both private and public schools. Arch Street is open to Greenwich students from 7th through 12th grade.

Celebrations

581 West Putnam Avenue, 618.1610

A night club for teens (ages 15-18) with a dance floor, guest D.J.s, a bar serving non-alcoholic drinks and two pool tables. The club owner, a former New York Giants player, provides a safe environment for teenagers. Hours: Every Friday and Saturday, 8 pm - 1 am.

Colonial Diner

69 East Putnam Avenue, 661.9067

The diner is open all night and provides a late-night spot for older high-school and returning college students to gather, meet friends, talk and eat. Hours: 24-hours a day, 7 days a week.

Educator Program

Bruce Museum, 1 Museum Drive, 869.0376

High school students are trained to teach young children in the Museum's Neighborhood Collaborative program. Topics covered relate to the Museum's exhibits, such as Japanese folk art, surrealism and Native American beadwork techniques.

TEENS/YOUNG ADULTS

Greenwich Cotillion

869.1979

Greenwich still has a Cotillion every year at the beginning of summer for young ladies who wish to debut. The Cotillion, sponsored by the Junior League of Greenwich, is often described as "a fun party with dignity," but perhaps is more accurately described as a series of dignified fun parties. Attendance is by open invitation on a first-come, first-serve basis. Some years you need to get your check and application in the moment it is received; other years there is less demand and the event fills up more slowly. To be included on the mailing list, contact the Junior League at 869.1979.

For private dance tutoring try Magic Dance, 622.0744 or Connoisseurs of Dance, 359.0076.

Midnight Basketball

YMCA, 50 East Putnam Avenue, 869.1630

From 10 pm to midnight, on the second and last Friday of every month, the Y provides supervised basketball for young adults ages 14 to 18.

Off-Center Stage

Contact: Moritz von Stuelpnagel, 622.9115

A summer theater company started in 1997 by Greenwich young people to give theatrical, hands-on opportunities to students in high-school and college. Students write, produce, stage and act in each summer's productions. Performances are held at the Bruce Museum and area public schools.

Safe Rides

869-8445

A service run by young people to keep other young people safe. Staffed Friday and Saturday nights from 10 pm - 2 am.

YWCA Teen Programs

869.6501 x 225

In addition to the Y's many traditional programs for teens they also offer the following winter programs:

Computer Cool Club: A program for children 10-14, provides a fun introduction to computers, animation and web site design.

Assets: A program for girls in 6th through 12th grades which trains them in leadership and team-building skills.

TRAVEL

AIRPORTS

The Bell Atlantic yellow pages has a handy airport map to La Guardia and JFK (or check the airport's web page).

Avistar Airport Valet Parking

800.621.7275   www.avistarparking.com

Avistar operates out of Kennedy, La Guardia and Newark. If you fly out of one airport, but return to another, they will transfer your car and have it waiting for you. Their web site has good instructions to each of their airport locations.

Kennedy Airport (JFK)

NYC, 718.244.444   www.panynj.gov/aviation/jfkframe.HTM

La Guardia Airport

NYC, 718.533.3400   www.panynj.gov/aviation/lgaframe.HTM

Newark Airport

Newark, NJ, 973.961.6000

www.panynj.gov/aviation/ewrframe.HTM

Leaving your car overnight at Kennedy and La Guardia is not recommended. Of the major New York City airports, Newark in New Jersey takes the longest to get to (80 minutes), but you can park your car there (in a private lot). Newark Airport is nicer and less congested than the other two. In addition, flights out of Newark are often less expensive. If you decide to drive to Newark, park at SKY/PARK; call 973.624.9000 for instructions.

Westchester County Airport

White Plains, NY, 914.285.4860

www.co.westchester.ny.us/airport

This airport is located on upper King Street. It is newly renovated and has good parking facilities. Commercial flights are limited and somewhat more expensive than those from the major NYC airports, but nothing could be easier or more convenient. Airlines that fly out of Westchester are American Airlines, US Air, Carnival, United (Chicago), Northwest & Business Express. If you have time, try the Sky Top Restaurant.

Directions: Glenville Road to King Street; R on King; L at light to Rye Lake Rd.

TRAVEL
AGENCIES

Empress Travel

7 West Putnam Ave, 622.1500

Run by friendly and well-liked Sheila and Les Russo. They have arranged many resident's vacations. They also do a lot of corporate travel business and are quite familiar with all of the US business destinations. They provide good personal service, including ticket delivery. They are most willing to search for a creative solution to get you a low cost airfare to your destination.

Hours: Weekdays, 9 am - 6 pm; Saturday, 10 am - 3 pm.

Liberty Travel

45 West Putnam Ave, 625.8170

Agents speak a number of languages. Because Liberty is a large operation with over 189 stores, they have big buying power for packages in the Caribbean and Florida. They are a good place to go to get a packaged tour for just about any purpose, intimate hotels, adventure trips, etc. If you don't quite know what you want, this could be a good bet. They are open every day, a real benefit if you are on a trip and need help immediately. They don't deliver tickets.

Hours: Monday - Thursday, 9 am - 7:30 pm; Friday, 9 am - 7 pm; Saturday, 10 am - 5 pm; Sunday, noon - 4 pm.

Unleashed Adventures of Greenwich

869.4522 or Unleashed@aol.com

This Greenwich business, founded by Kathleen Snoddon and Diane Terry, is for women only. They provide one-week adventure trips to exotic places. They cater to the civilized who will enjoy and benefit from an uncivilized experience. Returnees give their experience rave reviews.

TRAVEL

BUS

Connecticut Transit (CTtransit)
203.327.7433
www.cttransit.com
CTtransit provides frequent bus service from Greenwich and Old Greenwich to Port Chester, Stamford and Norwalk.

Norwalk Transit
800.982.8420
www.NorwalkTransit.com
Norwalk Transit provides two commuter bus routes around town.

CLUBS

Travel Club of Greenwich
56 Birch Hill Road, Newton CT 06470
Edith Szatai, President, 203.270.1285
Contact: Mary Jane Watson, Membership Chair, 203.637.9439
Virginia Obrig, Program Chair, 203.661.4456

TRAVEL

COMMUTING

See also: AUTOMOBILES and AUTOMOBILES, VEHICLE RENTALS

Travel Information

Local commuters can untangle their morning commutes by consulting the following commuter transportation web sites:

Metro-North Railroad: www.mta.nyc.ny.us/mnr/index.html
Offers the latest schedule information for all CT/NY/NJ MTA Metro North lines.

MetroPool: www.metropool.com
The site offers news and information on commuting in and around Fairfield and Westchester counties.

TravTips www.TravTips.net
The latest traffic information for Connecticut.

PASSPORT

Weekdays from 9 am to 4 pm, you can start the process of obtaining a new or renewed passport at the Greenwich Avenue Post Office. It normally takes twenty-five days to get your passport, although for a small fee you can expedite the process.

For passport photographs see PHOTOGRAPHY, PASSPORTS.

STORES

Parkers

43 Purchase Street, Rye, NY 10580, 914.921.6400

The ultimate travel store, run by Catherine Parker, a helpful and knowledgeable traveler. If you are planning an excursion or searching for a gift for a frequent traveler, this store is worth a trip—books on every conceivable destination, travel clocks, travel games, voltage converters, and an interesting selection of picnic and carry-on luggage.

Hours: Monday - Saturday, 9 am - 6 pm; Sunday, 11 am - 5 pm.

TRAVEL

TAXI/LIMOUSINE

CT Limousine Service

800.472.5466

If you are traveling alone, this may be your best way to get to La Guardia or Kennedy. Pick up at Greenwich Harbor Inn or the Hyatt Regency in Old Greenwich.

Eveready (Yellow) Cab Company

At Cos Cob RR Station, 869.1700

Greenwich Police

622.8006, 8015

A Greenwich off-duty policeman will drive you to any of the NY area airports and pick you up in your own car. This is often less expensive than a limousine service.

Greenwich Taxi

At Greenwich RR Station, 869.6000

An old stand-by for getting around town or to the train station - call ahead and make a reservation to be picked up. This is a good way to get to Westchester Airport. Greenwich Taxi is open until 1:30 am.

Orix, Limo-Car Service

203.322.7068

A very flexible auto service willing to pick you up at all hours. They will not only take you to the New York City theaters and airports, they will handle long distance trips to places such as Atlantic City. Hours: 24 hours a day.

Rudy's Limousine Service

869.0014

A comfortable, reliable service. When several people travel together, this is a wise choice. Their drivers are very professional and pleasant. Hours: 24 hours a day.

TRAVEL

TRAINS

Amtrak

800.USA.RAIL

www.amtrak.com

Operates from Stamford Station and connects to cities throughout the US and Canada.

Metro-North Commuter Railroad

800.638.7646 or 869.2663

www.mnr.org

Offers frequent service to Grand Central Station, New York City, Monday through Friday. Check weekend and holiday times.

Cos Cob Station
Sound Shore Drive, off Exit 4 of I-95

Greenwich Station
Railroad Ave, off Exit 3 of I-95

Old Greenwich Station
Sound Beach Ave, off Exit 5 of I-95

Riverside Station
Between exits 4 & 5 off I-95

INDEX

INDEX

INDEX

INDEX

INDEX

INDEX

INDEX

INDEX

INDEX

INDEX

INDEX

INDEX

INDEX

INDEX

INDEX

INDEX

INDEX

INDEX

NOTES

ABOUT THE AUTHORS

Carolyn and Jerry Anderson

At what age does one discover that the ordinary is extraordinary? For Jerry and Carolyn Anderson, it was when they returned to Greenwich. Jerry had been away at Harvard as an undergraduate, and then as a graduate at Columbia where he received his Masters in Business and Doctorate in Law. Carolyn had been at Boston University as an undergraduate and then at Columbia where she received her Masters. Jerry and Carolyn were introduced by a Greenwich friend, married, and in 1968 they bought their home on Clapboard Ridge Road in Greenwich. No other town was ever considered.

Jerry grew up in Deer Park and went to Brunswick. His youth was filled with sailing on the sound, playing tennis in the town tournaments and working on homework in the Greenwich Library. He learned to drive when Greenwich Avenue was a two-way street and dance lessons still required white gloves for boys as well as girls.

Carolyn is the President of Anderson Associates, a real estate firm specializing in Greenwich residential properties. She is a licensed appraiser and a professional member of the American Society of Interior Designers. Prior to opening Anderson Associates, she designed and renovated many restaurants and residences in Greenwich. In her spare time she writes cookbooks. Jerry and Carolyn rarely miss a new restaurant.

Their children, Clifford and Cheryl, were born in Greenwich Hospital. They thrived in the public school system, which launched them to successful college careers at Harvard and Princeton. Cheryl and Clifford enjoyed the benefits of Greenwich's many resources: water babies at the Y, scouting, running in town races, camping on Great Captain's Island and visiting the wonderful exhibits at Bruce Museum.

However, this book is not just the work of Carolyn and Jerry. It is the product of all of the Anderson Associates. The Anderson Associates are a diverse group - all ages and lifestyles, with one interest in common - Greenwich. They live in, work in and love Greenwich. Most grew up and went to school in Greenwich. Each in their own way, has come to the realization that Greenwich is extraordinary.

ABOUT THE AUTHORS

Cheryl Anderson

Cheryl Anderson is the daughter of Jerry and Carolyn Anderson. She attended school in Greenwich from kindergarten through high school, then attended The American University and Harvard. She currently attends medical school in Portland, Oregon. She writes from her own experience growing up in Greenwich.

Amy Zeeve

Amy is Vice President of Anderson Associates and the inspiration for the first Anderson Guide. Amy is an active participant in the Greenwich community and continues to be a strong contributor to the Guide.

ABOUT OUR ILLUSTRATOR

Vanessa Chow

Vanessa, a Greenwich resident, created the maps and drawings. She graduated from Greenwich High School, where she was one of their top art students, won awards at the Old Greenwich Art Society. Vanessa graduated magna cum laude from Connecticut College. She has studied art at Parsons School of Design, Silvermine, New York University, The Art Students League, The Chinese Academy of Fine Arts and Oxford University. She is a graphic designer in New York City.

AVOCET PRESS INC

Avocet Press Inc, the publisher of *The Anderson Guide to Enjoying Greenwich Connecticut,* is a small, independent publisher of a wide variety of quality literature, guidebooks and technical books. Their offerings range from important contemporary poetry to mysteries to beautifully written historical fiction.

You will find chapters and poems from their books on their website at www.avocetpress.com.

Poetry
The Various Reasons of Light
by Renee Ashley

Waking the Deaf Dog
by Michael Madonick

Memento Mori Mysteries
An Uncertain Currency
by Clyde Lynwood Sawyer, Jr and Frances Witlin

Maximum Insecurity
Deadly Sin
Matty Madrid mysteries by P. J. Grady

Dive Deep and Deadly
A Luanne Fogarty mystery by Glynn Marsh Alam

Literature
The Long Crossing
by Neva Powell

FEEDBACK FORM

We would appreciate your input.

IS THERE SOMETHING WE'VE MISSED?

_____

_____

_____

_____

HAVE YOU FOUND A MISTAKE?

_____

_____

_____

_____

HAVE YOU FOUND THIS BOOK USEFUL?
[ ] yes   [ ] no
Comments: _____

_____

_____

_____

Please mail this form to:
    Anderson Associates, Ltd.
    164 Mason Street
    Greenwich, CT 06830

ORDER FORM

Please send me ____ copies of The Anderson Guide to Enjoying Greenwich Connecticut 4th Edition

Total number of copies   _____ @ 15.00
          Price includes postage and sales tax.

Amount due $_____

I wish to pay by [   ] check or [   ] VISA or MasterCard

Name: _____

Address: _____

City: _____

State: _____   Zip: _____

Telephone: _____

Credit Card Number   _____ _____ _____ _____

Expiration Date: ___/___

Name on Card: _____

Signature: _____

You can fax, mail, email or phone your order to
Avocet Press Inc
19 Paul Court
Pearl River, NY 10965-1539
Toll free phone: 877-4-AVOCET
Fax number: 914-735-6807
Email   books@avocetpress.com